SCHAUM'S OUTLINE OF

Operating Systems

J. ARCHER HARRIS, Ph.D.

Department of Computer Science
James Madison University

Schaum's Outline Series

McGRAW-HILL
New York   Chicago   San Francisco   Lisbon
London   Madrid   Mexico City   Milan   New Delhi
San Juan   Seoul   Singapore   Sydney   Toronto

Dr. J. ARCHER HARRIS received his B.S. in Mathematics (with honors) from Denison University in 1973 and his M.S. and Ph.D. in Computer Science from SUNY at Stony Brook in 1975 and 1978. He currently is an associate professor of Computer Science at James Madison University where he has taught since 1985. His interests include operating systems, Unix, networks, and computer science education. Dr. Harris has also taught at Southern Illinois University and his consulting activities have included working with Tandon Corporation, the U.S. Immigration and Naturalization Service, BDS Corporation, TransAmerica Telemarketing, and Shenandoah Electronic Intelligence. Software developed by Dr. Harris includes NAMS (Network Account Management System), the *hed* editor, and the *sim* microprogram simulator.

Schaum's Outline of Theory and Problems of
OPERATING SYSTEMS

1 2 3 4 5 6 7 8 9 10 11 12 13 14 15 16 17 18 19 20 PRS PRS 0 9 8 7 6 5 4 3 2 1

ISBN 0-07-136435-8

Sponsoring Editor: Barbara Gilson
Production Supervisor: Elizabeth J. Shannon
Editing Supervisor: Maureen B. Walker
Compositor: TechSet

Library of Congress Cataloging-in-Publication Data applied for.

McGraw-Hill

A Division of The McGraw-Hill Companies

PREFACE

My first experience with operating systems was on a DEC PDP-11 computer running Unix Version 6. With the source code in hand, I learned about a fascinating piece of software which was both elegant and complex. An operating system is the ultimate challenge for a programmer, encompassing everything from low-level device manipulation, to concurrency, to object-oriented design.

This book explores the design principles found in modern operating systems. It is intended for those wishing to learn more about operating systems in general or for those with interest in a particular system who desire a broader perspective on its operation. As in all Schaum's Outline Series books, each chapter includes a concise presentation of the material and numerous solved problems. The book is suitable for use as a companion to a standard operating systems text, as a supplement to a course, or as a review guide for students preparing for graduate entrance or comprehensive exams.

The emphasis of this book is on design principles, not the detailed characteristics of any particular operating system. However, examples from various operating systems are cited, with DOS, Windows, and Unix being the most frequently referenced. The book concentrates on generally applicable design features and does not cover more specialized topics such as real-time or distributed systems.

I wish to thank all the staff at McGraw-Hill who helped produce this effort. I thank my students and my colleagues at James Madison University for their understanding and support. A special acknowledgment to Dr. Ramón Mata-Toledo for his part in bringing this book to life.

Finally, I express my profound gratitude to my wife and colleague, Nancy Harris. In addition to emotional support, her critical review was invaluable.

Although it is hoped all material in this book is accurate, the possibility does exist that some errors are present. Notification of errors, omissions, or suggested improvements should be sent to schaumos@mailgate.cs.jmu.edu. Updates on the book may be found at URL http://www.cs.jmu.edu/users/harrisja/schaumos.

J. ARCHER HARRIS

CONTENTS

CHAPTER 1

Introduction

Computer systems provide a capability for gathering data, performing computations, storing information, communicating with other computer systems, and generating output reports. Some of those capabilities are best implemented in hardware, others in software. An operating system is the software that takes the raw capabilities of the hardware and builds a more practical platform for the execution of programs. The operating system manages hardware resources, provides services for accessing those resources, and creates higher-level abstractions such as files, directories, and processes.

A typical computer system contains five major components: the hardware, the operating system, systems programs, application programs, and users (Fig. 1-1). The hardware does all the actual work and includes the memory, the **central processing unit** (CPU), and the input and output (I/O) devices. The operating system provides a set of services to programs. The user interacts with the operating system indirectly, through the programs. Systems programs are a set of utility programs supplied with an operating system to provide basic services for users. Examples of systems programs include a window manager for a **graphical user interface** (GUI), a command interpreter, and programs to rename, copy, or delete files. Application programs provide the computer with the functionality the users require. Examples of application programs include tax preparation software, a financial planner, a word processor, and a spreadsheet.

1.1 Machine Hardware

The CPU is the heart and brain of a computer system. It contains a number of special-purpose registers, an **arithmetic logic unit** (ALU), and the control logic necessary to decode and execute instructions (Fig. 1-2). Connected to the CPU by way of a communication **bus** are the memory and the I/O devices. The operation of the CPU is controlled by the instructions the CPU fetches from memory. The I/O devices, in turn, are commanded by the CPU.

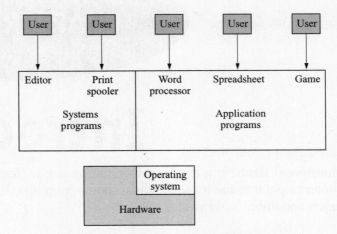

Fig. 1-1.   Computer system components.

The operation of a CPU can be described in terms of a simple loop, where each time through the loop one instruction is executed. The basic process by which instructions execute never varies.

- An instruction is fetched from the memory location specified by the special register called the ***program counter***. All instructions to be executed are fetched from main memory.

- The instruction is placed in a special register called the ***instruction register***.

- The program counter is incremented so it points to the next instruction to be executed.

- The instruction is decoded to determine what action is to be performed. The action is specified by the instruction's ***opcode*** (operation code) bits. The machine architecture defines which bits contain the opcode.

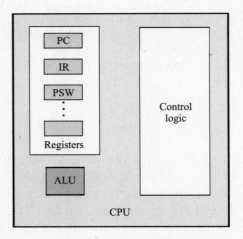

Fig. 1-2.   CPU organization.

- Depending on the operation to be performed, the value of one or more operands are fetched from memory.
- The operation specified in the opcode is performed. Five basic categories of operations exist.

  (1) **Movement**: Move a value from one location to another. The locations involved may be registers or memory locations.

  (2) **Computation**: Send one or more operand values to the ALU and have a computation performed.

  (3) **Conditional Branch**: If the branch condition is true, reset the program counter to point to the branch address. For an unconditional branch, the branch condition is always true.

  (4) **Procedure Call**: Save the current value of the program counter. Then reset the program counter to point to the beginning of a procedure. At the end of the procedure, a branch instruction specifying the saved program counter will allow the program to return to the current point of execution. The saved program counter may be stored in a register, in memory, or on the stack.

  (5) **Input/Output**: Transfer information concerning an input or output operation between the CPU and an I/O device.

- If required, a value is stored back into main memory.

1.1.1 TRAPS AND INTERRUPTS

Traps and *interrupts* are events that disrupt the normal sequence of instructions executed by the CPU. A trap is an abnormal condition detected by the CPU that usually is indicative of an error. Examples of trap conditions include dividing by zero, trying to access a memory location that does not exist or for which the program does not have access, executing an instruction with an undefined opcode, or trying to access a nonexistent I/O device.

An interrupt is a signal sent to the CPU by an external device, typically an I/O device. It is the CPU's equivalent of a pager, a signal requesting the CPU to interrupt its current activities to attend to the interrupting device's needs. A CPU will check interrupts only after it has completed the processing of one instruction and before it fetches a subsequent one.

The CPU responds to traps and interrupts by saving the current value of the program counter and resetting the program counter to a new address. This allows the CPU to return to executing at the point the trap or interrupt occurred, after it has executed a procedure for handling the trap or interrupt. The address the CPU jumps to is determined by the hardware architecture. On some machines, a unique address is associated with each trap and interrupt. More commonly, the architecture defines an address in memory to be the location of an *interrupt vector*. Each trap and interrupt is associated with an index into that vector. The branch address is determined by the contents of the memory location in the vector pointed to by the trap or interrupt's index.

Other state information is also typically saved when a trap or interrupt occurs. On many machines, that information is stored in a special *program status word* (PSW) register.

Interrupts may be associated with a hardware *priority level*. The CPU is also associated with a priority. Only interrupts with priorities higher than the CPU's are processed. An interrupt with a lower priority is left unprocessed until the CPU lowers its priority. CPU priority level is stored in the PSW and can be reset by changing the appropriate bits in the PSW.

One difference between traps and interrupts is traps are synchronous and interrupts are asynchronous. Given the same machine state and input data, a trap will occur at the exact same point of program execution each time a program runs. The occurrence of an interrupt, however, is dependent on the relative timing between the interrupting device and the CPU. Interrupts present a challenge to the debugging process since errors affected by the timing of the interrupt may not be easily repeatable.

1.1.2 MULTIMODE EXECUTION

To provide an operating system with privileges not granted to application programs, the hardware must support multiple modes of execution. Most commonly, two modes of execution are supported: *kernel* (or *supervisor*) *mode* and *user mode*. A single bit in the PSW records the system's execution mode. Attempts to perform certain activities while in user mode result in a trap. The restricted activities consist of those things normally reserved for the operating systems such as the execution of certain instructions (*privileged instructions*), accessing certain registers, and accessing I/O devices.

A system can enter kernel mode from user mode in one of three ways. A special instruction called a *supervisor call* (SVC) or a *system call* is similar to a procedure call except it sets the system's state to kernel mode. Unlike procedure call instructions, supervisor call instructions are not supplied with a branch address. The instruction's operand is a number that serves as an index into a vector similar to the interrupt vector. The branch address is determined by the contents of the memory location pointed to by the supervisor call operand. The vector is located in memory controlled by the operating system so the switch into kernel mode coincides with a jump to an operating system entry point.

Traps and interrupts are the other two mechanisms for switching into kernel mode. Like supervisor calls, the switch coincides with a jump to a kernel entry point. Application programs cannot change the system into kernel mode and remain executing in their own code.

On Unix systems, one user called the *superuser* is given special access privileges. The superuser may read or write any file and kill any process. The superuser should not be confused with kernel mode execution. Application programs running as the superuser are granted extraordinary access rights by the kernel, but those programs do not run in kernel mode and must use supervisor calls to request operating system services.

1.2   Operating System Structure

The operating system provides applications with a virtual machine. The supervisor calls implemented by the operating system expand the instruction set capability provided by the raw hardware. The supervisor calls support new abstractions such as processes and file systems.

In addition to providing the system call interface, the operating system has the responsibility for managing the underlying hardware resources. Applications cannot access I/O devices or execute privileged instructions. The operating system performs these tasks on behalf of the application programs. In doing so, it attempts to efficiently utilize the resources available to it and protect the integrity of the applications that must share those resources.

The tasks performed by an operating system can be divided into four areas.

- **Process Management:** A *process* is an executing program. Associated with a process are its code, its data, a set of resources allocated to it, and one or more "flows" of execution through its code. The operating system provides supervisor calls for managing processes and must manage the allocation of resources to processes. If multiple processes can exist simultaneously, the operating system must be capable of providing each process with an appropriate virtual environment in which it can run.

- **Memory Management:** At a minimum, memory must be shared by an application program and the operating system. On more sophisticated systems, memory can be shared by a number of processes. The operating system must manage the allocation of memory to processes and control the memory management hardware that determines which memory locations a process may access.

- **File System Management:** Computers process information. That information must be transmitted, processed, and stored. A file system object is an abstract entity for storing or transmitting a collection of information. The file system is an organized collection of file system objects. The operating system must provide primitives to manipulate those objects.

- **Device Management:** A computer communicates information through its input and output devices. Processes access those devices through the operating system supervisor calls provided for that purpose. The operating system attempts to manage those devices in a manner that allows them to be efficiently shared among the processes requiring them.

1.2.1   OPERATING SYSTEM TYPES

Users rarely had direct access to early computer systems. Computer input, both programs and data, was prepared on the input media, typically paper tape or punch cards. Users would hand their input to an operator and return minutes (if you were lucky) or hours later to pick up whatever output their program or "job" generated.

The operator would assemble the similar jobs into "batches" and run the batches through the computer. Each job had total control of the machine until it terminated.

A *batch* mode operating system manages a machine run in this manner. A batch operating system provides minimal functionality since it need not worry about the complications of sharing resources with multiple processes.

On *multiprogrammed batch* systems, jobs are read into a job pool stored on a disk. When one job is unable to execute because it is waiting for an I/O operation to complete, another job may be allowed to run. The sharing of computer resources by concurrently executing processes greatly increases operating system complexity.

Time-shared operating systems allow for interaction between user and process. In batch systems, all data is supplied at the time the program is input. This is fine for a program taking payroll information and printing weekly paychecks, but for programs that must interact with the user, the operating system must support an environment that allows programs to respond to user inputs in a reasonable amount of time. The operating system must not only share resources among the various processes, but it must create the illusion that processes are running simultaneously. It does this by shifting execution rapidly among all the active processes.

Increasingly, computers exist not as stand-alone entities but as part of a network of computers. At a basic level, this has limited impact on the operating system itself. An I/O device allows the computer to communicate on the network. However, network communications involve complex protocols and, for the reliability of the network, support for those protocols is built into a *networked* operating system. The general-purpose operating system of today is a networked time-shared system and is the focus of this book. Such systems may also have support for some form of batch processing.

A *real-time* operating system is designed to support execution of tasks within specific wall clock time constraints. Normally, users want the computer system to execute their programs as soon as possible, but no exact timing is required. In real-time systems, the correctness of a processing task is dependent on the wall clock time at which the processing occurred. For example, a real-time system sensing loss of coolant to a nuclear reactor may be required to initiate a backup system within a fraction of a second. The operating system must guarantee the task can be executed within a specified time constraint. Use of real-time systems is mostly limited to dedicated applications such as industrial control systems, weapon systems, and computer-controlled products.

What are desirable features in a time-shared system, resource sharing and management of I/O devices by the operating system, become detriments in a real-time system. Minimization of delays in the completion of tasks discourages resource sharing and encourages low-level access to hardware. For this reason, the design of general-purpose operating systems is much different from the design of real-time systems. The design of real-time systems will not be covered in this book.

Another specialized form of an operating system is a *distributed operating system*. With a network operating system, the resources on each machine on the network are managed by that machine's operating system. Operating system support facilitates communications among the machines. With a distributed operating system, the operating systems on all the machines work together to manage the collective network resources. A single collective distributed operating system manages the network resources provided by each network computer or *node*. Distributed operating systems are also beyond the scope of this book.

1.2.2 OPERATING SYSTEM KERNEL

The operating system *kernel* is the code designed to be executed while the hardware is executing in kernel mode. The kernel should not be considered a program. It is more accurately described as a subroutine library. One or more procedures in the library execute following a trap, an interrupt, or a supervisor call. At some point, the hardware is reset into user mode and control returns to a user program (although possibly not the same program that was executing when the kernel was entered).

To some, the kernel is the operating system. Each of the four areas of operating system management is implemented in the kernel, with supervisor calls triggering execution of functions in that area. In addition, device interrupts result in the execution of device management functions, and traps generated by memory management hardware activate memory management code. Every time the kernel is entered, the process scheduler may be called as the last step before returning control to a user program.

While systems featuring such large *monolithic* kernels are common, there has also been interest in *microkernel* operating systems. In these systems, the kernel contains minimal functionality. Essential functions such as control of memory management hardware, interprocess communications facilities, and interrupt and trap handling are provided by the kernel. Higher-level functions such as file system services are provided by server processes. A program seeking file system services would use interprocess communication system calls to send requests to the file system server process.

The use of server processes enhances flexibility. New servers can be activated without even rebooting the system. The small size of the microkernel simplifies the implementation and porting to new systems. Microkernels are well suited for distributed systems since, when using interprocess communication facilities, it makes little difference whether the process is on a local or remote system.

If the definition of an operating system is expanded to include some services provided by user-level processes, the distinction between system program and operating system becomes blurred. Services such as a print spooling system or a window manager are difficult to classify. An argument could be made for considering them part of the operating system's device management capabilities. In this book, the design features typically found in a monolithic kernel are explored. Although some of those features may be implemented outside the kernel, the design principles do not change. Higher-level services commonly considered to be systems programs, like print spooling systems, are not covered.

1.2.3 THE BOOT PROCESS

When power is first supplied to a computer system, a program in read-only memory (ROM) executes. After performing some diagnostic checks, a stage-0 boot program is executed. The program checks for the presence of one or more boot devices. On a PC, a boot device could be a floppy disk, a CD-ROM, or a hard disk. Once found, the stage-0 boot program reads the first sector from the boot device into main memory. The first sector of the boot device is known as the **boot sector** and should contain a stage-1 boot program. After it has been loaded into memory, the stage-0 boot program branches to the stage-1 boot program.

There is no guarantee the book sector will contain a boot program. If the boot sector has never been initialized, undefined values will be copied into memory. Before transferring control to the next stage in the boot process, the current boot program will check one or more bytes at the end of the boot sector for a "magic" bit pattern which is used to indicate that the sector contains a valid boot program.

On some systems, the stage-1 boot program then reads in the operating system. On others, a series of bootstrap programs must be copied into memory and executed. In either case, the operating system eventually gets copied into memory and the final boot program branches to the operating system's initialization entry point.

On a PC booting from a hard disk, the boot sector also contains a **partition table**. The disk may be divided into at most four primary partitions. The partition table contains the starting and ending location of each partition. The partition table also defines one partition as **active**. The stage-1 boot program reads the partition table and copies into memory the first sector of the active partition. The first sector of the active partition contains a stage-2 boot program designed to work with the operating system contained in that partition. It may also have capabilities for loading boot programs or operating systems from other partitions. At its simplest, the stage-2 boot program loads the partition's operating system into memory.

At the end of the boot process, the operating system has been loaded into memory and the boot program has branched to the operating system. The machine is executing in kernel mode. Any data structures (such as the interrupt vector), not set when the operating system was loaded, must be initialized. System registers and devices are initialized as is needed.

Once the operating system is ready to service processes, it creates any processes that provide operating systems services and also creates one or more processes to execute initialization system programs. On a simple system like DOS, this might only be a process to execute a command interpreter. On a more complicated system, an *init* system program may be provided that creates additional processes as specified in a configuration database. In either case, once the system is switched into user mode and control switches to the user mode processes, the operating system has completed its boot responsibilities and the system is running.

1.3   Outline of the Rest of This Book

Chapter 2, "Process Management," and Chap. 3, "Interprocess Communication and Synchronization," explore the design issues related to processes. Process characteristics, process scheduling, and supervisor calls for controlling processes are covered in Chap. 2. Chapter 3 covers those issues that arise when processes work cooperatively. Synchronization and communication primitives are discussed, as are ways of dealing with deadlock.

Chapter 4, "Memory Management," and Chap. 5, "Virtual Memory," discuss the allocation of memory to processes. The hardware support required to implement the various memory management options is discussed, as well as the operating system design issues. Chapter 5 focuses on those memory management schemes that allow the computer to operate as if it had more memory than it actually does.

Chapter 6, "File System Management," looks at the structure of both the overall file system and the individual files within the file system.

Chapter 7, "Device Management," covers the physical characteristics of key input/output devices and the operating system requirements for controlling those devices. Particular emphasis is placed on disks. A discussion of disk scheduling and RAID systems is included.

The book concludes with Chap. 8, "Security." In many ways, security is more of a management and policy issue than an operating system design issue. However, at the very least, operating system design and security are dependent on each other. Chapter 8 presents a brief look at security measures and the type of threats they are designed to deal with.

Solved Problems

1.1 What are the two main functions of an operating system?

Answer:

The two main functions of an operating system are managing system resources and providing application programs with a set of primitives that provide higher-level services.

1.2 What does the CPU do when there are no programs to run?

Answer:

There is always a program to run (as long as the computer is turned on). The cycle of fetching, decoding, and executing instructions never stops. When there are no user programs to run, the operating system will execute in a loop that does nothing (called a *busy-wait loop* or *idle loop*) until an interrupt occurs.

1.3 What characteristic is common to traps, interrupts, supervisor calls, and subroutine calls?

Answer:

Traps, interrupts, supervisor calls, and subroutine calls all save the current value of the program counter and branch to a new location in memory.

1.4 What characteristic is common to traps, interrupts, and supervisor calls, but different in subroutine calls?

Answer:

Traps, interrupts, and supervisor calls cause the machine to shift into kernel mode. A subroutine call does not change the execution mode.

1.5 Which of the following instructions should be privileged (can only be executed in kernel mode)?

(*a*) Change memory management registers

(*b*) Write the program counter

(*c*) Read the time-of-day clock

(*d*) Set the time-of-day clock

(*e*) Change processor priority

Answer:

(*a*) Yes

Changing memory management registers would allow a process to access memory locations it was not authorized to access.

(*b*) No

Writing the program counter is no different than executing on unconditional branch.

(*c*) No

Although direct access to devices is usually unwise, read access of the clock should not be harmful.

(*d*) Yes

Changing the clock could disrupt scheduled events and is typically not a right granted to a user process.

(*e*) Yes

Changing the processor's priority could cause interrupts to be lost.

1.6 An operating system could implement a memory I/O device. I/O operations to the device cause the corresponding memory location to be read or written. What is the disadvantage of providing such a device? Should it be accessible to users or just to system administrators?

Answer:

If users could access a memory device, they could read or write any memory location, subverting the operating system's protection mechanisms. The operating system itself could be overwritten, giving user programs the ability to execute instructions in kernel mode. Providing that capability to any user, even the system administrator, threatens the integrity of the operating system.

1.7   Classify the following applications as batch-oriented or interactive.

   (*a*)   Word processing

   (*b*)   Generating monthly bank statements

   (*c*)   Computing *pi* to a million decimal places

Answer:

   (*a*)   Interactive

   (*b*)   Batch

   (*c*)   Batch
   This job is almost 100% CPU-bound. A batch system without multiprogram-ming would attain nearly 100% CPU utilization running this program.

1.8   Why must a computer start in kernel mode when power is first turned on?

Answer:

When power is first turned on, the contents of memory is undefined. The boot program in ROM must read the code from the boot device to load into memory. To perform the input operation, the hardware must be in kernel mode. Since the operating system is not loaded, there are no supervisor calls the ROM boot program could use if it was in user mode.

1.9   What is the maximum size of the stage-1 boot program at the beginning of a hard disk, assuming a 2-byte bootstrap magic bit pattern and a 512-byte sector size?

Answer:

The stage-1 boot program must fit in the initial sector. Assuming a sector size of 512 bytes, and 2 bytes for the magic bit pattern, the maximum size of the boot program is 510 bytes. (On PC systems, which also store a partition table in the first sector, the boot program can be at most 446 bytes.)

Supplementary Problems

1.10   Name hardware features designed to explicitly assist the operating system.

1.11   What characteristic is common to traps, supervisor calls, and subroutine calls, but different in interrupts?

1.12   What characteristic do subroutine calls and supervisor calls have, but traps and interrupts do not?

1.13 Why must user programs be prohibited from writing to the memory locations containing the interrupt vector?

1.14 Which of the following instructions should be privileged (can only be executed in kernel mode)?

(a) Set mode to kernel mode

(b) Reboot

(c) Read the Program Status Word

(d) Disable interrupts

(e) Write the instruction register

1.15 Classify the following applications as batch-oriented or interactive.

(a) Generating personal 1040 tax returns

(b) Generating employee W-2 tax forms

(c) A flight simulator

1.16 Must the operating system and the book program that copies the operating system into memory be located on the same disk? Why?

 # Answers to Supplementary Problems

1.10 (1) Kernel/user mode operation

(2) Privileged instructions

(3) Supervisor call instructions

1.11 Traps, supervisor calls, and subroutine calls are all synchronous. A program repeatedly executed using the same input data will generate the same traps, supervisor calls, and subroutine calls at the same point on each run. Interrupts are asynchronous. A program repeatedly run with the same input data will not necessarily have interrupts occur at the same point on each run.

1.12 Subroutine and supervisor calls are instructions executable by user programs. Traps and interrupts are not; they are events triggered by the hardware.

1.13 If a program can write to the interrupt vector, the branch address used when an interrupt is received could be changed. At the least, the program could redirect the system so the interrupt was not properly handled. At worst, the interrupt could cause a branch to memory locations under the control of the application. The application would then be able to execute instructions in kernel mode.

1.14   (*a*)   Yes

(*b*)   Yes

(*c*)   No

(*d*)   Yes

(*e*)   No

1.15   (*a*)   Interactive

(*b*)   Batch

(*c*)   Interactive

1.16   No. The boot program needs to be able to read the operating system. Whether the operating system is on the same disk as the boot program is irrelevant. Installing on a floppy disk a boot program that reads the operating system from the hard disk can be useful protection in case the hard disk boot sector were to become corrupted. It is particularly useful on systems where the operating system is too large to fit on a floppy.

CHAPTER 2

Process Management

All activity on a computer system is centered around the execution of the instructions in computer programs. The term *process* refers to an executing set of machine instructions. The instructions themselves are a static entity. They exist on paper, in a file, or even as a conceptual idea in the mind of an individual. A process is that set of instructions brought to life, a dynamic entity performing actions as prescribed by the code.

Associated with a process are its code, its data, the operating resources allocated to it, and one or more *threads* of execution. A thread is a flow of execution through the process's code, with its own program counter, system registers, and stack.

Operating systems can be classified as one of three types of systems: single-process single-threaded, multiprocess single-threaded, or multiprocess multi-threaded. The simplest arrangement is single-process single-threaded where only one process can execute at a time. Once a process is allocated to the CPU, that process runs to completion before any other process can execute. DOS is an example of a single-process single-threaded operating system.

Multiprocessing systems are far more practical. They allow users to perform multiple concurrent tasks and they make more efficient use of computer resources. CPUs execute much faster than I/O devices. Millions of instructions can be executed in the time it may take to satisfy a single I/O request. In a single-process environment, the CPU sits idle, waiting for the I/O request to be satisfied. For a typical program, the CPU might be idle 50% of the time. Multiprocessing systems allow the CPU to be shared by multiple processes. The system interleaves the execution of the processes, allowing each one the opportunity to periodically use the CPU. If one process is idle, waiting for an I/O request to be satisfied, another process not waiting for I/O may be allocated to the CPU. With enough memory and careful tuning, CPU utilization approaching 100% can be achieved.

On multiprocessing single-threaded systems, like Unix, a single entity, the process, is the object upon which both resource allocation and CPU scheduling are performed. On multiprocessing multithreaded systems, resources are allocated to processes but CPU scheduling can be in terms of threads. Windows 2000, Mach, and Solaris are examples of multiprocessing multithreaded operating systems. To differentiate between single- and multithreading, the term *task* is sometimes used to refer to a multithreaded entity while a *heavyweight process* refers to a task with one thread. A thread is sometimes called a *lightweight process*.

On early batch systems, the term *job* was used to refer to one or more programs executed sequentially and treated by the system as a single entity. An executing job is a process, and the terms are sometimes used interchangeably.

2.1   Process Scheduling

On multiprocessing systems, scheduling is used to determine which process is given control of the CPU. Scheduling may be divided into three phases: long-term, medium-term, and short-term. Long-term scheduling, or *job scheduling*, determines which jobs or processes may compete for systems resources. Typically, once the job scheduler makes a job active, it stays active until it terminates. The main objective of the job scheduler is to provide the medium-term scheduler with an appropriate number of jobs. Too few jobs, and the CPU may sit idle because all jobs are blocked. Too many jobs, and the memory management system becomes overloaded, degrading system efficiency.

The medium-term scheduler, or *swapper*, swaps processes in and out of memory. Any memory management system that supports multiprocessing can use swapping to allow more processes to share a system than can physically fit in memory. Even memory management systems like paging may swap all of a process out of memory to limit the number of processes competing for memory.

The short-term scheduler, or *dispatcher*, allocates the CPU to a process that is loaded into main memory and ready to run. Typically, the dispatcher allocates the CPU for a fixed maximum amount of time. A process that must release the CPU after exhausting its time slot returns to the pool of processes from which the dispatcher selects the process to execute. On multithreaded systems, a variety of options exist for short-term scheduling. Instead of scheduling processes, the short-term scheduler can schedule threads. However, short-term scheduling can also be two-level scheduling: thread scheduling within process scheduling. Since threads within a process share memory and other resources, the overhead required to switch between threads in a process is less than the overhead when switching between heavyweight processes (or threads in different processes).

2.2   Process State

At its simplest, scheduling can consist of just short-term scheduling. On such a system a process exists in one of four states.

- *Blocked*: A process that is waiting for some event to occur before it can continue executing. Most frequently, this event is completion of an I/O operation. Blocked processes do not require the services of the CPU since their execution cannot proceed until the blocking event completes.

- *Ready*: A process that is not allocated to a CPU but is ready to run. A ready process could execute if allocated to a CPU.

- *Running*: A process that is executing on a CPU. If the system has n CPUs, at most n processes may be in the running state.

- *Terminated*: A process that has halted its execution but a record of the process is still maintained by the operating system (on Unix, these are referred to as *zombie* processes). The operating system may wish to retain information on a terminated process for a variety of reasons: the process has an I/O operation pending completion, it has child processes that are still executing and the system needs to retain information about the process that created them, or it has a parent or related process that in the future may request information about the terminated process.

Medium-term scheduling adds two additional process states

- *Swapped-Blocked*: A process that is waiting for some event to occur and has been swapped out to secondary storage.

- *Swapped-Ready*: A process that is ready to run but is swapped out to secondary storage. A swapped-ready process may not be allocated to the CPU since it is not in main memory.

On demand paged and segmented systems (discussed in Chap. 5), a process may have all or some of its pages or segments swapped out, yet still not be in a swapped state. The important characteristic of a process in a swapped state is its absence from the pool of processes considered for allocation to a CPU by the short-term scheduler.

Long-term scheduling adds the following state.

- *Held*: A process that has been created but will not be considered for loading into memory or for execution. Typically only new processes can become held processes. Once a process leaves the held state, it does not return to it.

Depending on the number of schedulers implemented, and therefore the number of states present, a number of different state models may be created to describe a system's behavior. Figure 2-1 depicts the complete seven-state model and the transitions that occur between the states.

- **Process Creation** → **Held**: Upon creation, a process is put into the held state.

- **Held** → **Swapped-Ready** or **Held** → **Ready**: Activate the process, making another process available for management by the medium-term scheduler. Since there may be insufficient memory for another swapped-in process, held processes may become swapped-ready processes. An operating system has the option of swapping in any new process and swapping out an older process if there is insufficient memory.

- **Swapped-Ready** → **Ready**: A process is swapped in when sufficient memory for it becomes available. This can happen for a number of reasons:

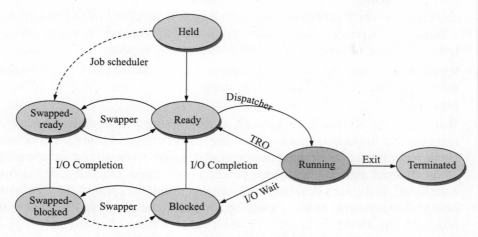

Fig. 2-1.   Process state transition diagram.

the medium-term scheduler made room available by swapping out other processes, processes released memory previously allocated to them, processes terminated releasing all memory allocated to them, or the amount of memory allocated to various processes is reduced based on changing system conditions. Note that on demand paged and segmented systems, it is not required that any memory be allocated to a process when it becomes ready. However, when the process enters the run state and attempts to execute an instruction, a fault will occur and the process will block as the required page or segment is swapped in.

- **Swapped-Blocked → Blocked**: A system can also decide to swap in blocked processes, although not all operating systems choose to make this transition. A blocked process cannot execute anyway, so placing it in memory appears to waste that resource. In some contexts, the decision may be appropriate: the process may be a high-priority process or the system may be lightly loaded with significant, unused memory available. In either case, moving a swapped-blocked process to the blocked state allows the process to execute sooner, once the blocking condition is satisfied.

- **Ready → Swapped-Ready** or **Blocked → Swapped-Blocked**: The medium-term scheduler swaps out processes to release memory resources for other processes. This may be done because other processes have requested additional memory or because the amount of memory that must be allocated to various processes has increased due to changing system conditions.

- **Swapped-Blocked → Swapped-Ready** or **Blocked → Ready**: A process in one of the blocked states is waiting for some event to occur. When that event occurs, the process is moved to the corresponding ready state.

- **Running → Ready**: Processes are allocated the CPU for maximum amount of time or **_time slice_**. If a process does not become blocked or voluntarily release the CPU prior to the end of its time slice, a timer runout (TRO) interrupt will transfer control to the operating system and the short-term scheduler. The short-term scheduler then moves the process to the ready state and chooses which process to run next. It is also possible that the transition of a high-priority process from a blocked to a ready state will trigger the short-term scheduler to preempt a low-priority running process.

- **Ready → Running**: When no process is allocated to the CPU, the short-term scheduler selects the next running process from the pool of ready processes.

- **Running → Blocked**: Tasks such as performing I/O operations, communicating with other processes, or waiting on system conditions are controlled by factors external to the process. In most of these cases, continued execution of the process must be suspended pending notification that the task has been completed or the specified condition has occurred. To prevent the CPU from being idle while the process waits on an event, the process is moved to the blocked state so the CPU may be allocated to a runnable process.

- **Running → Terminated**: Executing processes terminate by either performing some illegal action or by normally completing the execution of their code.

- **Any State → Terminated**: Although not illustrated in Fig. 2-1, a process can be terminated by some action external to the process. No matter what state a process is in, the operating system or another process may be able to terminate the process, moving it to the terminated state.

2.3   Scheduling Criteria

The goal of a scheduling algorithm is to identify the process whose selection will result in the "best" possible system performance. Best performance is a subjective evaluation that comprises a mix of a number of criteria of varying relative importance. The scheduling policy determines the importance of each of the criteria. A number of algorithms have been used extensively to implement a scheduling policy.

Listed below are some commonly used scheduling criteria. In some cases, the different criteria are complementary; they use different techniques to measure the same basic performance characteristics. In other cases, the criteria are contradictory; improving performance according to one criterion will adversely affect performance as measured by another. It is impossible to design an algorithm that optimizes all the criteria simultaneously.

- **CPU Utilization:** The percentage of time the CPU is executing a process. The load on the system affects the level of utilization that can be achieved; high utilization is more easily achieved on more heavily loaded systems. The importance of this criterion typically varies depending on the degree the system is shared. On a single-user system, CPU utilization is relatively unimportant. On a large, expensive, time-shared system, it may be the primary consideration.

- **Balanced Utilization:** The percentage of time all resources are utilized. Instead of just evaluating CPU utilization, utilization of memory, I/O devices, and other system resources are also considered.

- **Throughput:** The number of processes the system can execute in a period of time. Evaluation of throughput must consider the average length of a process. On systems with long processes, throughput will be less than on systems with short processes.

- **Turnaround Time:** The average period of time it takes a process to execute. A process's turnaround time includes all the time it spends in the system, and can be computed by subtracting the time the process was created from the time it terminated. Turnaround time is inversely proportional to throughput.

- **Wait Time:** The average period of time a process spends waiting. One deficiency of turnaround time as a measure of performance is the time a process spends productively computing increases the turnaround time, lowering the performance evaluation. Wait time presents a more accurate measure of performance because it does not include the time a process is executing on the CPU or performing I/O; it includes only the time a process spends waiting.

- **Response Time:** On interactive systems, the average time it takes the system to start responding to user inputs. On a system where there is a dialog between process and user, turnaround time may be mostly dependent on the speed of the user's responses and relatively unimportant. Of more concern is the speed with which the system responds to each user input.

- **Predictability:** Lack of variability in other measures of performance. Users prefer consistency. For example, an interactive system that routinely responds within a second, but on occasion takes 10 s to respond, may be viewed more negatively than a system that consistently responds in 2 s. Although average response time in the latter system is greater, users may prefer the system with greater predictability.

- **Fairness:** The degree to which all processes are given equal opportunity to execute. In particular, do not allow a process to suffer from *starvation*. A process is a victim of starvation if it becomes stuck in a scheduling queue indefinitely.

- **Priorities:** Give preferential treatment to processes with higher priorities.

2.4   Scheduling Algorithms

In the early days of computing, scheduling was mostly *nonpreemptive*; a process retained control of the CPU until the process blocked or terminated. This approach adequately served the needs of batch jobs where response time was of little or no concern. On today's interactive systems, *preemptive* scheduling is used. The scheduler may preempt a process before it blocks or terminates, in order to allocate the CPU to another process. This is a necessity on an interactive system, where lengthy execution without I/O by a process could monopolize the CPU, giving the processes in the ready queue no opportunity to respond to their users' inputs.

Six scheduling algorithms have seen widespread use.

2.4.1 FIRST-COME FIRST-SERVED

The simplest scheduling algorithm is *First-Come First-Served* **(FCFS)**. Jobs are scheduled in the order they are received. FCFS is nonpreemptive. Implementation is easily accomplished by implementing a queue of the processes to be scheduled or by storing the time the process was received and selecting the process with the earliest time.

FCFS tends to favor CPU-bound processes. Consider a system with a CPU-bound process and a number of I/O-bound processes. The I/O-bound processes will tend to execute briefly, then block for I/O. A CPU-bound process in the ready state should not have to wait long before being made runnable. The system will frequently find itself with all the I/O-bound processes blocked and the CPU-bound process running. As the I/O operations complete, the ready queue fills up with the I/O-bound processes. Their wait time increases while I/O device utilization plummets.

Under some circumstances, CPU utilization can also suffer. In the situation described above, once a CPU-bound process does issue an I/O request, the CPU can return to process all the I/O-bound processes. If their processing completes before the CPU-bound process's I/O completes, the CPU sits idle. An algorithm that provides a better mix of CPU- and I/O-bound processing usually performs better than FCFS.

2.4.2 SHORTEST JOB FIRST

Shortest Job First **(SJF)** is another nonpreemptive algorithm. It selects the job (process) with the shortest expected processing time. In case of a tie, first-come first-served scheduling can be used. Originally implemented in a batch-processing environment, SJF relied on a time estimate supplied with the batch job.

SJF has been modified for short-term scheduling use in an interactive environment. The algorithm bases its decision on the expected processor **burst time**. Expected burst time can be computed as a simple average of the process's previous burst times or as an exponential average. The exponential average for a burst can be computed using the equation

$$e_{n+1} = \alpha t_n + (1 - \alpha)e_n$$

where e_n represents the nth expected burst, t_n represents the length of the burst at time n, and α is a constant that controls the relative weight given to the most recent burst (if α is zero, the most recent burst is ignored; with α equal to one, the most recent purpose is the only consideration).

Clearly, SJF favors short jobs over long ones. In extreme cases, the constant arrival of small jobs can lead to starvation of a long job.

2.4.3 SHORTEST REMAINING TIME

Shortest Remaining Time (SRT) is a preemptive version of shortest job first. Any time a new process enters the pool of processes to be scheduled, the scheduler compares the expected value for its remaining processing time with that of the process currently scheduled. If the new process's time is less, the currently scheduled process is preempted. Like SJF, SRT favors short jobs, and long jobs can be victims of starvation.

2.4.4 ROUND ROBIN

Round Robin (RR) is a preemptive algorithm that selects the process that has been waiting the longest. After a specified time quantum, the running process is preempted and a new selection is made. Interrupts from an *interval timer* ensure that processing is suspended and control is transferred to the scheduling algorithm at the conclusion of the time quantum.

Round robin is used extensively in time-shared systems. Use of small time quantum allows round robin to provide good response time. However, short time quanta increase the number of switches between processes, decreasing efficiency. Hardware designed to perform rapid process switches facilitates use of round robin with a short time quantum.

2.4.5 PRIORITY

Priority scheduling requires each process to be assigned a priority value. The process selected is the one with the highest priority. First-come first-served can be used in case of a tie. Priority scheduling may be preemptive or nonpreemptive.

Priority assignment mechanisms vary widely and include basing the priority on a process characteristic (memory usage, I/O frequency), the user executing the process, usage cost (CPU time for higher-priority jobs costs more), or a user- or administrator-assignable parameter. Some of the mechanisms yield dynamically changing priorities (amount of time running), while others are static (the priority associated with a user).

Although it may be intuitively appealing to have the priority value directly proportional to its actual selection priority, on some systems the processes with the lowest-priority values are afforded the highest-selection priority.

2.4.6 MULTILEVEL FEEDBACK QUEUES

The major disadvantage with the five preceding algorithms is they basically treat all jobs the same. This results in each algorithm favoring certain kinds of processes. An algorithm using *Multilevel Feedback Queues* (MFQ) addresses this deficiency by customizing the scheduling of a process based on the process's performance characteristics.

An MFQ algorithm implements two or more scheduling queues. An entering process is inserted into the top-level queue. When selected, processes in the queue are allocated a relatively small time-slice. Upon expiration of the time-slice, the process is moved to the next lower queue (Fig. 2-2). Time-slices associated with the queues increase as the level lowers. If a process blocks before using its entire time-slice, it is either moved to the next higher-level queue or to the top-level queue.

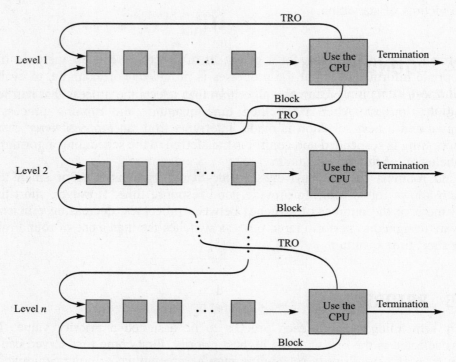

Fig. 2-2.   Multilevel feedback queue.

The process selected by MFQ is the next process in the highest-level nonempty queue. Typically, selection within a queue is FCFS. If a process enters a high-level queue while a process from a lower-level queue is executing, the low-level queue process may be preempted.

I/O-bound jobs remain in the higher-level queues where they receive higher priority over more CPU-bound processes in lower-level queues. However, the more CPU-bound jobs are granted longer time-slices. As with shortest job first and shortest remaining time, it is possible for a CPU-bound job to suffer from starvation. A possible remedy is to elevate a process to the next higher-level queue if it has remained idle in a queue for a certain amount of time.

The number of variables in a multilevel feedback queues system makes it both flexible and complex. The major options can be summarized as follows.

- The number of queues
- The time-slice associated with each queue
- The selection algorithms used to select a process from within each queue

- The condition(s) that will cause a process to sink to a lower-level queue
- The condition(s) that will cause a process to rise to a higher-level queue
- Whether arrival of a process into a higher-level queue will preempt a process from a lower-level queue
- The mechanism for determining which queue a new process enters into

2.5   Scheduling Algorithm Performance

Performance of an algorithm for a given set of processes can be analyzed if the appropriate information about the processes is provided. For example, to evaluate the Shortest Remaining Time algorithm, data on process arrival time and process execution time is required. Consider the set of four processes described in Table 2-1.

Table 2-1.   Process Scheduling Data.

Process	Arrival Time	Processing Time
A	0.0	5
B	1.0	2
C	2.0	5
D	3.0	3

At time 0, only process A has entered the system, so it is the process that executes. At time 1, process B arrives. At that time, process A has 4 time units left to execute, process B has 2. So process B starts executing at time 1. At time 2, process C enters the system. Process B continues executing; of the three processes it has the minimum number of time units. At time 3, process B terminates and process D enters the system. Of processes A, C, and D, process D has the smallest remaining execution time so it starts executing. When process D terminates at time 6, process A is restarted. When process A terminates at time 10, process C executes. Chart 2.1 illustrates the timing of the processes' execution.

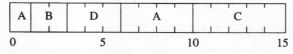

Chart 2.1.   Process execution timing.

Turnaround time for each process can be computed by subtracting the time the process entered the system from the time it terminated. The turnaround times for the processes described in Table 2-1 can be calculated as follows:

Process A: $10 - 0 = 10$
Process B: $3 - 1 = 2$
Process C: $15 - 2 = 13$
Process D: $6 - 3 = 3$

The average turnaround time is $(10 + 2 + 13 + 3)/4 = 7$.

The wait time can be computed by subtracting execution time from turnaround time, yielding the following four results for the processes in Table 2-2:

Process A: $10 - 5 = 5$
Process B: $2 - 2 = 0$
Process C: $13 - 5 = 8$
Process D: $3 - 3 = 0$

The average wait time is $(5 + 0 + 8 + 0)/4 = 3.25$.

Four jobs executed in 15 time units. So throughput is $4/15 = 3.75$ time units per job.

2.6   Process Attributes

The operating system stores information about a process in a *Process Control Block* (PCB). The PCB contains the information the operating system needs to know about a process: process state and scheduling information, memory management information, hardware run-state information, process signaling information, access control information, I/O and allocated resource information, and accounting information.

2.6.1   RUN STATE AND SCHEDULING

In addition to knowing the state of a process, the operating system must be able to quickly identify all the processes in a particular state. This usually involves maintaining separate lists or queues for each state. The PCB may contain a link to the appropriate state queue. For processes that are in the blocked state, information on the blocking event must be maintained. Information used by scheduling algorithms, such as priority level or time of last allocation to the CPU, can be found in the PCB.

2.6.2   MEMORY MANAGEMENT

Each time a process is given control of the CPU, the memory management hardware must be configured so only the memory locations allocated to that process may be accessed. For each process, the operating system must maintain a copy of the memory management configuration for that process. When a process obtains the CPU, a register is set to point to the process's configuration settings, or the configuration values are copied into special memory management registers.

2.6.3   HARDWARE STATE

On a multiprogrammed machine, when a process is given control of the CPU, various hardware registers must be restored to the values they had when the process was suspended. The operating system must store these values for each process that is not in the run state. Depending on the underlying hardware architecture, this may include values for the program counter, accumulator registers, general registers, stack pointers, index registers, arithmetic logic unit condition codes, and execution priority level. Resetting all the values when a new process takes control of the CPU is called a *context-switch*.

2.6.4 SIGNALING

An operating system may support some form of process signaling. A *signal* is a virtual interrupt created by the operating system. A signal may originate with a process or with the operating system and is sent to one or more processes. A process receiving a signal may respond by ignoring it, by terminating, or by executing a specified function. There may be a provision for scheduling a signal to be sent at some time in the future. Software timers are signals that a process sends to itself at some point in the future. The operating system must maintain information on how a process will respond should it receive signals. It also may need to maintain a list of signals that have been sent to a process but have not yet been serviced.

2.6.5 ACCESS CONTROL

Two types of access control information may be stored: information that determines the access rights of the process and information on the default access rights assigned to any object created by this process. Depending on the access control mechanism used, this information may be passwords, capabilities, or access control lists.

2.6.6 INPUT AND OUTPUT

The operating system must maintain information on files and devices allocated to a process or opened for I/O by a process. On most systems, a file or device must be opened before it can be accessed. An open file table stores information on each file or device opened by a process. Other information might include the current working directory of a process or a per-process root directory.

2.6.7 OTHER

Other information an operating system may maintain about a process includes the following.

- **Process id:** A process's unique identification number.
- **Parent process id:** The identification number of the *parent process*. The creation of new processes by existing processes creates an ancestral relationship. When a process is created, the creating process is the parent, the created process is the child.
- **Child process ids::** Process identification numbers of all of a parent's child processes.

- **Process group id(s):** A number that associates a process with a collection of processes that is independent of or in addition to the ancestoral relationship.
- **User id:** The identification number of the user running the process.
- **Effective user id:** User whose access rights will be in effect while running a particular program. For example, when user **bill** runs a program written and owned by user **mary**, it may be desirable for that process to run with **mary**'s access rights rather than **bill**'s.
- **Group id(s):** The mechanism for controlling access to system objects may incorporate the notion of groups of users who share a common set of access rights. On such a system, a process might be associated with one or more groups.
- **Effective group id(s):** Just as it may be desirable to substitute an effective user for the real user, it may be desirable to provide an effective group mechanism.
- **Account id:** While account and user could be synonymous, some systems may distinguish between a person (user) associated with a process and the accounting entity under which resource usage is recorded.
- **Priority level:** A factor in any of the scheduling decisions may be a process's priority level.
- **Elapsed CPU time:** Total CPU time used by a process to date.
- **Start time:** Wall clock time when the process was created and/or the time the process left the held state.
- **Scheduled start time:** Wall clock time a process should start its execution. A process with a scheduled start time should remain in the held state until that time.
- **Maximum CPU time:** Maximum amount of CPU time a process may use.
- **Memory allocation:** Total amount of memory allocated to a process.
- **Command:** The name of the executable file the process is executing and/or any arguments the process received when the process was created.
- **Terminal:** On systems where users interact with the system from terminal devices (monitor/keyboards, terminals, telnet sessions, etc.), an identification of the terminal associated with the process.
- **Termination status:** For a process that has terminated, the status value with which it terminated.

2.7   Process Supervisor Calls

The operating system must provide a mechanism for creating processes. When a process is created, the operating system must create a PCB for that process. Initial settings for information in the PCB may be determined from parameters specified in the supervisor call that created the process, values associated with the parent process, values associated with the user, or values determined by the operating system based on overall system load. Overall resources available to a process may be limited to a subset of those available to the parent process or to the user.

An initial hardware run-time state must be created for a new process. A memory image must be generated, and values for hardware registers, including the program counter, must be set. Two basic approaches to the initial state predominate.

In one approach, the *system* supervisor call specifies the file containing the program to be executed by the new process. The operating system must load memory based on the information stored in the file. The form of a file containing an executable program varies depending on the operating system. Even within a single operating system, multiple executable file formats may be supported. The *system* call may also allow arguments to be passed to the process as part of the initial run-time state.

In the other approach, process creation and execution of a program in a file are implemented as separate functions: *fork* and *exec*. The *fork* call creates a child process that is nearly an identical duplicate of the parent process; only a single register or memory location differs. For example, on Unix, only the *fork*'s return value differs in the two processes. In the child, the return value is zero, in the parent the return value is the process identification number of the child. By having the code in the processes test this value, the program can arrange for the parent and the child to branch to different code segments.

The *exec* call arranges for a process to execute the program stored in a file. This supervisor call overwrites the current run-time state of a process, replacing it with the state as specified in the file. By having a child process execute this supervisor call immediately after a *fork*, the effect of the *system* call is duplicated. However, the use of separate calls adds versatility to the system, allowing a process to overwrite itself without creating a child process or allowing multiple processing within a program.

Mechanisms for terminating a process include an *exit* supervisor call that terminates the calling process, an *abort* call that allows one process to terminate another, and operating system intervention should the process attempt some restricted activity. The processes that are permitted to *abort* another process are typically limited to the parent process, processes in the same group, processes associated with the same user, and/or processes associated with privileged system users.

It is possible for an operating system to suspend execution of a parent while its child executes. However, on most systems, the parent may execute concurrently with the child. On such systems, a *wait* call allows the parent to suspend itself until one or more of its children terminate. The *wait* may also provide a mechanism for a termination status to be passed back from the child to a parent.

On some systems, when a parent process terminates, all its children are automatically terminated. The children would then have their children terminated, a process known as ***cascading termination***.

In addition to calls to create and terminate processes, calls may exist for sending and controlling the receipt of software signals, for synchronizing concurrent processes, and for sending communications between processes. Interprocess synchronization and communication are covered in the next chapter.

Solved Problems

2.1   On a system with n CPUs, what is the maximum number of processes that can be in the ready, run, and blocked states?

Answer:

There is no limit to the number of processes that can be in the ready and blocked states. At most, n processes may be in the run state, since a process in the run state must be allocated to a CPU, and there are only n CPUs.

2.2   On a system with n CPUs, what is the minimum number of processes that can be in the ready, run, and blocked states?

Answer:

There can be zero processes in any of the three states. It is possible for all the processes to be blocked while waiting on I/O operations, leaving no processes in the ready and running states. All processes can be either in the ready or run state, leaving no processes blocked.

2.3   What is the principal advantage of multiprogramming?

Answer:

It increases CPU utilization. While one process is blocked, waiting for I/O to complete, the CPU may execute another process.

2.4   What is the principal disadvantage of too much multiprogramming?

Answer:

The overhead associated with managing too many processes can degrade performance. In particular, systems that use swapping may have insufficient memory resources to handle all the processes, leading to a condition known as *thrashing*.

2.5   The I/O wait percentage, ω, of a process is the percentage of time the process waits for I/O to complete when executed in a monoprogrammed environment. On a system using round-robin scheduling with n processes, all having the same I/O wait percentage, what percentage of the time will the CPU be idle (in terms of ω)?

Answer:

If the I/O wait percentage is ω, the probability at any instant that a process will be waiting is also ω (if a process spends 65% of its time waiting for I/O, the probability it is waiting for I/O at any instant is 65%). At first glance, it appears that if there are n processes, the probability they are all waiting for I/O is ω^n. But this is true only if there were a processor available for each process. The solution in a single-CPU system is a bit more complicated.

At any time, the system may have between 0 and n processes waiting on I/O. Let S_i represent the state where i processes are waiting on I/O. Let P_i represent the probability the system is in state S_i. Let λdt represent the probability that a running process will issue an I/O request in the next time instant. Let μdt represent the probability that a previously issued I/O request will be completed in the next time instant.

The probability that while in state S_i, the system will go into state S_{i+1} is the same as the probability, λdt, that the running process will issue an I/O request. The probability that while in state S_i, the system will go into state S_{i-1} is the same as the probability, $i\lambda dt$, that any of the i I/O requests will be completed. See Fig. 2-3.

If one looks at the transitions between states over time, the number of transitions $S_i \rightarrow S_{i+1}$ must match the number of transitions $S_{i+1} \rightarrow S_i$ (what goes up, must come done). Thus, the probability of either transition occurring must be the same, yielding the equation:

$$\lambda dt P_i = (i + 1)\mu dt P_{i+1}$$

Setting i to 0 yields

$$\lambda dt P_0 = \mu dt P_1$$

$$P_1 = \left(\frac{\lambda dt}{\mu dt}\right)P_0 = \left(\frac{\lambda}{\mu}\right)P_0$$

and

$$P_2 = \left(\frac{\lambda dt}{2\mu dt}\right)P_1 = \left(\frac{\lambda}{2\mu}\right)P_1 = \left(\frac{1}{2}\right)\left(\frac{\lambda}{\mu}\right)P_1$$

$$P_2 = \left(\frac{1}{2}\right)\left(\frac{\lambda}{\mu}\right)\left[\left(\frac{\lambda}{\mu}\right)P_0\right] = \left(\frac{1}{2}\right)\left(\frac{\lambda}{\mu}\right)^2 P_0$$

and

$$P_3 = \left(\frac{\lambda dt}{3\mu dt}\right)P_2 = \left(\frac{\lambda}{3\mu}\right)P_2 = \left(\frac{1}{3}\right)\left(\frac{\lambda}{\mu}\right)P_2$$

$$P_3 = \left(\frac{1}{3}\right)\left(\frac{\lambda}{\mu}\right)\left[\left(\frac{1}{2}\right)\left(\frac{\lambda}{\mu}\right)^2 P_0\right] = \left(\frac{1}{2 \times 3}\right)\left(\frac{\lambda}{\mu}\right)^3 P_0$$

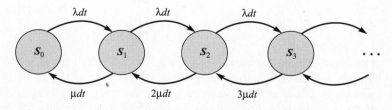

Fig. 2-3.　State transition diagram.

In general,

$$P_i = \left(\frac{1}{i!}\right)\left(\frac{\lambda}{\mu}\right)^i P_0 \qquad \text{(Eq. 2-1)}$$

We also know the system must be in one of the i states. That is, the sum of the state probabilities must be 1.

$$\sum_{i=0}^{n} P_i = 1$$

thus,

$$P_0 = 1 - \sum_{i=1}^{n} P_i$$

Substituting the result of Eq. 2-1 for P_i,

$$P_0 = 1 - \sum_{i=1}^{n} \left(\frac{1}{i!}\right)\left(\frac{\lambda}{\mu}\right)^i P_0$$

$$P_0 = 1 - P_0 \sum_{i=1}^{n} \left(\frac{1}{i!}\right)\left(\frac{\lambda}{\mu}\right)^i$$

$$P_0 + P_0 \sum_{i=1}^{n} \left(\frac{1}{i!}\right)\left(\frac{\lambda}{\mu}\right)^i = 1$$

$$P_0 = \frac{1}{1 + \sum_{i=1}^{n} \left(\frac{1}{i!}\right)\left(\frac{\lambda}{\mu}\right)^i}$$

Since $(1/0!)(\lambda/\mu)^0$ equals 1, the addition of 1 can be pulled into the summation by changing the lower bound for i to 0.

$$P_0 = \frac{1}{\sum_{i=0}^{n} \left(\frac{1}{i!}\right)\left(\frac{\lambda}{\mu}\right)^i}$$

By using Eq. 2-1, we get,

$$P_n = \left(\frac{1}{n!}\right)\left(\frac{\lambda}{\mu}\right)^n P_0$$

Substituting for P_0,

$$P_n = \frac{\left(\frac{\lambda}{\mu}\right)^n}{n! \sum_{i=1}^{n} \left(\frac{1}{i!}\right)\left(\frac{\lambda}{\mu}\right)^i} \qquad \text{(Eq. 2-2)}$$

The average time between I/O requests is $1/\lambda$. (If there is a 10% chance an I/O request will be issued, the average time between requests will be 10 time units.) The average length of an I/O operation is $1/\mu$. Dividing the average I/O time by the sum of the average I/O time and the average time between requests, yields the average wait time.

$$\omega = \frac{\dfrac{1}{\mu}}{\dfrac{1}{\mu} + \dfrac{1}{\lambda}}$$

$$\omega = \frac{\lambda}{\lambda + \mu}$$

$$\omega\lambda + \omega\mu = \lambda$$

$$\omega\mu = \lambda - \omega\lambda$$

$$\omega\mu = \lambda \times (1 - \omega)$$

$$\frac{\omega}{(1 - \omega)} = \frac{\lambda}{\mu}$$

Substituting for λ/μ in Eq. 2-2,

$$P_n = \frac{\left(\dfrac{\omega}{(1-\omega)}\right)^n}{n! \displaystyle\sum_{i=1}^{n} \left(\dfrac{1}{i!}\right)\left(\dfrac{\omega}{(1-\omega)}\right)^i}$$

2.6 For each of the following transitions between process states, indicate whether the transition is possible. If it is possible, give an example of one thing that would cause it.

(*a*) Run → ready

(*b*) Run → blocked

(*c*) Run → swapped-blocked

(*d*) Blocked → run

(*e*) Run → terminated

Answer:

(*a*) Possible, when a process's time quantum expires

(*b*) Possible, when a process issues an I/O request

(*c*) Not possible, although process could first go to the blocked state, then the swapped-blocked

(*d*) Not possible, although process could first go to the ready state, then to the run state

(*e*) Possible, when a process terminates itself

2.7 Given a system with n processes, how many possible ways can those processes be scheduled?

Answer:

This is a combinatorics problem of how many ways n objects can be ordered. When selecting the first object, one has n possible choices. For the second object, $n - 1$.

Each subsequent selection involves one less choice. The total number of possibilities is computed by multiplying all the possibilities at each point, making the answer *n*!.

2.8 On a system using round-robin scheduling, what would be the effect of including one process twice in the list of processes?

Answer:

In round robin, all ready processes are given equal access to the CPU. CPU time is divided equally among the processes. If a process was listed twice, it would be granted twice the CPU time of the other processes.

2.9 For the processes listed in Table 2-2, draw a chart illustrating their execution using:
(*a*) First-Come First-Served
(*b*) Shortest Job First
(*c*) Shortest Remaining Time
(*d*) Round Robin (**quantum = 2**)
(*e*) Round Robin (**quantum = 1**)

Table 2-2 Process Scheduling Data.

Process	Arrival Time	Processing Time
A	0.000	3
B	1.001	6
C	4.001	4
D	6.001	2

Answer:

(*a*) First-Come First-Served

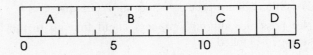

The processes are executed in the order they are received.

(*b*) Shortest Job First

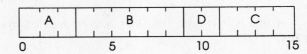

Process A starts executing; it is the only choice at time 0. At time 3, B is the only process in the queue. At time 9 when B completes, process D runs because it is shorter than process C.

(c)   Shortest Remaining Time

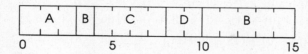

Process A starts executing; it is the only choice at time 0. It remains running when process B arrives because its remaining time is less. At time 3, process B is the only process in the queue. At time 4.001, process C arrives and starts running because its remaining time (4) is less than process B's remaining time (4.999). At time 6.001, process C remains running because its remaining time (1.999) is less than process D's remaining time (2). When process C terminates, process D runs because its remaining time is less than that of process B.

(d)   Round Robin **(quantum = 2)**

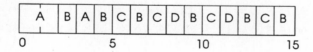

When process A's first time quantum expires, process B runs. At time 4, process A is restarted and process B returns to the ready queue. At time 4.001, process C enters the ready queue after process B. At time 5, process A terminates and process B runs. At time 6.001, process D enters the ready queue behind process C. Starting at time 7, processes C, D, B, and C run in sequence.

(e)   Round Robin **(quantum = 1)**

Process A runs for two time-slices since process B does not arrive until 1.001. Process B runs at time 4 since process C does not arrive until 4.001. Process B runs again at time 6 since process D does not arrive until 6.001. Process D enters the ready queue behind process C. From time 7 on, execution cycles through processes C, D, and B.

2.10   For the processes listed in Table 2-2, what is the average turnaround time (rounding to the nearest hundredth) using:

(a)   First-Come First-Served

(b)   Shortest Job First

(c)   Shortest Remaining Time

(d)   Round Robin **(quantum = 2)**

(e)   Round Robin **(quantum = 1)**

Answer:

Turnaround time is computed by subtracting the time the process entered the system from the time it terminated.

(a) $((3 - 0) + (9 - 1) + (13 - 4) + (15 - 6))/4 = 7.25$

(b) $((3 - 0) + (9 - 1) + (15 - 4) + (11 - 6))/4 = 6.75$

(c) $((3 - 0) + (15 - 1) + (8 - 4) + (10 - 6))/4 = 6.25$

(d) $((5 - 0) + (13 - 1) + (15 - 4) + (11 - 6))/4 = 8.25$

(e) $((4 - 0) + (15 - 1) + (14 - 4) + (12 - 6))/4 = 8.50$

2.11   For the processes listed in Table 2-2, what is the wait time (rounding to the nearest hundredth) for each process using:

(a)   First-Come First-Served

(b)   Shortest Job First

(c)   Shortest Remaining Time

(d)   Round Robin (**quantum = 2**)

(e)   Round Robin (**quantum = 1**)

Answer:

Wait time can be computed by subtracting a process's execution time from its turnaround time.

(a)   A: $(3 - 3) = 0$,   B: $(8 - 6) = 2$,   C: $(9 - 4) = 5$,   D: $(9 - 2) = 7$

(b)   A: $(3 - 3) = 0$,   B: $(8 - 6) = 2$,   C: $(11 - 4) = 7$,   D: $(5 - 2) = 3$

(c)   A: $(3 - 3) = 0$,   B: $(14 - 6) = 8$,   C: $(4 - 4) = 0$,   D: $(4 - 2) = 2$

(d)   A: $(5 - 3) = 2$,   B: $(12 - 6) = 6$,   C: $(11 - 4) = 7$,   D: $(5 - 2) = 3$

(e)   A: $(4 - 3) = 1$,   B: $(14 - 6) = 8$,   C: $(10 - 4) = 6$,   D: $(6 - 2) = 4$

2.12   For the processes listed in Table 2-2, what is the average throughput using:

(a)   First-Come First-Served

(b)   Shortest Job First

(c)   Shortest Remaining Time

(d)   Round Robin (**quantum = 2**)

(e)   Round Robin (**quantum = 1**)

Answer:

The answer is the same for all cases. Each algorithm completed 4 jobs in 15 time units or 3.75 time units per job.

2.13   For the processes listed in Table 2-3, draw a chart illustrating their execution using priority scheduling. A larger priority number has higher priority.

(a)   Preemptive

(b)   Nonpreemptive

Table 2-3. Process Scheduling Data.

Process	Arrival Time	Burst	Priority
A	0.0000	4	3
B	1.0001	3	4
C	2.0001	3	6
D	3.0001	5	5

Answer:

(*a*) Preemptive

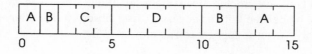

Process A runs until process B arrives. Process B preempts process A and runs until it is preempted by process C. After process C terminates, process D runs. After process D, the lower-priority process B and process A run.

(*b*) Nonpreemptive

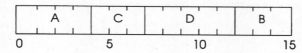

Process A runs to completion. When it terminates, the three other processes are all waiting to run. They run in the order of their priority: C, D, and B.

2.14 For the processes listed in Table 2-3, what is the turnaround time (rounding to the nearest hundredth) for each process?

(*a*) Preemptive

(*b*) Nonpreemptive

Answer:

(*a*) A: $15 - 0 = 15$,   B: $12 - 1 = 11$,   C: $5 - 2 = 3$,   D: $10 - 3 = 7$

(*b*) A: $4 - 0 = 4$,   B: $15 - 1 = 14$,   C: $7 - 2 = 5$,   D: $12 - 3 = 9$

2.15 For the processes listed in Table 2-3, what is the average throughput?

(*a*) Preemptive

(*b*) Nonpreemptive

Answer:

The answer is the same for all cases. Each algorithm completed 4 jobs in 15 time units or 3.75 time units per job.

2.16   On a system using multitlevel feedback queues, a totally CPU-bound process requires 40 seconds to execute. If the first queue uses a time quantum of 2 and at each level the time quantum increases by 5 time-units, how many times will the job be interrupted and on what queue will it be when it terminates?

Answer:

The process will be interrupted at time 2 in the first queue, time $2 + 7$ in the second queue, time $9 + 12$ the third queue, time $21 + 17$ the fourth queue, and will be running in the fifth queue when it terminates. There were four interrupts.

2.17   On a Unix system, the **nice** system call allows one to increase or decrease the priority value associated with a process. A user observes that after increasing their process's priority value, it appears to run slower. Why?

Answer:

On Unix, a high process priority value results in a lower selection priority. To increase a process's priority one must lower its priority value.

2.18   Is a nonpreemptive scheduling algorithm a good choice for an interactive system? Briefly, why?

Answer:

No. Once a process gains control of the CPU, it retains control until it blocks or it terminates. A process could execute for an extended period of time doing neither. Other processes on the system would not be able to execute, producing unacceptable response time.

2.19   A system uses the following preemptive priority scheduling algorithm (processes with larger priority numbers have higher priority). Processes enter the system with a priority of 0. While waiting on the ready queue, a process's priority changes at rate α. While running, a process's priority changes at rate β.

(a)   What is the algorithm that results from $\beta > \alpha > 0$?

(b)   What is the algorithm that results from $\alpha < \beta < 0$?

Answer:

(a)   While in the ready state, a process's priority increases. Thus, the process that has been in the ready state the longest will have the highest priority. The process that is running has its priority increased at a rate faster than any process in the ready state. So, no process in the ready state will ever preempt a running process. Running to termination, the process that has been in the ready state the longest is first-come first-served.

(b)   As soon as a process enters the system, its priority starts decreasing. A new process will have the highest priority and be immediately made runnable. When a running process terminates, the process that has been in the ready queue the shortest will have the highest priority. The algorithm is Last-In First-Out.

2.20 Given a system using the shortest-job-first algorithm for short-term scheduling and exponential averaging with $\alpha = 0.5$, what would be the next expected burst time for a process with burst times of 5, 8, 3, and 5, and an initial value for e_1 of 10?

Answer:

Solving for the various values of e:

$$e_1 = 10$$
$$e_2 = 0.5 \times 5 + 0.5 \times 10$$
$$e_2 = 7.5$$
$$e_3 = 0.5 \times 8 + 0.5 \times 7.5$$
$$e_3 = 7.75$$
$$e_4 = 0.5 \times 3 + 0.5 \times 7.75$$
$$e_4 = 5.375$$
$$e_5 = 0.5 \times 5 + 0.5 \times 5.375$$
$$e_5 = 5.1875$$

2.21 In what way is shortest-job-first scheduling just a particular form of priority scheduling?

Answer:

Shortest job first is priority scheduling with the expected processing time being the priority number. In this case, the process with the smallest priority number has the highest priority.

2.22 On a system using round-robin scheduling, let s represent the time needed to perform a process switch, q represent the round-robin time quantum, and r represent the average time a process runs before blocking on I/O. Give a formula for CPU efficiency given the following.

(a) $q = \infty$
(b) $q > r$
(c) $s < q < r$
(d) $s = q < r$
(e) q nearly 0

Answer:

(a) Processes will run until they block. For each cycle, s units of overhead will be needed to accomplish r units of useful work. CPU efficiency is $r/(r+s)$.

(b) Since processes will still run until they block, the answer is the same as for part (a).

(c) The number of switches required will be r/q, making the time wasted on switches sr/q. CPU efficiency is $r/(r+sr/q) = q/(q+s)$.

(*d*) Same answer as above except with $q = s$, the equation evaluates to $\frac{1}{2}$.

(*e*) Using the equation in part (*c*), as q goes to 0, CPU efficiency goes to 0.

2.23 To what degree do the following algorithms favor CPU-bound processes?

(*a*) First-Come First-Served

(*b*) Shortest Job First

(*c*) Shortest Remaining Time

(*d*) Round Robin

(*e*) Multilevel Feedback Queues

Answer:

First-come first-served is the only algorithm that favors CPU-bound jobs. I/O-bound jobs will only use the CPU briefly, blocking on I/O and releasing the CPU. CPU-bound jobs will have relatively short waits to obtain the CPU and will be able to retain use of the CPU for extended periods of time. Shortest job first and shortest remaining time favor short jobs. Being nonpreemptive, shortest job first will be more favorable to CPU-bound jobs than shortest remaining time, for the same reason first-come first-served favors them. Round robin and multilevel feedback queues generally treat all processes the same.

2.24 Give an example of a situation where it might be useful to have a program execute under the effective user of its owner rather than the real user executing the program.

Answer:

A program that allows users to schedule appointments for the program's owner. The program looks in a database that may only be modified by the program's owner, and schedules appointments into available time slots. The process executing the program requires write access to the scheduling database. The user executing the program should not be provided write access to that database; if they had it, they could erase other users' previously scheduled appointments.

Supplementary Problems

2.25 For each of the following transitions between process states, indicate whether or not the transition is possible. If it is possible, give an example of one thing that would cause it.

(*a*) Ready → run

(*b*) Ready → swapped-blocked

(*c*) Ready → held

(*d*) Blocked → ready

(*e*) Swapped-blocked → swapped-ready

2.26 Given a system that uses round-robin scheduling, assume it can perform a context-switch in zero time. Each process is allowed to run only one instruction before the next instruction is allocated to the CPU. The ready queue always contains n processes. If a process takes t seconds to execute in a uniprocessing environment, how long will it take to execute on this system?

2.27 On a system using nonpreemptive scheduling, processes with expected run times of 5, 18, 9, and 12 are in the ready queue. In what order should they be run to minimize wait time?

2.28 For the processes listed in Table 2-4, draw a chart illustrating their execution using:
  (a) First-Come First-Served
  (b) Shortest Job First
  (c) Shortest Remaining Time
  (d) Round Robin (**quantum = 2**)
  (e) Round Robin (**quantum = 1**)

Table 2-4. Process Scheduling Data.

Process	Arrival Time	Processing Time
A	0.000	4
B	2.001	7
C	3.001	2
D	3.002	2

2.29 For the processes listed in Table 2-4, what is the turnaround time (rounding to the nearest hundredth) of each process using:
  (a) First-Come First-Served
  (b) Shortest Job First
  (c) Shortest Remaining Time
  (d) Round Robin (**quantum = 2**)
  (e) Round Robin (**quantum = 1**)

2.30 For the processes listed in Table 2-4, what is the average wait time (rounding to the nearest hundredth) using:
  (a) First-Come First-Served
  (b) Shortest Job First
  (c) Shortest Remaining Time
  (d) Round Robin (**quantum = 2**)
  (e) Round Robin (**quantum = 1**)

2.31 For the processes listed in Table 2-5, draw a chart illustrating their execution using priority scheduling. A larger priority number has higher priority.

(*a*) Preemptive

(*b*) Nonpreemptive

Table 2-5. Process Scheduling Data.

Process	Arrival Time	Burst	Priority
A	0.0000	5	4
B	2.0001	4	2
C	2.0001	2	6
D	4.0001	4	3

2.32 For the processes listed in Table 2-5, what is the average wait time (rounding to the nearest tenth)?

(*a*) Preemptive

(*b*) Nonpreemptive

2.33 On a system using multilevel feedback queues, a totally CPU-bound process requires 50 seconds to execute. If the first queue uses a time quantum of 5, and at each lower level the time quantum doubles, how many times will the job be interrupted and on what queue will it be when it terminates?

2.34 Given a system using the shortest-job-first algorithm for short-term scheduling and exponential averaging with $\alpha = 0.4$, what would be the next expected burst time for a process with burst times of 2, 7, 4, and 5, and an initial value for e_1 of 5?

2.35 For nonpreemptive scheduling algorithms, prove shortest job first yields the lowest overall wait time.

2.36 On a system using multilevel feedback queues, what is the advantage of using a different time quantum in each queue?

2.37 Some scheduling algorithms are parameterized; their overall behavior is influenced by a parameter that may be tuned to obtain optimal performance. Indicate which of the following algorithms are fixed and which are parameterized.

(*a*) First-Come First-Served

(*b*) Shortest Job First

(*c*) Shortest Remaining Time

(*d*) Round Robin

(*e*) Multilevel Feedback Queues

2.38 Round-robin scheduling behaves differently depending on its time quantum. Can the time quantum be set to make round robin behave the same as any of the following algorithms? If so, how?

    (*a*) First-Come First-Served

    (*b*) Shortest Job First

    (*c*) Shortest Remaining Time

2.39 To what degree do the following algorithms favor short processes?

    (*a*) First-Come First-Served

    (*b*) Shortest Job First

    (*c*) Shortest Remaining Time

    (*d*) Round Robin

    (*e*) Multilevel Feedback Queues

Answers to Supplementary Problems

2.25 (*a*) Possible, when a process is selected by the short-term scheduler

    (*b*) Not possible

    (*c*) Not possible

    (*d*) Possible, when an I/O operation completes

    (*e*) Possible, when an I/O operation completes

2.26 *nt*

2.27 5, 9, 12, 18 (shortest job first)

2.28 (*a*) First-Come First-Served

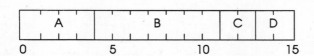

    (*b*) Shortest Job First

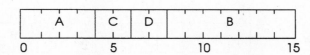

(c)　Shortest Remaining Time

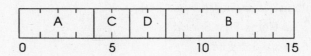

(d)　Round Robin **(quantum = 2)**

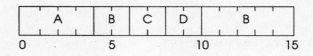

(e)　Round Robin **(quantum = 1)**

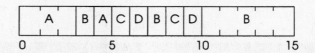

2.29　(a)　A: 4,　　B: 9,　　C: 10,　　D: 12
　　　　(b)　A: 4,　　B: 13,　　C: 3,　　D: 5
　　　　(c)　A: 4,　　B: 13,　　C: 3,　　D: 5
　　　　(d)　A: 4,　　B: 13,　　C: 5,　　D: 7
　　　　(e)　A: 5,　　B: 13,　　C: 6,　　D: 7

2.30　(a)　5.00
　　　　(b)　2.50
　　　　(c)　2.50
　　　　(d)　3.50
　　　　(e)　4.00

2.31　(a)　Preemptive

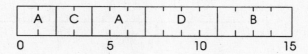

　　　　(b)　Nonpreemptive

2.32   (a)   3.50

          (b)   3.75

2.33   After three interrupts, the process will terminate in the fourth queue.

2.34 $e_5 = 4.7888$

2.35   Proof by contradiction. Assume some sequence of processes other than shortest job
           first yields the lowest overall wait time. There exist some processes in that sequence
           p_i and p_n with wait time w_i and w_n such that $(w_n - w_i) > 0$ with $i > n$. Let W be the
           sum of all w_X for $x > n$ and $x < i$. Now let's look what happens to overall wait time if
           we swap the scheduling of processes p_i and p_n. The wait times w_X, for all $x < n$ or
           $x > i$, will be unchanged. The wait time for the original p_n will increase by $W + w_i$.
           The wait time for the original p_i will decrease by $W + w_n$. The wait time for all w_X,
           $x > n$ and $x < i$, will change by $w_i - w_n$. The net change in wait time, c, can therefore
           be expressed by the equations:

$$c = ((n - i) - 1)(w_i - w_n) + (W + w_i) - (W + w_n)$$
$$c = ((n - i) - 1)(w_i - w_n) + w_i - w_n$$
$$c = (n - i)(w_i - w_n)$$

           Since $n > i$ and $w_i < w_n$, c must be negative. Swapping the order of the processes
           produced a lower overall wait time. This contradicts the assumption that there is some
           sequence of processes other than shortest job first that yields the lowest overall wait
           time. Thus, shortest job first yields the lowest overall wait time.

2.36   Jobs in the highest-level queues have the highest priority. The longer time quantum
           for the lower-level queues compensates for their lower priority providing a fairer
           distribution of CPU time to the different kinds of processes.

2.37   (a)   Fixed

          (b)   Fixed

          (c)   Fixed

          (d)   Parameterized

          (e)   Parameterized

2.38   (a)   A time quantum of ∞ yields first-come first-served scheduling.

          (b)   Not possible.

          (c)   Not possible.

2.39   (a)   First-come first-served is relatively unfriendly to short jobs. Short jobs that
                 follow long jobs must wait until the long job releases the CPU.

          (b)   Clearly favors short jobs.

(*c*) Favors short jobs even more than shortest job first since it will preempt a longer job currently running on the CPU.

(*d*) Neutral toward short jobs, treating all jobs equally.

(*e*) Generally neutral toward short jobs, although perhaps they fare slightly better in multilevel feedback queues than in round robin. Large CPU-bound jobs move to lower-priority queues where they can only execute if no other processes are ready.

CHAPTER 3

Interprocess Communication and Synchronization

Multiprogramming allows multiple processes to run concurrently, even on a system with only a single processor. Application developers may take advantage of this concurrent capability in the software solutions they develop. Operating systems that support multiprogramming provide support for these concurrent applications. Issues encountered in writing concurrent applications also occur in designing operating system code that must deal with concurrency in I/O devices and handling the interrupts those devices generate (not to mention operating system code for systems with multiple processors). Interprocess communication and synchronization primitives are important to operating system designers both for use within the operating system and as a service to provide to applications running on the operating system.

A *cooperating process* is one that shares information with or controls the sequence of instructions executed by another process. Information sharing may achieved by using shared memory locations, by passing information through shared files, or by using operating system services provided for that purpose.

3.1   Interprocess Communication

Files are the most commonly used mechanism for information sharing. Information written into a file by one process can be read by another. This mechanism is used by processes whether they execute concurrently or not. The amount of information that can be shared is limited only by the file size capacity of the file system.

Shared memory locations provide another mechanism for sharing information. On systems that support threads, shared memory is integral to the thread concept. Mechanisms also exist for sharing memory between processes. Some operating systems support a supervisor call that creates a shared memory space. On other systems, the file system allows for the creation of a RAM disk. A RAM disk is a virtual disk created from memory space. Files stored on the RAM disk are actually stored in memory.

A signaling mechanism (introduced in the previous chapter) can also be used to communicate information. Consider a system with two signaling primitives.

send_signal(pid,signalId)
Sends signal number *signalId* to the process with identification number *pid*.
react_signal(function,signalId)
Configures the process so if it should receive signal number *signalId*, it will respond by jumping to function *function*.

By associating a meaning with different signal numbers, processes can communicate information among themselves.

Many operating systems support an explicit messaging system for sending messages between processes. Some of the factors in designing a messaging system include the following.

- **To what kind of object is a message sent?**
  The destination object can be a process, a mailbox, or a communication buffer and can be identified by a name or an identification number.

- **How are processes associated with message objects?**
  The operating system can require any communication to be preceded by a primitive which establishes a connection with the destination object. Any process can be permitted to communicate with the destination object, or some restrictions could be imposed. If the destination object is a mailbox or a communication buffer, objects can be created automatically, a fixed number of predefined objects may exist or there may be a primitive to create the object.

- **How many processes may share a messaging object?**
  Separate limits can be placed on the number of processes which can read or write the message object. For example, any number of processes might be permitted to write to the object but only one could read messages from that object.

- **Is the messaging object bidirectional or unidirectional?**
  A process can be limited to either read or write access but not both. Bidirectional access can be permitted, allowing processes to both read and write to a message object.

- **How many messaging objects may a process access?**
  The operating systems may impose systemwide limits or limits on the number of objects that can be used for communications between two processes.

- **Are messages fixed or variable-sized?**
  If variable-sized, the operating system can impose a maximum size.

- **How many messages can be stored in a message object?**
  Message buffering can either be nonexistent, bounded, unbounded, or acknowledgement-based. Nonexistent buffering requires the send operation to block the sending process until the recipient receives the message. This type of transmission is called a *rendezvous*. Bounded buffering causes the send operation to block only if the buffer is full. With unbounded buffering, the sender is never blocked attempting to send a message. Acknowledgement buffering causes the sender to block until the receiver returns a special kind of acknowledgment reply. Both sender and receiver are free to continue their execution once the receiver has issued its reply.

- **Are messages sent by value or by reference?**
  Messages sent by reference require less overhead, but can be changed after they have been sent. For messages sent between processes, passing messages by reference violates the principle that each process should be provided an independent address space.

- **What happens if a process terminates while another process is blocked waiting on some action by the now terminated process?**
  Typically, either the blocking primitive returns with an error status indicating it failed or the blocked process is also terminated.

Consider the following three implementations of a message-passing system. The first is based on direct communication between processes.

int send_process(pid,message)
  Send *message* to the process with identification number *pid*. The message is copied into the receiver's message queue. Any process can send a message to any other process. This primitive never blocks because an unlimited number of messages can be queued for receipt. Messages are strings of any length. This primitive fails if the destination process does not exist.

int receive_process(pid,message)
  Receive the next message from the process with identification number *pid* and put that message in *message*. Messages are received in the order they are sent. If no messages are in the queue, block until a message is sent. If *pid* contains the special value of 0, receive a message from any process (the assumption is that no process may have an identification number of 0). The return value from this primitive is the process identification number of the sending process. This primitive fails if a sending process is specified and does not exist.

In the second scheme, message passing is accomplished indirectly through a mailbox.

int create_mailbox(mbx)
  Create a mailbox named *mbx*. This primitive fails if the mailbox already exists.
int delete_mailbox(mbx)
  Delete a mailbox named *mbx*. This primitive fails if the process issuing the primitive is not the owner of the mailbox or if the mailbox does not exist.
int send_mailbox(mbx,message)
  Send *message* to the mailbox with identification name *mbx*. The message is

copied into the mailbox. Any process can send a message to any mailbox. The sender is blocked until the message is received. Messages are a string of any length. This primitive fails if the mailbox does not exist.

int receive_mailbox(mbx,message)

Receive the message from the mailbox with identification name *mbx* and put that message in *message*. Messages are received in the order they are sent. If no messages are in the queue, block until a message is sent. This primitive fails if the process issuing the primitive is not the owner of the mailbox or if the mailbox does not exist.

The final example is based on a buffered communication channel called a *pipe*. Unlike the previous examples where the message destination was an identification number or a name that could be specified by any process, the sending and receiving primitives use a communication channel descriptor associated only with the process that created the pipe and the creating process's child processes.

void create_pipe(pdr,pdw)

Create a pipe. Store the value of a read descriptor in *pdr* and a write descriptor in *pdw*. This primitive never fails.

int close(pd)

For the process issuing this primitive, close the descriptor *pd*. The *pd* may be either a read or a write descriptor. This primitive fails if the descriptor is not open.

int send_pipe(pdw,byte)

Write *byte* into the pipe associated with write descriptor *pdw*. If the pipe already contains 4096 bytes, this primitive blocks until a read operation makes room for additional bytes in the pipe. This primitive fails if the descriptor is not open or if no processes have this pipe open for reading.

int receive_pipe(pdr,byte)

Read a byte into *byte* from the pipe associated with read descriptor *pdr*. Bytes are read in the order they were written into the pipe. If the pipe is empty and no processes have the pipe open for writing, return a special value indicating the pipe is empty. Otherwise, the receiving process should block if the pipe is empty. This primitive fails if the descriptor is not open.

Cooperating processes face two major problems: starvation and *deadlock*. Just as some scheduling algorithms may indefinitely delay a process the opportunity to execute, the exact nature of the cooperation between processes may also result in starvation. Consider, for example, an implementation of mailboxes that allowed multiple processes to read from a mailbox and did not service read requests in first-come first-served order. If one process issued a steady stream of read requests and all its requests were satisfied first, it would be possible for the request of another process to never be satisfied.

Deadlock occurs when two or more processes block waiting for an event under the control of the other blocked process, for example, an application where process *A* sends messages to process *B* through one mailbox, and process *B* sends messages to process *A* through a second mailbox. Consider what would happen if both processes attempt to read an incoming message before they send a message. Both will block waiting for the other process to send, a condition that can never be satisfied.

In addition to starvation and deadlock, processes that share data face the problem of data inconsistency. Consider, for example, two processes, each accomplishing some task, then concurrently attempting to increment a shared variable that maintains a count of the number of tasks performed by the cooperating processes. If the value of the count had been 10, after incrementing by both processes, the count should be 12. But if both processes access the value of the count at the same time, both will be incrementing 10, and both will be storing 11 back in the count variable. The code functions correctly only if no process accesses the shared variable in the middle of another process's attempt to increment the variable.

3.2   Process Synchronization

Situations where the correctness of the computation performed by cooperating processes can be affected by the relative timing of the processes' execution is called a *race condition*. To be considered correct, cooperating processes may not be subject to race conditions.

When cooperating processes run on a system with a single processor, concurrency is simulated by the processes sharing the CPU. The scheduling algorithm determines the relative timing of cooperating processes. The result may differ widely from an idealized perception of parallel execution. Not only is timing dependent on the scheduling algorithm used, it is also dependent on the system load created by other processes on the system. On multiprocessor systems, there is no guarantee all processors work at equivalent speeds. Depending on which processes are allocated to which processors, timing can differ drastically.

3.2.1 CRITICAL SECTION

Code executed by a process can be grouped into sections, some of which require access to shared resources, and others that do not. The sections of code that require access to shared resources are called *critical sections*. To avoid race conditions, a mechanism is needed to appropriately synchronize the execution within critical sections.

Mechanisms to control access to critical sections will be assumed to operate under the following conditions.

- **Relative Speed:** No assumptions may be made about the relative execution speeds of the cooperating processes except execution of each process proceeds at some nonzero speed.

- **No Indivisibility:** No assumptions may be made about the indivisibility of machine instructions except that which is included as part of the definition of a synchronizing primitive. Instructions may be broken up into a number of atomic actions; execution of other processes may be interleaved among those atomic actions. However, it may be assumed that access to shared memory locations is serialized so that no two processes may be reading or writing to a memory location simultaneously.

- **Bounded Use:** A process only executes in its critical section for some finite time and may not terminate while in its critical section.

To ensure correctness, mechanisms to control access to critical sections should satisfy the following requirements.

- **Mutual Exclusion:** When one process is in a critical section that accesses a set of shared resources, no other process may be in a critical section that accesses any of those shared resources. (It is possible for processes to have multiple critical sections, each accessing independent resources. In such a case, one process could safely execute in a critical section that accesses the first resource while another process was in a critical section that accesses the second resource. In this book, however, it will be assumed all critical sections access the same set of shared resources. Such an assumption simplifies the treatment of the material significantly, and extension of the principles to situations containing independent critical sections is obvious.)

- **Progress:** When no process is in its critical section, and one or more processes are waiting to enter the critical section, the decision as to which process will enter the critical section will involve only those waiting processes and must be made within a finite amount of time. A process that terminates outside its critical section may not prevent other processes from entering their critical sections.

- **Bounded Wait:** When a process requests access to a critical section, a decision that grants it access may not be delayed indefinitely. A process may not be denied access because of starvation or deadlock.

A number of mechanisms have been used to implement mutual exclusion. The mechanisms include hardware-supported solutions, operating system primitives, software solutions, and constructs implemented in programming languages.

For most of the mechanisms presented, two implementation details affect their utility: blocking and wait lists. When a process is blocked from entering a critical section, it can wait until the blocked event is satisfied by either executing instructions that do nothing (*busy-waiting*) or by entering a blocked state. Obviously, busy-waiting makes use of the CPU less efficient. However, the blocking technique used is irrelevant to the proper function of the mutual exclusion mechanism.

When a process leaves its critical section, and one or more processes are blocked awaiting entrance to their critical sections, the mutual exclusion mechanism must select which blocked process will enter its critical section next. The selection mechanism should ensure no process suffers from starvation.

3.2.2 INTERRUPT DISABLING

On a single-CPU system, processes do not actually execute in parallel. Concurrency is achieved by interleaving the execution of the ready processes. Once a process gains control of the CPU, it can only lose that control when execution is transferred to code within the operating system. A process can prevent the operating system from executing by not issuing any supervisor call instructions, not executing any instructions that cause a trap, and by disabling interrupts.

Mutual exclusion can be achieved by implementing operating system primitives to disable and enable interrupts. Access to a critical section can be controlled by calling those primitives.

```
DisableInterrupt()
```

```
// Critical Section
```

```
EnableInterrupt()
```

Provided no supervisor calls are issued in the critical section and no traps occur, the process that enters the critical section will retain control of the CPU while in the critical section, guaranteeing its mutually exclusive access. This mechanism is easily implemented and easily incorporated into software. However, it also has important disadvantages.

- It only works in a single-processor environment.
- Interrupts can be lost if not serviced promptly. A process remaining in its critical section for any longer than a brief time would potentially disrupt the proper execution of I/O operations.
- Exclusive access to the CPU while in the critical section could inhibit achievement of the scheduling goals.
- A process waiting to enter its critical section could suffer from starvation.

3.2.3 *TestAndSet* INSTRUCTION

The *TestAndSet* instruction executes as an indivisible atomic action and can be defined as follows.

```
boolean TestAndSet (boolean locked)
{
  if (locked)
    return true;
  else
  {
    locked = true;
    return false;
  }
}
```

TestAndSet can be implemented in a multiprocessor environment. Since it executes as an atomic action, a *TestAndSet* instruction executed on one CPU must complete before another *TestAndSet* can be executed on any other CPU.

A partial solution to controlling critical section access uses a single shared variable.

```
shared boolean lock = false;
// ...
```

```
while (TestAndSet(lock))
    DoNothing();
```

```
// Critical Section
```

```
lock = false;
```

However, this partial solution does leave processes subject to starvation. Additional complexity is needed in the full solution.

```
shared boolean waiting[MAX_PID] = false;
shared boolean lock = false;
int pid = ThisProcessPid();
boolean ts;
int nextPid;
// ...
```

```
waiting[pid]=true;
ts=true;
while (waiting[pid] and ts)
    ts=TestAndSet(lock);
waiting[pid]=false;
```

```
// Critical Section
```

```
nextPid=(pid+1) mod MAX_PID;
while (nextPid !=pid && waiting[nextPid] == false)
    nextPid=(pid+1) mod MAX_PID;
if (nextPid == pid)
    lock = false;
else
    waiting[nextPid] = false;
```

Proof that mutual exclusion is preserved, and starvation is prevented, is left as exercises (Problems 3.3 and 3.22).

3.2.4 SWAP INSTRUCTION

Another instruction, *Swap*, can also be used to implement mutual exclusion. Like *TestAndSet*, it must execute atomically.

```
boolean void Swap(boolean a, boolean b)
{
    boolean temp;
    temp = b;
    b = a;
    a = temp;
}
```

Mutual exclusion is achieved as follows.

```
shared boolean lock = false;
boolean key;
// ...
```

```
key = true;
do
    Swap (lock, key);
while (key);
```

```
// Critical Section
```

```
lock = false;
```

As with *TestAndSet*, a more complete solution that prevents starvation may also be created from the swap instruction.

3.2.5 WAIT AND SIGNAL

The hardware solutions described previously share the disadvantage of using busy-waiting. If, instead of busy-waiting, a process becomes blocked when *TestAndSet* returns *true*, obvious performance benefits can be obtained. The operating system can implement the primitives *Wait* and *Signal* to create that functionality. Assumed in their implementation is a *ProcessQueue* object with operations *Insert* and *Remove*. The *Insert* operation places an object at the tail of queue and changes the process's state to blocked. The *Remove* operation selects the process that has been in the queue the longest and changes its state from blocked to ready (if the queue is empty, *Remove* does nothing).

```
struct WaitSignalVar
{
   boolean lock;
   ProcessQueue queue;
};
void Wait(WaitSignalVar var)
{
   if (TestAndSet(var.lock))
      Var.ProcessQueue.Insert();
}
void Signal(WaitSignalVar var)
{
   var.ProcessQueue.Remove();
   var.lock = false;
}
```

Wait and *Signal* are atomic operations, with *Wait* considered to be terminated when a process is inserted into the queue and blocked.

3.2.6   SEMAPHORES

Controlling synchronization by using an abstract data type called a ***semaphore*** was proposed by Dijkstra in 1965. Semaphores are easily implemented in operating systems and provide a general-purpose solution to controlling access to critical sections.

A semaphore is a nonnegative integer variable upon which two atomic operations are defined: *P* and *V* (named for the Dutch words *proberen* [to test] and *verhogen* [to increment]).

```
Struct semaphore
{
   int count;
   ProcessQueue queue;
};
void P(semaphore s)
{
   if (s.count > 0)
      s.count = s.count - 1;
   else
      s.queue.Insert(); // Block this process
}
void V(semaphore s)
{
   if (s.queue.empty())
      s.count = s.count + 1;
   else
      s.queue.Remove();     // Schedule a process, if any,
                            // blocked on 's'
}
```

Semaphore operations are also sometimes known by the names of *Down* and *Up* or *Wait* and *Signal*. When instantiated, a semaphore's count value may be initialized to any nonnegative value. With an initial value of 1, a semaphore ensures mutually exclusive access if *P* is executed before entering a critical section and *V* upon exiting. By setting the semaphore's initial value to *n*, *P* and *V* can be used to allow up to *n* processes in their critical sections.

A ***binary semaphore*** is a semaphore whose count may only take on the values of 1 or 0.

```
void P(semaphore s)
{
   if (s.count == 1)
     s.count = 0;
   else
     s.queue.Insert();    // Block this process
}
void V(semaphore s)
{
   if (s.queue.empty())
     s.count = 1;
   else
     s.queue.Remove();    // Schedule a process, if any,
     blocked on 's'
}
```

To more clearly distinguish between the types of semaphores, those which can take on any nonnegative value may be referred to as ***general semaphores*** or ***counting semaphores***.

Mutual exclusion is achieved by initializing a semaphore variable to one, executing a *P* operation before entering the critical section, and executing a *V* operation after leaving the critical section.

```
shared semaphore s = 1;
// ...
```

```
P(s);
```

```
// Critical Section
```

```
V(s);
```

3.2.7 DEKKER'S ALGORITHM

Dekker developed an algorithm for two processes based solely on software; no hardware or operating system support was required.

```
// -------------------
// Dekker's Algorithm
```

CHAPTER 3   Interprocess Communication

```
// -------------------
shared boolean wantIn[2] = false;
shared int favored = 1;
int myPid = 0;        // For process 0. Set to 1 for process 1.
int otherPid = 1 - myPid;
```

```
wantIn[myPid] = true;
while (wantIn[otherPid])
{
   if (favored == otherPid)
   {
     wantIn[myPid] = false;
     while (favored == otherPid)
       DoNothing();
     wantIn[myPid] = true;
   }
}
```

```
// Critical Section
```

```
favored = otherPid;
wantIn[myPid] = false;
```

3.2.8 PETERSON'S ALGORITHM

Peterson developed a solution for two processes that was simpler and easier to prove
than Dekker's.

```
// ---------------------
// Peterson's Algorithm
// ---------------------
shared boolean wantIn[2] = false;
shared int turn = 1;
int myPid = 0;        // For process 0. Set to 1 for process 1.
int otherPid = 1 - myPid;
```

```
wantIn[myPid] = true;
turn = otherPid;
while (wantIn[otherPid] && turn == otherPid)
     DoNothing();
```

```
// Critical Section
```

```
wantIn[myPid] = false;
```

Proof that Petersons' algorithm satisfies the requirements of a mechanism to control
access to a critical section is left as an exercise (Problem 3.24).

3.2.9 BAKERY ALGORITHM

Lamport proposed the bakery algorithm, a software solution for N processes.

```
//--------------
/ Bakery Algorithm
//--------------
shared boolean choosing[N] = false;
shared int number[N] = 0;
int myPid = 0;          // For process 0. Set to X for process X.
int jj;
```

```
choosing[myPid] = true;
number[myPid] = MAX(number) + 1;
choosing[myPid] = false;
for (jj=0; jj<N; jj=jj+1)
{
   while (choosing[jj])
     DoNothing();
   while (number[jj] != 0 && ((number[jj] < number[myPid])
 || (number [jj] == number[myPid] && j < i))
     DoNothing();
}
```

```
// Critical Section
```

```
number[myPid] = 0;
```

Proof that the bakery algorithm satisfies the requirements of a mechanism to control access to a critical section is left as an exercise (Problem 3.6).

3.2.10 MONITORS

Although semaphores provide a general-purpose mechanism for controlling access to critical sections, their use does not guarantee that access will be mutually exclusive or deadlock will be avoided. Programming errors, such as omitting a *P* operation before a process enters its critical section, can result in program malfunctions. However, those malfunctions may manifest themselves only if particular execution timing patterns occur. This makes error detection during testing problematic. Even if an error is detected, inability to repeat the error may make locating its cause difficult.

A ***monitor*** is a programming language construct that guarantees appropriate access to critical sections. The code placed before and after a critical section, to control access to that critical section, is generated by the compiler. Controlled access is provided by the language, not the programmer.

Inside a monitor is a collection of initialization code, shared data objects, and functions that may access those objects. Processes that wish to access the shared data may do so only through the execution of monitor functions. Access to the functions is controlled so that only a single process may be executing within the monitor at any time. A process will be placed on an entrance queue and blocked if it calls a monitor function while another process is executing in the monitor. The general form of a monitor is illustrated in Fig. 3-1.

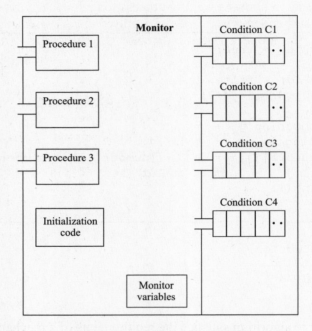

Fig. 3-1. Structure of a monitor.

Actual monitor syntax could look something like the code below.

```
monitor sample
{
    // variable declarations
    int i;
    condition c;
    // function declarations
    void CriticalSectionEntryPoint1 ()
    {
        // function code
    }
    void CriticalSectionEntryPoint2 ()
    {
        // function code
    }
```

```
    sample
    {
     // initialization code
    }
}
```

The *condition* type is a part of the monitor construct. Two operations are permitted on *condition* variables: *cwait* and *csignal*. The *cwait* operation suspends the process invoking it and places that process on a queue associated with that variable. Waiting processes are not considered to be in the monitor.

The *csignal* operation allows a waiting process to reenter the monitor at the point its execution was suspended. However, since only one process may execute in the monitor at a time, the monitor construct cannot allow the signaled process to be restarted while the signaling process is still executing within the monitor. Three possibilities have been proposed for dealing with this situation.

- The signaling process is suspended until the signaled process leaves the monitor.
- The signaled process must wait until the signaling process leaves the monitor.
- The signaling operation may only be executed as the last statement before leaving the monitor. The signaled process may execute immediately.

The third definition will be used in this book.

The major disadvantage of the monitor concept is its lack of implementation in most commonly used programming languages. While semaphores are not included in most languages either, P and V operations are easily added as independent subroutines or as operating system supervisor calls. Monitors cannot easily be added if they are not natively supported by the language.

3.3   Deadlock

Deadlock occurs when each process in a set of processes controls a resource that another process in the set has requested. Each process blocks, waiting for its requested resource to become available. For deadlock to occur, four conditions must hold.

- **Mutual Exclusion**: Each resource may be allocated to only one process at any instant.
- **Hold and Wait**: Processes do not release previously granted resources while waiting for pending requests to be granted.
- **No Preemption**: Previously granted resources may not be taken away from the processes holding them.
- **Circular Wait**: There exists a chain of two or more processes such that each process in the chain holds a resource requested by the next process in the chain.

3.3.1 DEADLOCK PREVENTION

Deadlock can be prevented by never allowing all four conditions to hold. By implementing a policy that makes one of the conditions impossible, the system will be assured to be deadlock-free. However, implementing such a policy may introduce more problems than it solves, as the following analysis shows.

Eliminating mutually exclusive access to any resource is not a practical solution. Some resources cannot be shared. However, in some cases, apparently nonshareable resources can be shared if direct access is not required. For example, a printer appears to be a nonshareable resource. Two users cannot print on the printer simultaneously. However, the exact time that the printing takes place is typically not important. A spooling system allows processes to access a virtual printer simultaneously. The print jobs are sent to the actual printer in a nonshared sequential fashion. Unless direct access to the actual printer is required, spooling eliminates the mutually exclusive access condition for the printer resource.

The hold-and-wait condition will never apply if requests for resources can only be made by processes holding no resources. One strategy enforces this restriction by requiring all resources to be requested before a process starts executing. There are two major disadvantages to this policy. First, a process may not know what resources it will require. The resources needed may depend on its computation. A process requesting every resource it may conceivably need may request resources it never actually uses. Even if the resources are used, forcing the request to occur before the process starts may result in the process holding resources long before they are actually needed. This can lead to poor system performance due to low resource utilization. This strategy is also very susceptible to starvation. A process requesting a number of popular resources may never find them all available at one time.

Another hold-and-wait prevention strategy is to require processes to release all held resources when a request is made. Unfortunately, in most cases this strategy is not practical. For example, after a process has written data to a disk, to release the disk to request a printer jeopardizes the data on the disk. If the disk is allocated to another process, all the stored data could be lost.

Eliminating the non-preemption condition is even less practical than eliminating mutual exclusion. Preempting a resource is essentially forced sharing. Preemption can be applied to devices whose state can be saved and then later restored. For example, a process can be preempted from using a CPU by saving the CPU state. However, the device characteristics necessary to do this are essentially the same as the characteristics needed for creating a shared virtual device for which mutually exclusive access is not required.

Elimination of the circular-wait condition is perhaps the most promising of the prevention techniques. One method for breaking the cycle is to associate each resource with a unique priority number. Processes may only request a resource if its priority is higher than all currently held resources. Using this strategy, any resource can be requested. If the resource does not have a higher priority than all currently held resources, the currently held resource with a higher priority must first be released. In those situations, this approach is similar to the one used to eliminate the hold-and-wait condition, but this strategy is more flexible, allowing resources to be held under some circumstances when an additional request is made. If the priority numbers are chosen wisely, this system may accommodate the needs of many processes. However, it will not work in all cases. There typically is no priority number that will match the needs of all processes.

3.3.2 DEADLOCK AVOIDANCE

Rather than prevent one of the conditions that must be present for deadlock to exist, deadlock can be avoided by never allocating a resource if it may eventually lead to deadlock. A simple way to do this is to allocate resources to only one process at a time. Although not efficient, deadlock clearly cannot occur. In the future, a more generous allocation policy can be implemented with additional information about potential resource needs of all processes.

A system is said to be in a *safe* state if there is a *safe execution sequence*. An execution sequence is an ordering for process execution such that each process, when executed, runs until it terminates or is blocked, and all requests for resources are immediately granted if the resource is available. A safe execution sequence is an execution sequence in which all processes run to completion.

An *unsafe* state is a state that is not safe, not necessarily a deadlocked state (Fig. 3-2). An unsafe state may currently not be deadlocked, but there is at least one sequence of requests from processes that would make the system deadlocked. If that sequence of requests occurs, no set of responses to those requests would allow the operating system to avoid a deadlocked state.

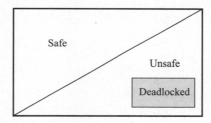

Fig. 3-2.   Relationship between safe, unsafe, and deadlock states.

An algorithm for determining whether or not a state is safe must be supplied with the following information: the current allocation of resources to each process, the maximum number of each resource a process might request, and the total number of each resource currently available in the system. The algorithm for a system with P processes and R resources can be summarized as follows.

```
// -----------------------------------------------
// Algorithm to determine if a system is in a safe state.
// -----------------------------------------------
int max[P][R];
int current [P][R]
int avail[R];
```

```
int done[P] = false;
boolean safe;
int pp = 0;
while (pp<P)
{
    if (done[pp]) continue;
    // -------------------------------------------
    // If only this process's requests are granted, could
    // it run to completion?
    // -------------------------------------------
    for (int rr=0; rr<R; rr++)
    {
        if (max[pp][rr] - current[pp][rr] <= avail[rr])
        {
            // -----------------------------------
            // No. Not enough of resource rr is available.
            // Go to next process.
            // -----------------------------------
            pp = pp+ 1;
            continue 2; // Go to next iteration of outer loop
        }
    }
    // ---------------------------------------------
    // Yes. Reset system to the state it would be in if this
    // process did run to completion, releasing all its
    // resources. Then start all over.
    // ---------------------------------------------
    for (int rr=0; rr<R; rr++)
        avail[rr] = avail[rr] + current[pp][rr];
    done[pp] = true;
    pp = 0;
}
// ------------------------------------
// If all processes could run to completion,
// system state is safe.
// ------------------------------------
safe = true;
for (int pp=0; pp<P; pp++)
    if (! Done[pp]) safe = false;
```

The **banker's algorithm** makes decisions on granting a resource based on whether or not granting the request will put the system into an unsafe state. When a request is received, the algorithm first checks that the process is not requesting more resources than its specified maximum allocation, raising an error exception for an invalid request. Given a valid request, the number of resources requested is compared to the number of resources available. If not enough resources are available, the request is denied. If sufficient resources are available, the algorithm creates a modified version of the current state that reflects the effect of granting the request. The algorithm then checks if the modified version of the system state is safe. The resource is granted if and only if the modified version of the system state is safe.

While very elegant in design, the banker's algorithm has one major disadvantage. It requires knowledge of the maximum number of resources each process might request. Such information is not available on most systems. Thus, few systems use the banker's algorithm.

3.3.3 DEADLOCK DETECTION

Instead of trying to prevent or avoid deadlock, systems could allow deadlock to happen (hoping it occurs infrequently), and recover from deadlock when it does occur. Such a strategy requires mechanisms for detecting and recovering from deadlock.

A resource allocation graph may be used to model the state of resource allocations and requests. In such a graph, processes are drawn as circles, resources as rectangles. Within a resource rectangle, a dot is drawn for each instance of that resource. For each pending resource request, a direct arrow is drawn from the process to the resource rectangle. For each granted request, a direct arrow is drawn from a resource dot to the process. Figure 3-3 shows the resource graph for the system described in Table 3-1.

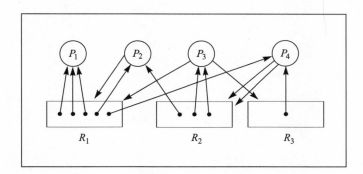

Fig. 3-3.   Resource allocation graph.

Table 3-1.   Resource Usage.

Process	Current Allocation			Outstanding Requests			Resources Available		
	R_1	R_2	R_3	R_1	R_2	R_3	R_1	R_2	R_3
P_1	3	0	0	0	0	0			
P_2	1	1	0	1	0	0	0	0	0
P_3	0	2	0	1	0	1			
P_4	1	0	1	0	2	0			

A reduced resource allocation graph can be used to determine whether or not deadlock exists. To reduce a resource allocation graph, the arrows associated with each process and each resource are checked.

- If a resource has only arrows pointing away from it (meaning it has no requests pending), erase all its arrows.
- If a process has only arrows pointing toward it (meaning all its requests have been granted), erase all its arrows.
- If a process has arrows pointing away from it, but for each such request arrow there is an available resource dot (a dot without an arrow leading from it) in the resource the arrow points to, erase all the process's arrows.

If, in checking all the processes, at least one process was found for which its arrows could be erased, go back and reiterate the process. Continue until there are either no arrows remaining, or no process can have its arrows removed. The system is deadlocked if and only if no arrows remain. Figure 3-4 shows the reduced version of the resource allocation graph in Fig. 3-3.

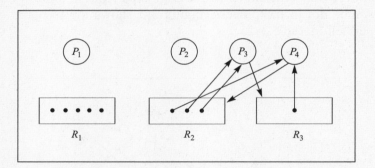

Fig. 3-4. Reduced resource allocation graph.

While a reduced resource allocation graph provides a useful depiction of the system's state to human beings, a computer system is better suited to an algorithmic approach. The algorithm for determining deadlock is similar to the algorithm for detecting if the system is in a safe state.

```
// ------------------------------------------------
// Algorithm to determine if a system is in a deadlocked
   state.
// ------------------------------------------------
int request[P][R];
int current[P][R]
int avail[R];
int done[P] = false;
boolean deadlock;
int pp = 0;
```

```
while (pp < P)
{
   if (done[pp]) contine;
   // ---------------------------------------
   // Can the requests of this processes be granted?
   // ---------------------------------------
   for (int rr=0; rr<R; rr++)
   {
        if (request[pp][rr] <= avail[rr])
        {
          // ---------------------------------------
          // No. Not enough of resource rr is available.
          // Go to next process.
          // ---------------------------------------
          pp = pp + 1;
          continue 2;    // Go to next iteration of outer loop
        }
   }
   // ---------------------------------------
   // Yes. Reset system to the state it would be in if
   // this process ran to completion without issuing
   // any additional requests, releasing all its
   // resources. Then start all over.
   // ---------------------------------------
   for (int rr=0; rr<R; rr++)
     avail[rr] = avail[rr] + current[pp][rr];
   done[pp] = true;
   pp = 0;
}
// ---------------------------------------
// If all processes can run to completion,
// system state is deadlock free.
// ---------------------------------------
deadlock = false;
for (int pp=0; pp<P; pp++)
   if (! done[pp]) deadlock = true;
```

3.3.4 RECOVERY FROM DEADLOCK

Three approaches to recover from deadlock are automatic preemption, automatic termination, or manual intervention.

With **automatic preemption** the operating system preempts a subset of the allocated resources. Three major issues must be resolved to implement such a strategy.

- **Selection:** Which resources from which processes are to be preempted? If the decision is made to preempt one resource from a process, should all its other resources also be preempted? Other factors in making the decision could include:

(1)   A process's priority

(2)   How long a process has been executing

(3)   How long a process still needs to execute

(4)   How many resources a process currently holds

(5)   The size of the different sets of resources that, if released, would break the deadlock

(6)   How many processes would be affected

- **Consequence:** What happens to the processes that have resources preempted? Can the system maintain state information about processes such that if they are victims of preemption, they can be rolled back to an earlier state? Maintaining such information can be costly in terms of both time and storage space. Even rolling a process back to its starting state may not be practical. Some input data may be unrecoverable. Unless that data was captured and saved when the process was first run, the ability to process that information will have been lost.

- **Starvation:** If the same process is repeatedly a victim of preemption, constant rollbacks could preclude it from terminating. Will the selection mechanism preclude the possibility of starvation? One solution is to use a *preemption counter*. Each time a process is rolled back, the preemption counter is incremented. Should deadlock occur, no resources would be preempted from the process with the highest preemption counter.

Instead of preempting resources, **automatic termination** eliminates deadlock by terminating processes. All deadlocked processes could be terminated, or the system could select a subset of the deadlocked processes to terminate. Although more drastic, terminating all processes can be done quickly on systems where fast resolution is important. If only a subset of processes are to be terminated, the same factors encountered in automatic preemption may be considered in selecting the processes to be terminated. It should also be noted that the termination of one process may have effects beyond that process. Processes dependent on the terminated process's computation may be adversely affected, and partially updated files may be left in inconsistent states.

The **manual intervention** approach turns responsibility for resolving the problem over to the system operator. Given the limitations of the automatic approaches, in many cases this is an attractive option. But some systems run without a full-time (or even part-time) operator and others must react to a deadlock situation within moments of its detection. In such cases, manual intervention is not a practical solution.

3.3.5   OSTRICH ALGORITHM

All the mechanisms for dealing with deadlocks presented thus far have had one or more serious drawbacks. The fact of the matter is there is no good way of dealing with deadlocks. For most operating systems, deadlock is a rare occurrence. So in many cases, the problem of deadlock is ignored, like an ostrich sticking its head in the sand and hoping the problem will go away.

Computer systems fail for wide variety of reasons. In each case, designers must consider if the cost of the solution is justified by the magnitude of the problem to be fixed. Do the frequency of and damage caused by power outages justify the cost of an uninterruptable power supply? Do the frequency of and damage caused by disk failures justify the cost of a RAID disk array? By the same token, do the frequency of and damage caused by deadlock justify the cost of implementing a strategy for dealing with deadlock? In many cases, the answer has been no.

Solved Problems

3.1   Show how the *send_mailbox* and *receive_mailbox* primitives could be used to implement a system for printing files. Processes wishing to print would send the name of the file to be printed to mailbox *printer*. The print spooler would print any file whose name was found in the mailbox.

Answer:

```
// --------------------
// Process wishing to print
// --------------------
char filename[]; // Contains name of file to be printed
status = send_mailbox("printer", filename);
if (status < 0)
{
    // Failure
}
// -----------
// Print Spooler
// -----------
char filename[]; // Contains name of file to be printed
while (true)
{
    status = receive_mailbox ("printer", filename);
    if (status < 0)
    {
        // Failure
    }
    print (filename); // Print the file
}
```

3.2   Indicate how mutual exclusion could be implemented using mailboxes with nonblocking *send_mailbox* and blocking *receive_mailbox* primitives. Assume the primitives are executed as indivisible atomic operations.

Answer:

After creating and initializing a mailbox *mutex* to have a single message, any process wishing to enter its critical section must attempt to receive a message. Only when a process actually receives a message can it enter its critical section. When it leaves its critical section, it returns the message it received back to the mailbox. Since there is only one message, only one process can be in its critical section at a time.

```
receive_mailbox(mutex,message);
```

```
// Critical Section
```

```
send_mailbox(mutex,message);
```

3.3 Show that the *TestAndSet* solution presented in Section 3.2.3 guarantees mutual exclusion.

Answer:

A process may enter its critical section only if either *ts* or *waiting[pid]* is *false*. For *ts* to be *false, TestAndSet* must have executed and returned *false*, setting *lock* to *true* in doing so. Since *lock* is reset to *false* only after a process has left its critical section, any attempts to execute *TestAndSet* while a process is in its critical section will yield return values of *true*. Thus, *ts* cannot grant access to the critical section while another process is in its critical section.

The variable *waiting[pid]* can also only become *false* when some process leaves its critical section. Exiting from the critical section can only set one element in *waiting* to *false* and only if it does not set *lock* to *false*. Thus, only one process may enter the critical section because its element in *waiting* is *false*, and no other process may have *ts* set to *false* at the same time. Mutual exclusion is assured.

3.4 Show how the following problem does not satisfy the requirements of a mechanism to control access to a critical section.

```
shared int turn = 1;
int myPid = 0;    // For process 0. Set to 1 for process 1.
int otherPid = 1 - myPid;
```

```
while (turn !=myPid)
DoNothing();
```

```
// Critical Section
```

```
turn = otherPid;
```

Answer:

This solution fails the progress requirement. It requires alternating access to the critical section. A process terminating outside its critical section eventually prevents the other process from entering its critical section.

3.5   Show the Dekker's algorithm satisfies the requirements of a mechanism to control access to a critical section.

Answer:

Mutual Exclusion: First look at the case where one process, P_i, is in its critical section and the other, P_j, wishes to enter. If P_i is in its critical section, *wantIn[i]* must be *true*. The *while* condition will remain *false* for P_j until P_i leaves its critical section, so mutual exclusion for this case is preserved.

The other case is if both processes execute *wantIn[myPid] = true* before the other enters its critical section. The variable *favored* must be either *i* or *j* and will not change until one process is granted access to its critical section and subsequently leaves. If *favoured* is *n*, *wantIn[n]* cannot change because the *if* statement will always evaluate to *false*. Thus the process other than P_n may not enter the critical section until after P_n has left its critical section, guaranteeing mutual exclusion.

Progress: No process is in its critical section. First consider the case that only one process is attempting to enter its critical section. The variable *wantIn[otherPid]* is *false* and a decision is made. If both processes are attempting to enter their critical section and *favored* is *n*, *favored* will not change in value and *wantIn[n]* will remain *true*. Within finite time, P_m (!$m = n$) will execute its *if* statement and reset *wantIn[m]* to *false*. P_m will then enter a busy-wait loop, preventing *wantIn[m]* from changing to *true* until *favored* changes. Since *favored* cannot change until P_n leaves its critical section, *wantIn[m]* cannot change until P_n leaves its critical section. Within a finite time after *wantIn[m]* is set to *false*, P_n will execute *while(wantIn[otherPid])* and the decision will be made.

Bounded Wait: If a process, P_i, is denied entrance to the critical section, then either P_j is in its critical section or will be granted access to its critical section (since it has already been shown a decision will be made). When P_j leaves its critical section, *favored* will be reset to *i*. It was previously shown that with *favored* set to *n* and P_n attempting to enter its critical section, a decision to grant P_n access to its critical section will occur in finite time. Using $n = i$, P_i must enter its critical section in finite time.

3.6   Show how the bakery algorithm satisfies the requirements of a mechanism to control access to a critical section.

Answer:

Lemma: If P_i is in the critical section and P_j has chosen a value for *number[k]*, then (*number[i] < number[k]*) or (*number[i] = = number[k]*)&&($i < k$) for all !$i = k$.

Proof: If P_i set *number[i]* before P_j executed *choosing[myPid] = true*, then when P_j computes *MAX(number)*, *MAX(number) > number[i]* and therefore *number [i] < number[k]*. If P_i set *number[i]* after P_j executed *choosing[myPid] = true*, P_i could not get past the *while(choosing[jj])DoNothing( )* for *jj = k* until after *number[k]* had been set. If P_i is in its critical section, then when P_i executed the next *while* statement, (*number[i] < number[k]*) or (*number[i] = = number [k]*)&&($i < k$) must be true or execution could not have proceeded past that loop. Since P_j had already set *number[k]*, *number[k]* has not changed and the expression must still be *true*.

Mutual Exclusion: Assume two processes, P_i and P_j, are in their critical sections. Then the lemma must hold for both. But it cannot. So the assumption is false.

Progress: Some process or processes must have the smallest value for *number[i]*. Any processes setting *number[myPid]* after the value has been set in one process will have a larger value. Of all the processes with the same value in *number[i]*, one must have the lowest value for *i*. Let that process be P_n. For P_n, the second *while* will always be false. Since any *choosing[i]* may only remain *true* for a finite time and cannot become *true* again until a decision has been made to grant some process access to the critical section, process P_n cannot be delayed by the first *while* statement for an indefinite period of time. Thus, some process P_n will be granted access within finite time.

Bounded Wait: For any process P_i that has executed *choosing[myPid]* = *false*, any process P_j subsequently executing *choosing[myPid]* = *true* will have a larger value in *number[k]* and by the lemma cannot enter the critical section while P_i is waiting to enter. Since at most a finite number of processes may be waiting to enter the critical section, and any requesting entry in the future cannot gain entry before P_i, P_i will be able to gain entry within finite time.

3.7 Implement general semaphores using the *TestAndSet* instruction. You may use *ProcessQueue* objects as defined earlier in the chapter, with the additional provision that the *Insert* function may be passed a boolean flag which will be set to *false* after the process state has been set to blocked.

Answer:

Since the semaphore primitives are atomic actions, access to *P* and *V* must be controlled by a *TestAndSet* lock variable. The *Insert* function must clear the lock to allow other processes access to the semaphore primitives.

```
struct semaphore
    {
    int lock = false;
    int count;
    ProcessList queue;
    }
void P (semaphore s)
    {
    while (TestAndSet(s.lock))
        DoNothing();
    if (s.count == 0)
    {
        s.count = s.count - 1;
        s.lock = false;
    }
    else
        s.queue.Insert(s.lock);
    }
void V (semaphore s)
    {
```

```
        while (TestAndSet(s.lock))
            DoNothing();
    if (s.queue.empty())
        s.count = s.count + 1;
    else
        s.queue.Remove();
    s.lock = false;
    }
```

3.8   *The Dining Philosophers Problem:* Five philosphers are sitting at a round table. In the center of the table is a bowl of rice. Between each pair of philosphers is a single chopstick. A philosopher is in one of three states: thinking, hungry, or eating. At various times, a thinking philosopher gets hungry. A hungry philosopher attempts to pick up one of the adjacent chopsticks, then the other (not both at the same time). If the philosopher is able to obtain the pair of chopsticks (they are not already in use), then the philosopher eats for a period of time. After eating, the philosopher puts the chopsticks down and returns to thinking. Write a monitor for the dining philosphers problem.

Answer:

```
monitor philosphers
{
    type (thinking, hungry, eating): state[5];
    condition needChop[5];
    int inc (int ii) { return (ii+1) % 5; }
    int inc (dec ii) { return (ii+4) % 5; }
    getChop(int person)
    {
        state[person] = hungry;
        if (state[inc(person)] == eating
        || state[dec(person)] == eating)
            needChop[person].cwait();
        state[person] = eating;
    }
    doneEating(int person)
    {
        int right = inc(person);
        int left = dec(person);
        state[person] = thinking;
        if (state[right] == hungry
        && state[inc(right)] != eating)
            needChop[right].csignal();
        else if (state[left] == hungry
        && state[inc(left)] != eating)
            needChop[left].csignal();
    }
}
```

3.9 *Sleeping Barber Problem:* There is a barber shop with *n* chairs for waiting customers, one barber's chair, and one barber. If a customer enters the store and there are no free chairs, the customer leaves. If a customer enters the store and the barber is sleeping, the customer wakes up the barber and gets a haircut. Otherwise, a customer enters the store, takes a seat, and waits. If the barber finishes a haircut and there are waiting customers, the barber cuts the hair of the next customer. Otherwise, the barber goes to sleep in his chair. Using semaphores, write the functions to control the actions of customers and the barber.

Answer:

```
shared semaphore cutHair = 0;
shared semaphore waiting = 0;
shared semaphore countMutex = 1;
shared int count = 0;
void barber ()
{
    while (true)
    {
        P(cutHair);
        GiveHaircut();
    }
}
void customer()
{
    P(countMutex);
    if (count == n+1)      // N chairs plus the barbers chair.
        exit();
    count = count + 1;
    if (count > 1)
    {
        // -----------
        // Take a chair
        // ----------
        V(countMutex);
        P(waiting);
    }
    else
        V(countMutex);
    // ----------------
    V(cutHair);
    ReceiveHaircut();
    // ----------------
    P(countMutex);
    count = count - 1;
    if (count > 0)
        V(waiting);
    V(countMutex);
    }
}
```

3.10   Show that by assigning a unique priority number to each resource, and prohibiting a process from requesting a resource with a priority less than or equal to the priority of any held resource, deadlock can be avoided.

Answer:

Assume $P_1, P_2, \ldots, P_n$ are an ordered list of the deadlocked processes such that P_i is waiting on a resource, R_i, held by P_{i+1} (P_0 is holding the resource requested by P_n). Thus, P_i is holding resource R_{i-1} while requesting R_i. Let S_i be the selection priority number of resource R_i. We know $S_{i-1} < S_i$. So $S_0 < S_1 < \cdots < S_n < S_0$. But this is impossible, so our assumption must be false.

3.11   Gridlock is a traffic problem (Fig. 3-5) in which further movement by traffic is impossible. Show that the four conditions of deadlock apply.

Answer:

- **Mutual Exclusion:** Only one car may be occupying a particular spot on the road at any instant.
- **Hold and Wait:** No car ever backs up.
- **No Preemption:** No car is permitted to push another car out of the way.
- **Circular Wait:** Each corner of the city block contains vehicles whose movement depends on the vehicles blocking the next intersection.

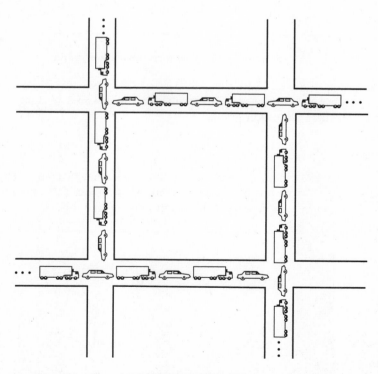

Fig. 3-5.   Gridlock.

3.12 Given process resource usage and availability as described in Table 3-2, draw the resource allocation graph.

Table 3-2.   Resource Usage.

Process	Current Allocation			Outstanding Requests			Resources Available		
	R_1	R_2	R_3	R_1	R_2	R_3	R_1	R_2	R_3
P_1	2	0	0	1	1	0			
P_2	3	1	0	0	0	0	0	0	0
P_3	1	3	0	0	0	1			
P_4	0	1	1	0	1	0			

Answer:

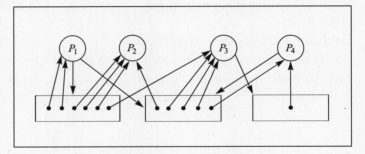

Solution 3-12.   Resource allocation graph.

3.13 Given process resource usage and availability as describe in Table 3-2, draw the reduced resource allocation graph.

Answer:

P_2 has only links pointing toward it, so all those links may be erased. The requests for R_1 and R_2 by P_1 may now be granted, leaving P_1 with arcs that only point toward it. Those arcs can be erased leaving the graph looking like this.

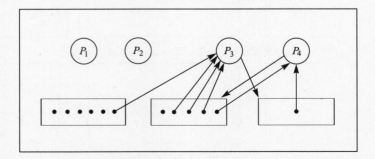

Solution 3-13(a).   Partially reduced resource allocation graph.

The request for R_3 by P_4 may now be granted and all the arcs pointing toward P_4 may be erased. Similarly, the arcs for P_3 can be erased and the reduced graph has no arcs.

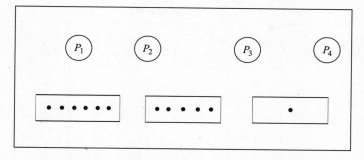

Solution 3-13(b).   Reduced resource allocation graph.

3.14   Given process resource usage and availability as described in Table 3-2, is the system deadlocked?

Answer:

No. A reduced resource allocation graph with no arcs means there is no deadlock.

3.15   What is the minimum number of resources needed to be available for the state described in Table 3-3 to be safe (note the question is asking for the number of resources **available**, not how many resources exist):

Table 3-3

Process	Current Allocation	Maximum Allocation
	R_1	R_1
P_1	1	3
P_2	1	2
P_3	3	9
P_4	2	7

Answer:

If one instance of R_1 was available, process P_2 could be guaranteed of running to completion. It could then release the resource it is currently using, making two of R_1 available. This would allow P_1 to run to completion, increase the number of R_1's available to three. With only three R_1's, P_3 and P_4 could still deadlock if they both request their maximum potential allocation. If there were three R_1's to start instead of one, P_4 would now have five R_1's available to it and could run to completion. Adding its two R_1's to the pool allows P_3 to run. The minimum number of available resources needed for the state to be safe is three.

3.16 Is the state described in Table 3-4 safe or unsafe?

Table 3-4

Process	Current Allocation		Maximum Allocation		Resources Available	
	R_1	R_2	R_1	R_2	R_1	R_2
P_1	1	2	4	2	1	1
P_2	0	1	1	2		
P_3	1	0	1	3		
P_4	2	0	3	2		

Answer:

The state is safe. Allocating both available resources allows P_2 to run to completion, leaving one R_1 available and two R_2's. This allows P_4 to run, leaving three R_1's and two R_2's. P_1 may now run, leaving four R_1's and four R_2's. P_3 may now run, so the state is safe.

Supplementary Problems

3.17 A system has a jukebox CD-RW. The jukebox is loaded with blank CD-ROM media, and can load and burn a CD-Rom without human intervention. A spooling program controls access to the CD-RW. Applications wishing to burn CD-ROMs send a message to the spooler which hands over control of the CD-RW to that application. The spooler takes all the messages it receives from the application and writes them to the CD-RW. A message of length 0 closes the session. The application retains control of the CD-RW until it closes the session. The spooler returns a message to the application indicating whether the CD-ROM was burned successfully. Show how *send_process* and *receive_process* could be used to implement this software.

3.18 Write a program that creates two child processes. Each child process reads from a different serial line and sends the characters read back to the parent process through a pipe. The parent process outputs all characters received. A child terminates when an exclamation point character is received. The parent terminates after both children have terminated. Use the *send_pipe* and *receive_pipe* primitives.

3.19 An application that produces and consumes data is to be written using two processes. Process 1 executes the function *produce* to generate data, and process 2 executes the function *consume* to consumer the data. Using functions *send_signal* and *react_signal*, write the code for the two processes such that process 1's calls to *produce* alternate with process 2's calls to *consume*.

3.20 Show how a *TestAndSet* primitive could be implemented by disabling interrupts.

3.21 Implement a pool of 20 semaphores using a monitor. The argument to the *P* and *V* functions will be the semaphore number. Include an *Init* function to set a semaphore's initial value.

3.22 Show that the *TestAndSet* solution presented in Section 3.2.3 prevents starvation.

3.23 Show how the following code does not satisfy the requirements of a mechanism to control access to a critical section.

```
shared boolean wantIn[2] = false;
int myPid = 0;    // For process 0. Set to 1 for process 1.
int otherPud = 1 - myPid;
```

```
wantIn[myPid] = true;
while (wantIn[otherPid])
  DoNothing();
```

```
// Critical Section
```

```
wantIn[myPid] = false;
```

3.24 Show that Peterson's algorithm satisfies the requirements of a mechanism to control access to a critical section.

3.25 *The Readers and Writers Problem:* Any number of readers may simultaneously be reading from a file. Only one writer at a time may write to a file, and no reader can be reading while a writer is writing. Using semaphores, write a solution to the readers and writers problem that gives priority to readers.

3.26 *The Thirsty Person Problem (adapted from the Cigarette Smokers Problem):* To drink, a thirsty person must have three things: water, ice, and a glass. There are three thirsty people, each having a different one (and only one) of the three required items. A fourth person, a server, has an unlimited supply of all three items. If nobody is drinking, the server places two of the three items (chosen at random) onto a table. The thirsty person who can make a drink from those two items will pick them up and drink a glass of ice water. When done, the thirsty person will notify the server and the process will repeat. Write a monitor to control the thirsty people and the server in the following program.

```
// -------
// Server
// -------
while (true)
{
    drinkers.Serve();
}
// -----------------------
```

```
// Drinker (type is water or ice or glass)
// ------------------------
while (true)
{
    drinkers.GetIngredients(type);
    drink();
    drinkers.NotifyServer(type);
}
```

3.27 Given the resource allocation graph in Fig. 3-6, fill in the resource usage table (see Table 3-5).

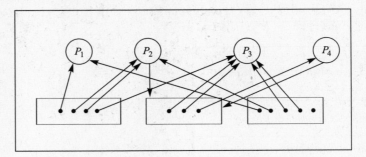

Fig. 3-6. Resource allocation graph.

Table 3-5

Process	Current Allocation			Outstanding Requests			Resources Available		
	R_1	R_2	R_3	R_1	R_2	R_3	R_1	R_2	R_3
P_1 P_2 P_3 P_4									

3.28 Is the following state described in Table 3-6 safe or unsafe?

Table 3-6

Process	Current Allocation		Maximum Allocation		Resources Available	
	R_1	R_2	R_1	R_2	R_1	R_2
P_1	7	2	9	5		
P_2	1	3	2	6	2	1
P_3	1	1	2	2		
P_4	3	0	5	0		

3.29   For the system described in Table 3-7, draw the resource allocation graph.

Table 3-7.   Resource Usage.

Process	Current Allocation			Outstanding Requests			Maximum Allocation			Resources Available		
	R_1	R_2	R_3	R_1	R_2	R_3	R_1	R_2	R_3	R_1	R_2	R_3
P_1	2	0	0	1	0	0	2	0	1			
P_2	1	2	0	0	0	1	2	5	2	0	2	0
P_3	0	1	1	0	0	0	1	4	2			
P_4	0	0	1	0	0	1	2	0	1			

3.30   For the system described in Table 3-7, draw the reduced resource allocation graph.

3.31   For the system described in Table 3-7, is the system deadlocked?

3.32   For the system described in Table 3-7, is the system in a safe or unsafe state?

Answers to Supplementary Problems

3.17
```
// ----------------
// Application process
// ----------------
while (moreDataToProduce)
{
    // Produce data
    send_process(spoolerPid, data);
}
send_process(spoolerPid, "");
receive_process(spoolerPid, status);
if (status == "error")
{
    // Failure
}
// ----------------
// CD-RW Spooler
// ----------------
while (true)
{
    appPid = receive_process(0, data);
    status = LoadBlankMedia();
```

```
        while (data != "")
        {
                if (status == noError)
                        status = BurnData(data);
                receive_process(appPid, data);
        }
        if (status == noError)
                send_process(appPid, "success");
        else
                send_process(appPid, "error");
}
```

3.18
```
int pdr, pdw;
string port;
char inChar;
create_pipe(pdr,pdw);
child1 = fork();
if (childl != 0)
        child2 = fork();
if (child1 == 0)
        port = "COM1";
else if (child2 == 0)
        port = "COM2";
if (childl == 0 || child2 == 0)
{
    // Both children
    close (pdr);
    inChar = input(port);
    while (inChar != '!')
    {
            send_pipe(pdw, inChar);
            inChar = input(port);
    }
    close (pdw)
    exit(0);
}
else
{
  // Parent
  int status;
  close (pdw);
  status = receive_pipe(pdr,inChar);
  while (status != 0)
  {
          output(inChar);
          status = receive_pipe)pdr,inChar);
  }
  close (pdr)
  exit(0);
}
```

3.19
```
// Process 1
int    produce_flag = 1;
int    proceed()
{
    produce_flag = 1;
}

int main ()
{
    react_signal(proceed, 1);
    while (1)
    {
        while (produce_flag == 0)
            ;
        produce();
        produce_flag = 0;
        send_signal (process2, 2);
    }
}
// Process 2
int    consume_flag = 0;
int    proceed()
{
    consume_flag = 1;
}
int main ()
{
    react_signal(proceed, 2);
    while (1)
    {
        while (consume_flag == 0)
            ;
        consume();
        consume_flag = 0;
        send_signal (process1, 1);
    }
}
```

3.20
```
boolean TestAndSet (boolean locked)
{
    boolean status;
    // DisableInterrupts
    if (locked)
        status = true;
    else
    {
        locked = true;
        status = false;
    }
    //EnableInterrupts
    return status;
}
```

3.21

```
monitor semaphore
{
        condition queue[20];
        int queueCnt[20];
        int count[20];

        boolean P (int sema)
        {
            if (count[sema] == -1)
                count[sema] == -1;
            if (count[sema] > 0)
                count[sema] = count[sema] - 1;
            else
            {
                queueCnt[sema] = queueCnt[sema] + 1;
                queue[sema].cwait();
            }
         }
        boolean V (int sema)
        {
            if (count[sema] == -1)
                count[sema] == -1;
            if (queueCnt[sema] == 0)
                count[sema] = count[sema] + 1;
            else
            {
                queueCnt[sema] = queueCnt[sema] - 1;
                queue[sema].csignal();
            }
        }
        boolean init (int sema, int value)
        {
            if (count[sema] != -1)
                return false;
            else
            {
                count[sema] = value;
                return true;
            }
        }
        semaphore
        {
          for (int ii=0; ii<20; ii++)
            {
                queueCnt[sema] = 0;
                count[sema] = -1;
            }
        }
}
```

3.22 Let some process i enter its critical section after some other process n has been blocked from entering. The processes from $i+1$ to n (using modulo MAX_PID arithmetic) form an ordered (based on process identification number) list of processes, S_i. When process i leaves its critical section, $waiting[k]$ must be $true$ for some value of k, $i > k$, and $k <= n$. Element k of $waiting$ will be set to $false$ and process P_k will be permitted to enter its critical section. Thus, the next process to enter the critical section will be some process from S_i. If k is not n, the same analysis applies to P_k. However, S_k must contain P_n and be a subset of S_i. Since the set of processes from which the next process to enter its critical section gets progressively smaller, and must contain P_n, eventually P_n must be chosen. Since n may be any process, starvation can never occur.

3.23 This solution fails the bounded wait requirement given the following execution sequence.

Time	P_1	P_2
0	wantln[myPid] = true	
1		wantln[myPid] = true
2	while (wantln[otherPid])	
3		while (wantln[otherPid])

The processes are now deadlocked.

3.24 **Mutual Exclusion:** First look at the case where one process, P_i, is in its critical section and the other, P_j, wishes to enter. If P_i is in its critical section, $wantIn[i]$ must be $true$. The variable $turn$ will be set to i and the $while$ condition will remain $true$ for P_j until P_i leaves its critical section. Mutual exclusion for this case is preserved.

The other case is if both processes execute $wantIn[myPid] = true$ before the other enters its critical section. Let P_j execute $turn = otherPid$ second. P_i must have already set $wantIn[myPid]$ to $true$ and executed $turn = otherPid$. The $while$ condition for P_j will evaluate to $false$ and cannot change until P_i leaves the critical section. Mutual exclusion for this case is preserved.

Progress: No process is in its critical section. First, consider the case that only one process is attempting to enter its critical section. The variable $wantIn[otherPid]$ is $false$ and a decision is made. If both processes are attempting to enter their critical section, within finite time both will have executed $turn = otherPid$. After that point, for at least one of them, the $while$ must evaluate to $false$ and that process will be able to move into its critical section.

Bounded Wait: If a process, P_i, is denied entrance to its critical section after executing $turn = otherPid$, then either P_j is in its critical section or will be granted access to its critical section (since it has already been shown a decision will be made). After P_j leaves its critical section, $wantIn[myPid]$ will be set to $false$. If P_i executes its $while$ statement before P_j tries to reenter its critical section, P_i will be granted access. If P_i executes its $while$ statement after P_j tries to reenter its critical section, under mutual exclusion it was shown that if P_j executes $turn = otherPid$ after P_i, then P_j must wait for P_i to enter its critical section before P_j can enter its critical section. Thus, the next process to enter its critical section will be P_i and that decision will be made in finite time.

3.25
```
shared semaphore rSem = 1;
shared semaphore wSem = 1;
shared int readCount = 0;
void readers()
{
    P(rSem);
        readCount = readCount + 1;
        if (readCount == 1)
            P(wSem);
    V(rSem);
    READ();
    P(rSem);
        readCount = readCount - 1;
        if (readCount == 0)
            V(wSem);
    V(rSem);
}
void writers()
{
    P(wSem);
        WRITE();
    V(rSem);
}
```

3.26
```
monitor drinkers()
{
    condition iceWater, iceGlass, waterGlass;
    condition server();
    boolean suppliedIce = false;
    boolean suppliedWater = false;
    boolean suppliedGlass = false;
    typedef requirements (water, ice, glass);
    int drinkers = 0;
    boolean first = true;
Serve()
{
    if (first == false)
        server.cwait();
    first = false;
    rr = random(3);
    if (rr == 0)
    {
        suppliedIce = true;
        suppliedWater = true;
        iceWater.csignal();
    }
    else if (rr == 1)
    {
        suppliedGlass = true;
        suppliedIce = true;
```

```
            iceGlass.csignal();
        }
        else
        {
            suppliedGlass = true;
            suppliedWater = true;
            waterGlass.csignal();
        }
    }
GetIngredients(requirements has)
{
    if (has == glass)
    {
      if (suppliedIce == false || suppliedWater == false)
          iceWater.cwait();
    }
    else if (has == water)
    {
      if (suppliedIce == false || suppliedGlass == false)
          iceGlass.cwait();
    }
    else
    {
      if (suppliedGlass == false || suppliedWater == false)
          waterGlass.cwait();
    }
    suppliedIce = false;
    suppliedWater = false;
    suppliedGlass = false;
    }
    NotifyServer()
    {
        server.csignal();
    }
}
```

3.27

Process	Current Allocation			Outstanding Requests			Resources Available		
	R_1	R_2	R_3	R_1	R_2	R_3	R_1	R_2	R_3
P_1	1	0	1	0	0	0			
P_2	2	0	1	0	1	0	0	0	1
P_3	1	2	2	0	0	0			
P_4	0	1	0	0	1	0			

3.28 No.

3.29

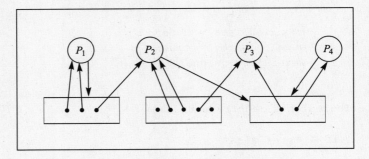

Solution 3-29.   Resource allocation graph.

3.30

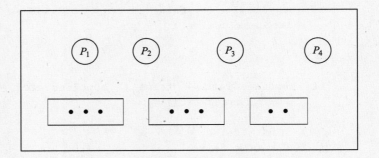

Solution 3-30.   Reduced resource allocation graph.

3.31 No.

3.32 Unsafe.

CHAPTER 4

Memory Management

The operating system must co-reside in main memory with one or more executing processes. Memory management is responsible for allocating memory to processes and for protecting the memory allocated to each process from undesired access by other processes. It is also responsible for protecting the memory allocated to the operating system from unauthorized access.

Memory management is not just a software task. The operating system requires hardware support to implement any of the nontrivial memory management schemes. Thus, some operating system design issues are also hardware design issues. Memory management hardware is typically protected from user access; the operating system is solely responsible for its control.

4.1   Single Absolute Partition

The simplest memory management scheme requires no hardware support. Memory space is divided into two partitions by convention; one partition is allocated to the operating system and the other to an executing process. So-called "well-behaved" programs limit themselves to accessing the memory locations in the process's partition. Without hardware support, however, there is nothing to prevent programs from corrupting the operating system. Early DOS systems used a variant of this scheme, allowing misbehaving user programs to crash the entire system (which they frequently did).

When a program is loaded into a partition, the addresses in the loaded code must correspond to the appropriate addresses in the partition. Addresses in the code may be *bound* to particular memory addresses at either compile time or load time. Programs that have been bound to memory locations at compile time are said to contain *absolute code*. If the binding occurs when the program is loaded into memory, the program is said to contain *relocatable code*. For a program to contain relocatable code, some mechanism must exist to identify the bytes in the program that refer to memory addresses. Although this adds complexity to the compiling and loading process, it has the obvious advantage of freeing the program to be loaded into any available memory locations.

Protection can be incorporated into an absolute partition scheme by adding a hardware *base register*. The operating system loads the base register with the lowest address accessible by the user program. The hardware then compares each address generated by the user program to the contents of the base register (Fig. 4-1). Addresses less than the address stored in the base register cause a memory-fault trap into the operating system.

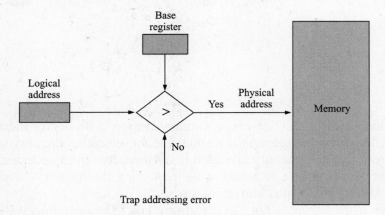

Fig. 4-1.   Base register addressing.

4.2   Single Relocatable Partition

Far more useful than base register systems are systems that contain a *relocation register*. As with a base register, the relocation register is loaded by the operating system with the starting address of the process. But instead of comparing the relocation register's contents to the address generated by the process, its contents are added. The program now operates in a *logical* address space. It is compiled as if it would be allocated to memory starting at location 0. The memory management hardware converts logical addresses into actual *physical* addresses.

4.3   Multiprogramming

Single-partition schemes limit a computer to executing one program at a time. Such monoprogramming systems are increasingly rare. To load multiple processes, the operating system must divide memory into multiple partitions for those processes.

4.4   Muliple Partitions

In a multiple-partition scheme, multiple partitions are created to allow multiple user processes to be resident in memory simultaneously. A second hardware register, to be used in conjunction with the relocation register, marks the end of a partition. This register may contain either the size of the partition or the last address in the partition. Typically, the register contains the partition's size and is referred to as the *size register* or the *limit register* (Fig. 4-2).

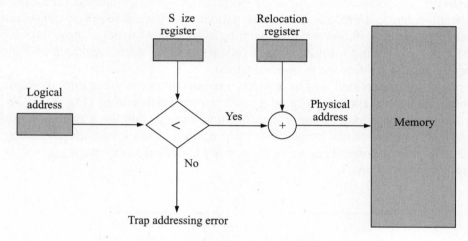

Fig. 4-2.   Relocation and size registers.

4.4.1   MULTIPLE FIXED PARTITIONS

If all the partitions are the same size, the operating system need only keep track of which partition is allocated to each process. The partition table stores either the starting address for each process or the number of the partition allocated to each process. If the partition number is stored and the partition size is a power of 2, the starting address can be generated by concatenating the appropriate number of zeros to the partition number. The limit register is set at boot time and contains the partition size. Each time a process is allocated control of the CPU, the operating system must reset the relocation register.

Space at the end of a partition that is unused by a process is wasted. Wasted space within a partition is called *internal fragmentation*. One method for reducing internal fragmentation is to use partitions of different sizes. If this is done, the operating system must also reset the limit register each time a process is allocated to the CPU. The partition size must be either stored in the partition table or deduced from the partition number.

Having different-size partitions complicates process management. Each time a different process is given control of the CPU, the operating system must reset the size register in addition to the relocation register. The operating system must also make decisions on which partition it should allocate to a process. Obviously, a process cannot be allocated to a partition smaller than the size of the process. But should a smaller process be allocated to a large partition if it will fit in a smaller partition, even though the smaller partition is currently occupied by another process?

4.4.2 MULTIPLE VARIABLE PARTITIONS

Instead of dividing memory into a fixed set of partitions, an operating system can choose to place processes into whichever memory locations are unused. The amount of space allocated to a process is the exact amount of space it requires, eliminating internal fragmentation. However, the operating system must manage more data. The exact starting and ending location of each process must be stored, and data on which memory locations are free must be maintained.

As processes are created and terminated, memory usage evolves into alternating sections of allocated and unallocated space, or *checkerboarding* (Fig. 4-3). As a result, although there may be more memory unallocated than the size of a waiting process, that memory cannot be used for the process because it is scattered among a number of memory *holes*. This wasted space not allocated to any partition is called *external fragmentation*.

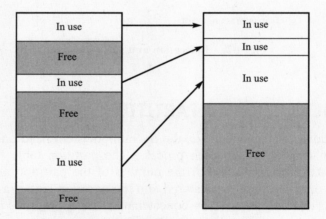

Fig. 4-3.   Checkerboarding and compaction.

A bit map can be used to keep track of what memory has been allocated. Memory is divided into allocation units and each bit in the map indicates whether or not the corresponding unit is allocated. Increasing the size of the allocation unit decreases the size of the bit map, but increases the amount of memory wasted when the process size is not a multiple of the size of the allocation unit.

A linked list can also be used to keep track of free memory. Each hole will contain an entry indicating the hole's size and a pointer to the next hole in the list. The operating system needs only a pointer to the first hole in the list. The list may be maintained in memory order, size order, or in no particular order.

Compaction may be used to make more efficient use of memory. By moving processes in memory, the memory holes can be collected into a single section of unallocated space. The question is whether the extra overhead taken to move the processes justifies the greater efficiency gained by making better use of memory space.

4.4.2.1   Partition Selection Algorithms

In situations where multiple memory holes are large enough to contain a process, the operating system must use an algorithm to select which hole the process will be loaded into. A variety of algorithms have been studied.

- **First Fit**: The operating system looks at all sections of free memory. The process is allocated to the first hole found that is larger than the size of the process. Unless the size of the process matches the size of the hole, the hole continues to exist, reduced by the size of the process.

- **Next Fit**: In first fit, since all searches start at the beginning of memory, holes at the beginning of memory are considered for allocation more frequently than those at the end. Next fit attempts to improve performance by distributing its searches more evenly over the entire memory space. It does this by keeping track of which hole was last allocated. The next search starts at the last hole allocated, not at the beginning of memory.

- **Best Fit**: Best fit searches the entire list of holes to find the smallest hole whose size is greater than or equal to the size of the process.

- **Worst Fit**: In situations where best fit finds an almost perfect match, the hole that remains is virtually useless because it is so small. To prevent the creation of these useless holes, worst fit works the opposite of best fit; it always picks the largest remaining hole.

4.4.3   BUDDY SYSTEM

A buddy system offers a compromise between fixed-size and variable-size allocation. Memory is allocated in units that are a power of 2. Initially there is a single allocation unit that comprises all of memory. When memory must be allocated to a process, the process is allocated a unit memory whose size is the smallest power of 2 larger than the size of the process. For example, a 50K process would be placed in a 64K allocation unit. If no allocation units exist of that size, the smallest available allocation larger than the process will be split into two "buddy" units half the size of the original. Splitting continues with one of the buddy units until an allocation unit of the appropriate size is created. When a process releasing memory causes two buddy units to both be free, the units are combined to form a unit twice as large. Figure 4-4 shows how allocation units would be split and joined as memory is allocated and released.

Given a memory size of 2^N, a buddy system maintains a maximum of N lists of free blocks, one for each size. (Given a memory size of 2^8, allocation units of size 2^8 through 2^1 are possible.) With a separate list of available blocks for each size, the

Action	Memory					
S tart	1M					
Request A, 150Mb	A	256K			512K	
Request B, 100Mb	A	B	128K		512K	
Request C, 50Mb	A	B	C	64K	512K	
Release B	A	128K	C	64K	512K	
Request D, 200Mb	A	128K	C	64K	D	256K
Request E, 60Mb	A	128K	C	E	D	256K
Release C	A	128K	64K	E	D	256K
Release A	256K	128K	64K	E	D	256K
Release E	512K				D	256K
Release D	1M					

Fig. 4-4. Buddy system.

allocation or release of memory can be processed efficiently. However, the buddy system does not use memory efficiently because of both internal and external fragmentation.

4.5 Simple Paging

On a system that uses *simple paging*, memory is divided into fixed-size blocks called *page frames*. Processes are divided into blocks called *pages* which are the same size as the page frames. The size of a page frame (and page) is determined by the hardware. When a process is loaded into memory, the operating system loads each page into an unused page frame. The page frames used need not be contiguous.

For each process, a *page table* stores the number of the page frame allocated for each page. Thus, the number of the page frame into which page N was loaded is stored in the Nth entry in the page table. The page size is a power of 2. Thus, if a logical address contains L bits, and the page size is 2^P bytes, P bits of an address specify offset within a page, and the remaining $L - P$ bits specify the page number. The hardware generates the physical address by appending the page offset to the page frame number extracted from the page table (Fig. 4-5). The translation of the logical address into a physical address, including the division of the logical address into page number and offset, is totally transparent to the process.

In a paged system, a size register may be used to trap out-of-bounds addresses. But more typically, the page table entry contains a valid/invalid bit. For a process with only n pages, only the first n page table entries would be marked as valid. On some systems, one or more protection bits may also be included in a page table entry. However, protection capabilities are more commonly associated with segmented systems.

On systems where processes can have a large number of pages, a multilevel system may be used (Fig. 4-6). The page number may be broken into two or more components. The first component serves as an index into the top-level page table. The entry in that table points to the table at the next level. The next component in the page number serves as an index into that table. The process continues until the

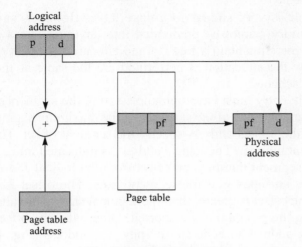

Fig. 4-5.   Simple paging.

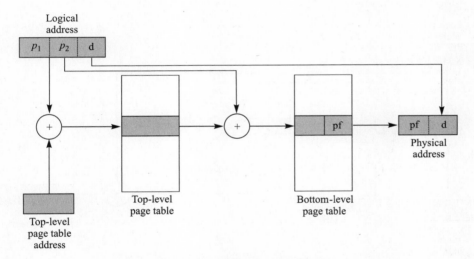

Fig. 4-6.   Multilevel page tables.

entry in the bottom-level table is accessed. That entry will contain the frame number associated with the page.

4.6   Simple Segmentation

Segmentation, like paging, divides a program into a number of smaller blocks called **segments**, each of which is allocated to memory independently. Unlike paging, segments are variable-size. Responsibility for dividing the program into segments lies with the user (or compiler); the operating system is uninvolved. The hardware sets an upper limit on the size of any segment.

A segment table is very similar to a page table. However, since segments are variable-size, memory cannot be predivided into anything like a page frame. The operating system must maintain a free list and allocate segments to memory holes. The issues of how the allocation is performed are the same as those found in the variable partition scheme.

A segment table entry must have fields for storing the segment's starting address in main memory and the size of the segment. If the maximum segment size is m bits, the last m bits of the logical address specify the segment offset. The remaining bits specify the segment number. The logical address is translated into a physical address by extracting the segment number and offset from the logical address. The segment number is used as an index into the segment table. The offset is compared to the segment size. If the offset is greater than the segment size, an invalid-address fault is generated, causing the program to be aborted. Otherwise, the offset is added to the segment's starting address to generate the physical address (Fig. 4-7). To increase speed, the size check and the physical address generation can be performed concurrently.

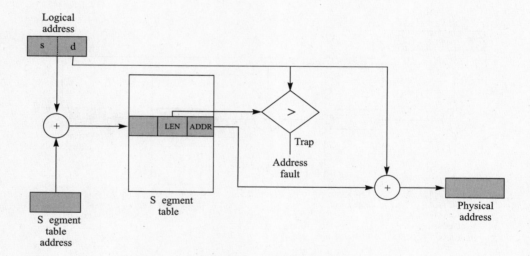

Fig. 4-7. Simple segmentation.

Because segments are user-defined, it is possible to define certain segments to be read-only. By adding a read-only bit into a segment table entry, the memory management system can check for write operations to read-only segments and generate a fault if such an operation is detected.

If support for read-only segments is present, it may also be possible for multiple processes to share read-only segments, thereby decreasing memory usage. Typically, this occurs when two processes are executing the same program, and the code for that program is designated to be in one or more read-only segments.

Shared segments may also be used by processes executing different programs but using the same subroutine library. In this situation, care must be taken that addresses within the shared segment will work with both programs. For addresses to locations within the segment, the simplest solution is to use relative addressing. Relative addressing uses the offset from the current value of the program counter to generate the destination address. For all addresses, indirect addressing though a register pointing to the appropriate segment is also a possibility. Direct addressing, which specifies the segment and offset of the destination address, is possible only if all programs use the same segment number for the segment being accessed.

4.7 Segmentation with Paging

Segmentation can be combined with paging to provide the efficiency of paging with the protection and sharing capabilities of segmentation. As with simple segmentation, the logical address specifies the segment number and the offset within the segment. However, when paging is added, the segment offset is further divided into a page number and a page offset. The segment table entry contains the address of the segment's page table. The hardware adds the logical address's page number bits to the page table address to locate the page table entry. The physical address is formed by appending the page offset to the page frame number specified in the page table entry (Fig. 4-8).

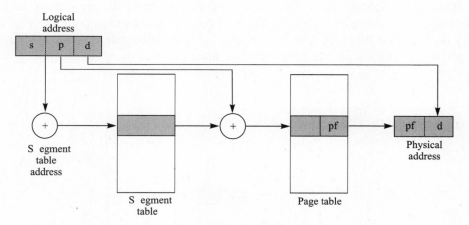

Fig. 4-8. Segmentation with paging.

4.8 Page and Segment Tables

Each process has its own paging and/or segment tables which the operating system stores in memory. On some systems, a memory management register points to the segment or page table for the currently executing process. When a new process is given control of the CPU, just the one register needs to be reset to switch to the new process's logical address space.

If the page tables are small enough, the memory management unit may have a set of registers to hold the page table. The registers are typically faster than regular memory, speeding the process of address translation.

4.8.1 ASSOCIATIVE MEMORY

On systems with extremely large page tables, *associative memory* (or *translation lookaside buffer*) may be used. Each element in an associate memory is identified by an index value. Unlike ordinary memory, associative memory is not referenced by address. Instead, it is presented with a search value and it searches all its elements, looking for one with a corresponding index value. The search of all the elements occurs in parallel, so access time is the time to access a single element.

Paging systems use small, high-speed associative memories to improve performance. An entry in the associative memory would be identical to a page table entry, except it would also contain a field for the page number. When a page is specified, the associative memory is searched at the same time the regular page table is accessed. If an entry in the associative memory is found with the matching page number, the regular page table access is aborted and the associative memory entry is used. If a match in the associative memory is not found, the page table entry is used (Fig. 4-9).

At the same time the logical address is being translated, the associative memory replaces one of its entries (typically the least recently used entry) with the page table entry for the page currently being accessed. Thus, the associative memory maintains a copy of the entries for the most recently used pages.

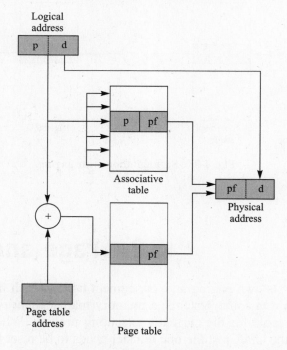

Fig. 4-9.   Associative memory.

When a new process is given control of the CPU, the memory management unit must not use associative memory entires from a previous process. The easiest way to prevent this is by the operating system marking each entry in the associative memory as invalid. Alternatively, the associative memory could add a field to hold a process identification number. For each attempted access, a match would also require the process identification number to match the value in a special register holding the current process's identification number.

The greatest performance improvement is achieved when the associative memory is significantly faster than the normal page table lookup and the *hit ratio* is high. The hit ratio is the ratio between accesses that find a match in the associative memory and those that do not.

4.8.2   INVERTED PAGE TABLE

On paged systems with a large virtual address space that uses an associative memory, an inverted page table may be used to reduce page table size. Instead of the page table containing an entry for each of a very large number of pages, the table contains an entry for each page frame. The entry stores the page number allocated to that frame. When an address cannot be resolved with an entry in the associative memory, the inverted table is searched for the entry containing the page number. *Hashing* is used to speed the search.

4.9   Swapping

Swapping may be used to increase the number of processes sharing the CPU. In addition to the processes stored in the main memory, one or more processes may be temporarily copied out of memory to a backing store. As space becomes available in main memory (possibly because a process is swapped out explicitly to make room for a process to be swapped in), swapped-out processes may be returned to memory. To execute on the CPU, a process must be in main memory. Decisions on which process to swap out and which process to swap in are made by the operating system's process scheduler.

4.10   Overlaying

In all the previous memory management schemes, the amount of memory available to a process is limited by the amount of physical memory. *Overlaying* allows a process to execute despite the system having insufficient physical memory. The programmer defines two or more overlay segments within the program such that no two overlay segments need be in memory at the same time. The operating system would then manage swapping overlay segments, reducing the amount of physical memory required by the program.

The major disadvantage of overlaying is the extensive programmer involvement in the process. Identifying overlay segments is neither a simple nor a reliable process. A far superior solution is to use a memory management scheme that frees the user from the limitations of physical memory. Such systems are called virtual memory systems and are covered in the next chapter.

 # Solved Problems

4.1   In each of the listed memory management schemes, briefly describe the functions performed by the operating system software.

(a)   Single Absolute Partition (with base register)
(b)   Multiple Variable Partitions
(c)   Buddy System
(d)   Simple Paging

Answer:

(a)   Single Absolute Partition (with base register)
When the system is booted, the operating system loads the base register with the address of the lowest memory location that can be accessed by a user program.

(b)   Multiple Variable Partitions
The operating system must keep track of which memory locations are in use and which are free. When a process is created or a process terminates, the operating system must update the memory allocation data. Before allocating a process to memory, the operating system must decide where to place it in memory. When a process is given control of the CPU, the operating system must load both the process's starting address and its size into the relocation and size registers.

(c)   Buddy System
The operating system must keep track of which memory allocation units are in use and which are free. When a process is created, the operating system must assign it to a memory allocation unit, splitting allocation units as necessary. When a process terminates, its allocation unit must be marked free, and allocation units must be combined where possible. When a process is given control of the CPU, the operating system must load both the process's starting address and its size into the relocation and size registers.

(d)   Simple Paging
The operating system must keep track of which page frames are in use and which are free. When a process is created, the operating system must allocate a set of page frames to the process. When the process terminates, the operating system must free the page frames allocated to the process. When a process is

given control of the CPU, the operating system must set the page table registers appropriately for the process.

4.2   In each of the listed memory management schemes, briefly describe the functions performed by the memory management hardware.

(*a*)   Single Absolute Partition (with base register)

(*b*)   Multiple Variable Partitions

(*c*)   Buddy System

(*d*)   Simple Paging

Answer:

(*a*)   Single Absolute Partition (with base register)
Each time a memory location is referenced, its address is compared to the address in the base register. An address smaller than the address in the base register results in a memory-fault trap.

(*b*)   Multiple Variable Partitions
Each time a memory location is referenced, its logical address is compared to the address in the size register. An address larger than the address in the size register results in a memory-fault trap. The logical address is also added to the address in the relocation register to generate the memory location's physical address.

(*c*)   Buddy System
The hardware for the buddy system works the same way as the hardware for multiple variable partitions.

(*d*)   Simple Paging
Each time a memory location is referenced, the paging hardware translates the logical address into the physical address. The page number bits in the logical address are used as an index into the page table. The logical address page offset bits are appended to the page frame number, obtained from the appropriate page table entry, to form the physical address.

4.3   A program containing relocatable code was created, assuming it would be loaded at address 0. In its code, the program refers to the following addresses: 50, 78, 150, 152, 154. If the program is loaded into memory starting at location 250, how do those addresses have to be adjusted?

Answer:

All addresses need to be adjusted upward by 250. So the adjusted addresses would be 300, 328, 400, 402, and 404.

4.4   How is an absolute partition scheme using relocatable code similar to a relocatable partition scheme? How are they different?

Answer:

Both schemes use a single partition. In both schemes, the program is relocatable so that its code may be loaded anywhere in memory. However, in an absolute partition scheme, the addresses in the code must be adjusted and bound to the actual memory addresses at the time the program is loaded into memory. In a relocatable partition scheme, each address is bound to the actual memory location during execution at the time the memory location is referenced.

4.5 On a system with 2^{24} bytes of memory and fixed partitions, all of size 65,536 bytes, what is the minimum number of bits needed in an entry in the process table to record the partition to which a process has been allocated?

Answer:

65,536 is 2^{16}. Dividing the number of bytes of total memory by the size of each partition yields the number of partitions, $2^{24}/2^{16} = 2^8$. Eight bits are needed to store one of 2^8 partition numbers.

4.6 On a system with 2^{24} bytes of memory and fixed partitions, all of size 65,536 bytes, how many bits must the limit register have?

Answer:

The total amount of memory on the system is irrelevant. Since 65,536 is 2^{16}, the largest valid address is $2^{16} - 1$. In binary, $2^{16} - 1$ is 16 ones. The limit register must have 16 bits.

4.7 On a system using fixed partitions with sizes 2^{16}, 2^{24}, and 2^{32}, how many bits must the limit register have?

Answer:

Since the system has only one limit register, it must be large enough to accommodate addresses in any partition. The largest possible partition is 2^{32}. Therefore, the limit register must have 32 bits.

4.8 On a system using first-fit allocation, assume memory is allocated as specified in Fig. 4-10 before additional requests for 20K, 10K, and 5K (in that order) are received. At what starting address will each of the additional requests be allocated?

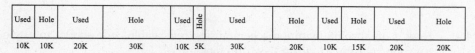

Used	Hole	Used	Hole	Used	Hole	Used	Hole	Used	Hole	Used	Hole
10K	10K	20K	30K	10K	5K	30K	20K	10K	15K	20K	20K

Fig. 4-10. Variable partition memory allocation.

Answer:

First-fit searches for the first hole larger than or equal to 20K. The first hole is too small (10K). The second hole (30K) can accommodate the request. So the first request would be allocated at the start of the second hole, location 40K. This would reduce the size of the second hole to 10K. Memory would now look as follows.

used	hole	used	hole	used	hole	used	hole	used	hole	used	hole
10K	10K	40K	10K	10K	5K	30K	20K	10K	15K	20K	20K

The second request for 10K would be allocated into the first hole at starting location 10K, eliminating the first hole. Memory would now look as follows.

used	hole	used	hole	used	hole	used	hole	used	hole
60K	10K	10K	5K	30K	20K	10K	15K	20K	20K

For the final request, the first hole not smaller than 5K starts at location 60K.

4.9   On a system using best-fit allocation, assume memory is allocated as specified in Fig. 4-10 before additional requests for 20K, 10K, and 5K (in that order) are received. At what starting address will each of the additional requests be allocated?

Answer:

Best fit searches for the smallest hole larger than or equal to 20K. The fourth hole is exactly 20K, making it the best fit. That hole starts at location $10K + 10K + 20K + 30K + 10K + 5K + 30K = 115K$. Memory would now look as follows.

used	hole	used	hole	used	hole	used	hole	used	hole
10K	10K	20K	30K	10K	5K	60K	15K	20K	20K

The second request for 10K would be allocated into the first hole at starting location 10K, eliminating the first hole. Memory would now look as follows.

used	hole	used	hole	used	hole	used	hole
40K	30K	10K	5K	60K	15K	20K	20K

The final request of 5K would be allocated to the hole of 5K that starts at location $60K + 10K + 10K = 80K$.

4.10 On a system using worst-fit allocation, assume memory is allocated as specified in Fig. 4-10 before additional requests for 20K, 10K, and 5K (in that order) are received. At what starting address will each of the additional requests be allocated?

Answer:

Worst fit always allocates the largest hole, so the first request would be allocated to the second hole, 30K. The second hole starts at location 40K. Memory would now look as follows.

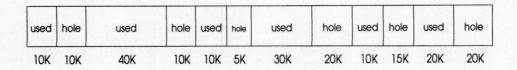

used	hole	used	hole	used	hole	used	hole	used	hole	used	hole
10K	10K	40K	10K	10K	5K	30K	20K	10K	15K	20K	20K

The fourth hole is now the largest and would be allocated to the second request. (The sixth hole is also 20K. It would be equally correct to derive a solution based on worst fit choosing the sixth hole instead of the fourth hole.) This hole starts at location $10K + 10K + 40K + 10K + 10K + 5K + 30K = 115K$. Memory would now look as follows.

used	hole	used	hole	used	hole	used	hole	used	hole	used	hole
10K	10K	40K	10K	10K	5K	40K	10k	10K	15K	20K	20K

Now the largest hole is the last one. The final request would be allocated starting at location $10K + 10K + 40K + 10K + 10K + 5K + 40K + 10K + 10K + 15K + 20K = 180K$.

4.11 On a system using next-fit allocation, assume memory is allocated as specified in Fig. 4-10 before additional requests for 20K, 10K, and 5K (in that order) are received. At what starting address will each of the additional requests be allocated?

Answer:

Next fit searches for the first hole larger than or equal to 20K. The first hole is too small (10K). The second hole (30K) can accommodate the request. So the first request would be allocated at the start of the second hole, location 40K. This would reduce the size of the second hole to 10K. Memory would now look as follows.

used	hole	used	hole	used	hole	used	hole	used	hole	used	hole
10K	10K	40K	10K	10K	5K	30K	20K	10K	15K	20K	20K

For the next request, next fit starts searching with the last allocated block. Starting the search with the second hole, the second hole is found to be able to accommodate the 10K request. Thus, the second request would be allocated starting at location 60K. Memory would now look as follows.

used	hole	used	hole	used	hole	used	hole	used	hole
10K	10K	60K	5K	30K	20K	10K	15K	20K	20K

The search for a hole for the third request would start at location 80K; the hole at that location would be selected for the third request.

4.12 On a system with 1Mb of memory using the buddy system, draw a diagram showing the allocation of memory after each of the following events.

(a) Process A, request 50K

(b) Process B, request 150K

(c) Process C, request 60

(d) Process D, request 60

(e) Process E, request 60

(f) Process D, exit

(g) Process C, exit

(h) Process E, exit

(i) Process A, exit

(j) Process F, request 125

(k) Process G, request 150

(l) Process F, exit

(m) Process G, exit

(n) Process B, exit

Answer:

(a) Process A, request 50K
Since initially only a 1Mb block is available for the 50Kb request, the 1Mb blocks will be divided into two 512K blocks. The 512K block at location 0 will be further subdivided into two 256K blocks. The 256K block at location 0 is

similarly split, as is the resulting 128K block at location 0. This leaves the system with the following five blocks.

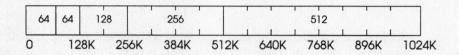

Process A is allocated to the first 64K block.

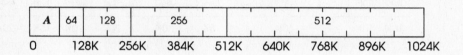

(b) Process B, request 150K
A 150K request must be allocated to a 256K block. Such a block is available at location 256K.

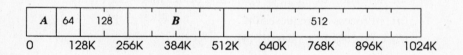

(c) Process C, request 60
A 60K request must be allocated to a 64K block. Such a block is available at location 64K.

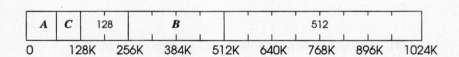

(d) Process D, request 60
The 128K block must be split to form two 64K blocks. The request is allocated to the block at location 128K.

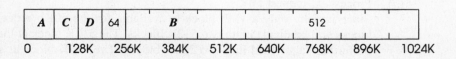

(e)   Process E, request 60
       The request is allocated to the 64K block at location 192K.

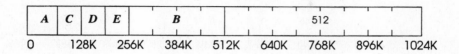

(f)   Process D, exit
       The 64K block at location 128K is marked as being available. Since that
       block's buddy (the 64K block at location 194K) is in use, no further action is
       taken.

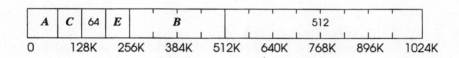

(g)   Process C, exit
       The 64K block at location 64K is marked as being available. Since that block's
       buddy (the 64K block at location 0K) is in use, no further action is taken. Note
       that two adjacent 64K blocks are available but they are not combined into a
       128K block because they are not buddies.

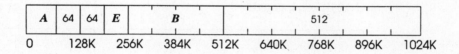

(h)   Process E, exit
       The 64K block at location 64K is marked as being available. Since that block's
       buddy (the 64K block at location 128K) is also free, the two blocks are
       combined to form a free 128K block at location 128K. Since the buddy block
       at location 0K is split, no further action is taken.

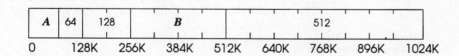

(i)   Process A, exist
       The 64K block at location 0K is marked as being available. Since that block's
       buddy (the 64K block at location 64K) is also free, the two blocks are
       combined to form a free 128K block at location 0K. Now, both the 128K

block at location 0K and the 128K block at location 128K are free, so they are combined to form a 256K block at location 0K. Since the buddy block at location 256K is in use, no further action is taken.

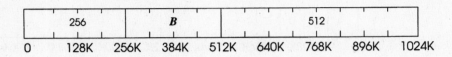

(j) Process F, request 125
Since no 128K blocks are available, the 256K block at location 0K is split to form two 128K blocks. Process F is allocated to the first one.

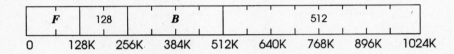

(k) Process G, request 150
Since no 256K blocks are available, the 512K block at location 512K is split to form two 256K blocks. Process G is allocated to the first one.

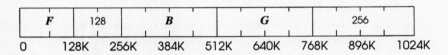

(l) Process F, exit
The block at location 0K is freed and the buddy 128K blocks at locations 0K and 128K are merged.

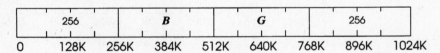

(m) Process G, exit
The block at location 512K is freed and the buddy 256K blocks at locations 512K and 768K are merged.

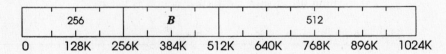

(n) Process B, exit
The block at location 256K is freed and the buddy 256K blocks at locations 0K and 256K are merged. The two 512K blocks are then merged, leaving a single 1024K block.

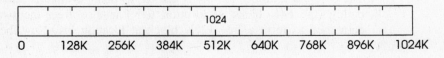

4.13 On a system with 1Mb of memory using the buddy system, what is the first request that will fail in the following string of requests due to lack of available memory? Requests: 50K, 150K, 90K, 130K, 70K, 80K, 120K, 180K, 60K.

Answer:

Memory blocks will be adjusted for each request as follows:

Req	0	128K	256K	384K	512K	640K	768K	896K	1024K
50K	X	64	128	256		512			
150K	X	64	128	X		512			
90K	X	64	X	X		512			
130K	X	64	X	X		X		256	
70K	X	64	X	X		X		X	128
80K	X	64	X	X		X		X	X

The next request for 120K could not be satisfied.

4.14 In the previous problem, at the time of the failed request, how much memory is wasted due to internal fragmentation and how much is wasted due to external fragmentation?

Answer:

There is one 64K block that is unallocated but unusable. Thus, external fragmentation is 64K. Of the remaining $1024K - 64K = 960K$ of allocated space, only $50K + 150K + 90K + 130K + 70K + 80K = 570K$ has been requested. Thus, $960K - 570K = 390K$ is wasted due to internal fragmentation.

4.15 Why are page sizes always a power of 2?

Answer:

All addresses are binary and are divided into page or page frame number and offset. By making the page size a power of 2, the page number, the page frame number, and the offset can be determined by looking at particular bits in the address; no mathematical calculations are required. The physical address can be generated by concatenating the offset to the frame number.

4.16 In paging (assuming the page size is a power of 2), why is it not necessary to add the page offset to the starting address of the page frame to generate a physical address?

Answer:

The starting address of an n-bit page frame is a multiple of 2^n. Thus, the bit pattern of the frame's starting address consists of the frame number followed by n 0's. An addition operation of an n-bit offset would be adding only the offset to the 0's in the starting address. Rather than add, it is far more efficient to simply append the offset to the frame number.

4.17   On a simple paging system with 2^{24} bytes of physical memory, 256 pages of logical address space, and a page size of 2^{10} bytes, how many bits are in a logical address?

Answer:

The logical address space contains $256 = 2^8$ pages of 2^{10} bytes, making the total logical address space $2^{10} \times 2^8 = 2^{18}$ bytes. An 18-bit address is required to cover a 2^{18}-byte address space.

4.18   On a simple paging system with 2^{24} bytes of physical memory, 256 pages of logical address space, and a page size of 2^{10} bytes, how many bytes are in a page frame?

Answer:

The page frame size is the same as the page size. Therefore, the page frame size is 2^{10} bytes.

4.19   On a simple paging system with 2^{24} bytes of physical memory, 256 pages of logical address space, and a page size of 2^{10} bytes, how many bits in the physical address specify the page frame?

Answer:

A 24-bit address is required to cover the 2^{24}-byte physical address space. Since pages, and therefore page frames, are 2^{10} bytes, the last 10 bits in the physical address specify the page offset. The remaining 14 bits specify the page frame number.

4.20   On a simple paging system with 2^{24} bytes of physical memory, 256 pages of logical address space, and a page size of 2^{10} bytes, how many entries are in the page table (how long is the page table)?

Answer:

The page table must contain an entry for each page. Since there are 256 pages in the logical address space, the page table must be 256 entries long.

4.21   On a simple paging system with 2^{24} bytes of physical memory, 256 pages of logical address space, and a page size of 2^{10} bytes, how many bits are needed to store an entry in the page table (how wide is the page table)? Assume each page table entry contains a valid/invalid bit in addition to the page frame number.

Answer:

Each entry contains 1 bit to indicate if the page is valid and 14 bits to specify the page frame number.

4.22   On a simple paging system with a page table containing 64 entries of 11 bits (including valid/invalid bit) each, and a page size of 512 bytes, how many bits in the logical address specify the page number?

Answer:

Since there are $64 = 2^6$ pages, 6 bits of the logical address are required to specify the page number.

4.23   On a simple paging system with a page table containing 64 entries of 11 bits (including valid/invalid bit) each, and a page size of 512 bytes, how many bits in the logical address specify the offset within the page?

Answer:

Since a page is $512 = 2^9$ bytes long, 9 bits are required to specify the offset within the page.

4.24   On a simple paging system with a page table containing 64 entries of 11 bits (including valid/invalid bit) each, and a page size of 512 bytes, how many bits are in a logical address?

Answer:

The 6 most significant bits of the logical address would specify the page number, the 9 least significant bits would specify the page offset, making the total number of bits 15.

4.25   On a simple paging system with a page table containing 64 entries of 11 bits (including valid/invalid bit) each, and a page size of 512 bytes, what is the size of the logical address space?

Answer:

In the previous problem, the logical address was determined to have 15 bits. A 15-bit address creates an address space of $32,768 = 2^{15}$.

4.26   On a simple paging system with a page table containing 64 entries of 11 bits (including valid/invalid bit) each, and a page size of 512 bytes, how many bits in the physical address specify the page frame number?

Answer:

A page table entry contains the frame number and a valid/invalid bit. If the total number of bits is 11, the number of bits in a page frame number are 10.

4.27 On a simple paging system with a page table containing 64 entries of 11 bits (including valid/invalid bit) each, and a page size of 512 bytes, how many bits in the physical address specify the offset within the page frame?

Answer:

The page frame offset is the same as the page offset, a 9-bit value.

4.28 On a simple paging system with a page table containing 64 entries of 11 bits (including valid/invalid bit) each, and a page size of 512 bytes, how many bits are in a physical address?

Answer:

The 10 most significant bits of the physical address would specify the page frame number, the 9 least significant bits would specify the page offset, making the total number of bits 19.

4.29 On a simple paging system with a page table containing 64 entries of 11 bits (including valid/invalid bit) each, and a page size of 512 bytes, what is the size of the physical address space?

Answer:

A 19-bit address creates an address space of 2^{19}.

4.30 On a simple paged system, can the logical address space be larger than the physical address space? Can it be smaller.

Answer:

The logical address space may be the same size as the physical address space or it may be smaller. Making the logical address space smaller prevents one process from monopolizing all of memory. The logical address may not be larger than the physical address space. If the logical address space is larger than the physical address space, all pages could not be resident in physical memory. Simple paging has no capability for dealing with references to pages that are not in memory. Demand paging (covered in the next chapter) allows for a process whose memory requirements exceed that of actual physical memory present.

4.31 A system that uses a two-level page table has 2^{12}-byte pages and 32-bit virtual addresses. The first 8 bits of the address serve as the index into the first-level page table.

(a)   How many bits specify the second-level index?

(b)   How many entries are in a level-one page table?

(c)   How many entries are in a level-two page table?

(d)   How many pages are in the virtual address space?

Answer:

(a)   12 bits

Given a page size of 2^{12} bytes, 12 bits are needed to specify the offset. That leaves $32 - (12 + 8) = 12$ bits.

(b) 2^8

Eight bits can specify up to 2^8 entries.

(c) 2^{12}

Twelve bits can specify up to 2^{12} entries.

(d) 2^{20}

Twenty bits can address 2^{20} pages. Or, if you prefer, 2^8 level-one page table entires each access a level-two page table with 2^{12} entries. $2^8 \times 2^{12} = 2^{20}$.

4.32   A computer has a 32-bit virtual address space and 1024-byte pages. A page table entry takes 4 bytes. A multilevel page table is used because each table must be contained with a page. How many levels are required?

Answer:

A page table can contain $1024/4 = 256 = 2^8$ entries. Given the page size of 2^{10}, $32 - 10 = 22$ bits specify the page number. Each level of page table can handle 8 of the 22 bits, so three levels would be required. Tables at two of the levels would have 2^8 entries; the table size at the other level would be only 2^6.

4.33   In the preceding problem, which would require less space allocated to page tables, having the 2^6 table size at the top or the bottom level? Assume a page allocated for use as a page table can be used only for that page table.

Answer:

Having the smaller table at the top level would save space. With a 2^6 top-level table, there would be only 2^6 second-level tables and $2^6 \times 2^8$ bottom-level tables. In total, $2^{14} + 2^6 + 1 = 16,449$ pages would be required for the tables. If the bottom-level tables were 2^6, there would be 2^8 second-level tables and $2^8 \times 2^8$ bottom-level tables. In total, $2^{16} + 2^8 + 1 = 65,793$ pages would be required for the tables.

4.34   On a simple paged system, associative registers hold the most active page entries and the full page table is stored in the main memory. If references satisfied by the associative registers take 90 ns, and references through the main memory page table take 220 ns, what is the effective access time if 60% of all memory references find their entries in the associative registers.

Answer:

The average (or effective) access time is computed by summing the products of the various values and their probabilities. References through the associative registers take 90 ns and have a probability of 0.60. References through the page table take 220 ns and have a probability of $1.00 - 0.60 = 0.40$. The effective access time is $90 \times 0.60 + 220 \times 0.40 = 142$ nsec.

4.35   On a simple paged system, associative registers hold the most active page entries and the full page table is stored in the main memory. If references satisfied by the associative registers take 100 ns, and references through the main memory page table take 180 ns, what must the hit ratio be to achieve an effective access time of 125 ns?

Answer:

If h is the hit ratio, then $100h + 180 \times (1 - h) = 125$. Solving for h,

$$100h + 180 - 180h = 125$$
$$180 = 125 + 80h$$
$$55 = 80h$$
$$55/80 = h$$
$$0.6875 = h$$
$$68.75\% = h$$

4.36   What advantage does segmentation offer over multiple variable partitions?

Answer:

Because programs are being divided into segments, the size of the object being allocated memory is smaller in segmentation than it is in multiple variable partitions. This increases the chances for filling small memory holes, decreasing external fragmentation.

4.37   On a system using simple segmentation, compute the physical address for each of the logical addresses, given the following segment table. If the address generates a segment fault, indicate so.

Segment	Base	Length
0	330	124
1	876	211
2	111	99
3	498	302

   (a) 0,99

   (b) 2,78

   (c) 1,265

   (d) 3,222

   (e) 0,111

Answer:

(a) 429

Offset 99 is less than the segment length of 124. Segment 0 begins at location 330, so offset 99 is at physical address $99 + 330 = 429$.

(b) 177

Offset 78 is less than the segment length of 99. Segment 2 begins at location 111, so offset 78 is at physical address $78 + 111 = 189$.

(c) Fault

Offset 265 is greater than the segment length of 211. This address results in a segment fault.

(d) 720

Offset 222 is less than the segment length of 302. Segment 3 begins at location 498, so offset 222 is at physical address $222 + 498 = 720$.

(e) 441

Offset 111 is less than the segment length of 124. Segment 0 begins at location 330, so offset 111 is at physical address $111 + 330 = 441$.

4.38 On a system using paging and segmentation, the virtual address space consists of up to 8 segments where each segment can be up to 2^{29} bytes long. The hardware pages each segment into 256-byte pages. How many bits in the virtual address specify the:

(a) Segment number?

(b) Page number?

(c) Offset within page?

(d) Entire virtual address?

Answer:

(a) 3

Since $8 = 2^3$, 3 bits are needed to specify the segment number.

(b) 21

With $256 = 2^8$ byte pages, a 2^{29}-byte segment can have $2^{29}/2^8 = 2^{21}$ pages. Thus, 21 bits are needed to specify the page number.

(c) 8

To specify the offset into the 2^8-byte page, 8 bits are needed.

(d) 32

$3 + 21 + 8 = 32$.

4.39   Why is paging faster than segmentation?

Answer:

In segmentation, the offset must be added to the starting segment address. With paging, no addition need be performed. The page frame number and the offset are concatenated to form the physical address. Concatenating the two bit patterns is faster than adding them.

4.40   What are the two major differences between segmentation and paging?

Answer:

(1)   In segmentation, the program is divided into variable-size segments. In paging, the program is divided into fixed-size pages.

(2)   In segmentation, the user (or compiler) is responsible for dividing the program into segments. In paging, the division into pages is performed by the operating system and is transparent to the user.

 # Supplementary Problems

4.41   In each of the listed memory management schemes, briefly describe the functions performed by the operating system software.

(*a*)   Single Relocatable Partition

(*b*)   Multiple Fixed Partitions

(*c*)   Simple Segmentation

4.42   In each of the listed memory management schemes, briefly describe the functions performed by the memory management hardware.

(*a*)   Single Relocatable Partition

(*b*)   Multiple Fixed Partitions

(*c*)   Simple Segmentation

4.43   A program containing relocatable code was created, assuming it would be loaded at address 100. In its code, the program refers to the following addresses: 135, 160, 164, 220, 224. If the program is loaded into memory starting at location 500, to what do those addresses have to be changed?

4.44   On a system with 2^{32} bytes of memory and fixed partitions, all of size 2^{20} bytes, what is the minimum number of bits needed in an entry in the process table to record the partition to which a process has been allocated?

4.45   In a multiple variable partition scheme,

(*a*)   If the register marking the end of the partition contains the size of the partition, how does the hardware use that register?

(b) If the register marking the end of the partition contains the last physical address of the partition, how does the hardware use that register?

(c) What is the principal advantage of storing the size of the partition over the maximum address in the partition?

4.46 On a system using fixed partitions with sizes 2^8, 2^{24}, and 2^{64}, how many bits must the limit register have?

4.47 On a system using fixed partitions, all of size 2^P, how many bits must the limit register have?

4.48 On a system using first-fit allocation, assume memory is allocated as specified in Fig. 4-11 before additional requests for 10K, 25K, and 20K (in that order) are received. At what starting address will each of the additional requests be allocated?

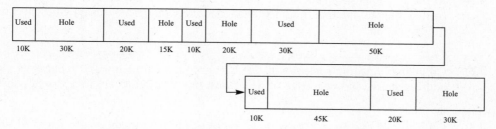

Fig. 4-11. Variable partition memory allocation.

4.49 On a system using best-fit allocation, assume memory is allocated as specified in Fig. 4-11 before additional requests for 10K, 25K, and 20K (in that order) are received. At what starting address will each of the additional requests be allocated?

4.50 On a system using worst-fit allocation, assume memory is allocated as specified in Fig. 4-11 before additional requests for 10K, 25K, and 20K (in that order) are received. At what starting address will each of the additional requests be allocated?

4.51 On a system using next-fit allocation, assume memory is allocated as specified in Fig. 4-11 before additional requests for 10K, 25K, and 20K (in that order) are received. At what starting address will each of the additional requests be allocated?

4.52 On a system with 1Mb of memory using the buddy system, draw a diagram showing the allocation of memory after each of the following events:

(a) Process A, request 150K

(b) Process B, request 40K

(c) Process C, request 80

(d) Process D, request 210

(e) Process B, exit

(f) Process E, request 60

(g) Process C, exit

(h) Process A, exit

(i) Process E, exit

(j) Process F, request 115

(k) Process G, request 150

(l) Process F, exit

(m) Process G, exit

(n) Process D, exit

4.53 On a system with 1Mb of memory using the buddy system, what is the first request that will fail in the following string of requests, due to lack of available memory? Requests: 150K, 70K, 260K, 40K, 70K, 180K, 50K, 120K, 60K.

4.54 In the previous problem, at the time of the failed request, how much memory is wasted due to internal fragmentation and how much is wasted due to external fragmentation?

4.55 On a simple paging system with 2^{32} bytes of physical memory, 2^{12} pages of virtual address space, and page size of 512 bytes, how many bits are in a virtual address?

4.56 On a simple paging system with 2^{32} bytes of physical memory, 2^{12} pages of virtual address space, and page size of 512 bytes, how many bytes are in a page frame?

4.57 On a simple paging system with 2^{32} bytes of physical memory, 2^{12} pages of virtual address space, and page size of 512 bytes, how many bits in the physical address specify the page frame?

4.58 On a simple paging system with 2^{32} bytes of physical memory, 2^{12} pages of virtual address space, and page size of 512 bytes, how many entries are in the page table (how long is the page table)?

4.59 On a simple paging system with 2^{32} bytes of physical memory, 2^{12} pages of virtual address space, and page size of 512 bytes, how many bits are needed to store an entry in the page table (how wide is the page table)? Assume each page table entry contains a valid/invalid bit in addition to the page frame number.

4.60 On a simple paging system with a page table containing 512 entries of 16 bits (including valid/invalid bit) each, and a page size of 1024 bytes, how many bits in the logical address specify the page number?

4.61 On a simple paging system with a page table containing 512 entries of 16 bits (including valid/invalid bit) each, and a page size of 1024 bytes, how many bits in the logical address specify the offset within the page?

4.62 On a simple paging system with a page table containing 512 entries of 16 bits (including valid/invalid bit) each, and a page size of 1024 bytes, how many bits are in a logical address?

4.63 On a simple paging system with a page table containing 512 entries of 16 bits (including valid/invalid bit) each, and a page size of 1024 bytes, what is the size of the logical address space?

4.64 On a simple paging system with a page table containing 512 entries of 16 bits (including valid/invalid bit) each, and a page size of 1024 bytes, how many bits in the physical address specify the page frame number?

4.65 On a simple paging system with a page table containing 512 entries of 16 bits (including valid/invalid bit) each, and a page size of 1024 bytes, how many bits in the physical address specify the offset within the page frame?

4.66 On a simple paging system with a page table containing 512 entries of 16 bits (including valid/invalid bit) each, and a page size of 1024 bytes, how many bits are in a physical address?

4.67 On a simple paging system with a page table containing 512 entries of 16 bits (including valid/invalid bit) each, and a page size of 1024 bytes, what is the size of the physical address space?

4.68 A system that uses a two-level page table has 32-bit virtual addresses. The first 8 bits of the address serve as the index into the first-level page table, and the next 10 bits specify the level-two page table entry.

(a) How many bytes in a page?

(b) How many entries in a level-one page table?

(c) How many entries in a level-two page table?

(d) How many pages in the virtual address space?

4.69 A computer has a 64-bit virtual address space and 2048-byte pages. A page table entry takes 4 bytes. A multilevel page table is used because each table must be contained with a page. How many levels are required?

4.70 On a simple paged system, associative registers hold the most active page entries, and the full page table is stored in main memory. If references satisfied by the associative registers take 60 ns and references through the main memory page table take 200 ns, what is the effective access time if 40% of all memory references find their entries in the associative registers?

4.71 On a simple paged system, associative registers hold the most active page entires, and the full page table is stored in main memory. If reference satisfied by the associative registers take 90 ns and references through the main memory page table take 190 ns, what must the hit ratio be to achieve an effective access time of 120 ns?

4.72 Simulate in a 'C' function the memory management hardware in a simple segmented system. Write the function 'Trans', which takes a segmented virtual address and translates it into a physical address, returning the physical address as an **int**. You may assume the function *Fault* handles segment faults and has already been written. The 'segTable' variable contains the segment table.

```
struct SegTableType
        {       int     loc;     /* Starting segment addr        */
                int     len;     /* Length of segment in bytes   */
        };
struct VirtualAddressType
        {       int     seg;     /* Portion of address specifying
                                                        segment */
                int     off;     /* Portion of address specifying
                                                        offset  */

        };
struct SegTableType segTable[NUMBER_SEGMENTS];
void Fault ();          /* Processes a segment fault. */
```

4.73 On a system using simple segmentation, compute the physical address for each of the logical addresses, given the following segment table. If the address generates a segment fault, indicate so.

Segment	Base	Length
0	1100	500
1	2500	1000
2	200	600
3	4000	1200

(a)   0,300

(b)   2,800

(c)   1,600

(d)   3,1100

(e)   1,1111

4.74 On a system using paging and segmentation, the virtual address space consists of up to 16 segments where each segment can be up to 2^{16} bytes long. The hardware pages each segment into 512-byte pages. How many bits in the virtual address specify the following?

(a)   Segment number

(b)   Page number

(c)   Offset within page

(d)   Entire virtual address

Answers to Supplementary Problems

4.41   (*a*)   Single Relocatable Partition
When the system is booted, the operating system loads the relocation register with the address of the lowest memory location that can be accessed by a user program.

(*b*)   Multiple Fixed Partitions
When the operating system is booted up, it must load the size of a partition into the size register. The operating system must keep track of which partitions are in use and which are free. When a process is created or a process terminates, the operating system must update the partition usage data. Before allocating a process to memory, the operating system must check that the process is smaller than the partition size. When a process is given control of the CPU, the operating system must load the process's starting address into the relocation register.

(*c*)   Simple Segmentation
The operating system must keep track of which memory locations are in use and which are free. When a process is created, the operating system must allocate the segments to memory and create a segment table for the process. When a process terminates, the operating system must reset its memory locations as free. When a process is given control of the CPU, the operating system must load the process's segment table into the memory management registers. If a segment fault occurs, the operating system must handle the fault.

4.42   (*a*)   Single Relocatable Partition
Each time a memory location is referenced, its address is added to the address in the relocation register to form the physical address.

(*b*)   Multiple Fixed Partitions
Each time a memory location is referenced, its logical address is compared to the address in the size register. An address larger than the address in the size register results in a memory-fault trap. At the same time, the logical address is added to the address in the relocation register to generate the physical address.

(*c*)   Simple Segmentation
Each time a memory location is referenced, the segmentation hardware translates the logical address into the physical address. The segment number bits in the logical address are used an index into the segment table. The logical address segment offset bits are added to the segment's starting address, obtained from the appropriate segment table entry, to form the physical address.

4.43   535, 560, 564, 620, 624

4.44   12 bits

4.45   (*a*)   Each logical address generated by a program is compared to the size (or limit) register. Any address greater than the size register results in a memory-fault trap.

(b) Each logical address is added to the relocation register to generate a physical address. The physical address is then compared to the maximum physical address. Any address greater than the maximum physical address results in a memory-fault trap.

(c) The comparison of the logical address to the size can occur at the same time that the relocation register is being added to the logical address. The comparison of the physical address to the maximum physical address must occur after the addition. By doing the comparison concurrently, the mapping from virtual to physical address can be accomplished faster.

4.46 64

4.47 P

4.48 10K, 135K, 20K

4.49 60K, 10K, 85K

4.50 135K, 185K, 10K

4.51 10K, 135K, 160K

4.52 (a) Process A, request 150K

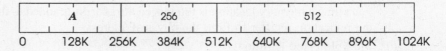

(b) Process B, request 40K

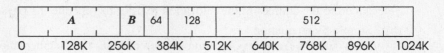

(c) Process C, request 80

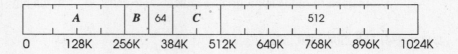

(d) Process D, request 210

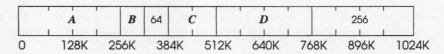

(e) Process B, exit

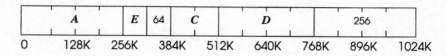

(f) Process E, request 60

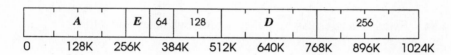

(g) Process C, exit

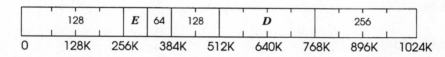

(h) Process A, exit

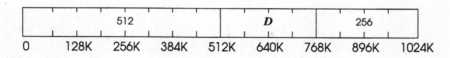

(i) Process E, exit

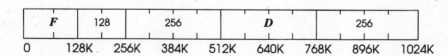

(j) Process F, request 115

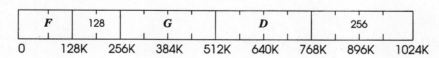

(k) Process G, request 150

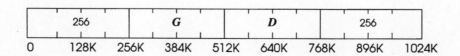

(l) Process F, exit

(*m*)   Process G, exit

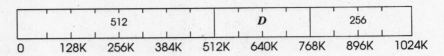

(*n*)   Process D, exit

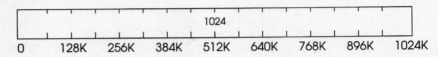

4.53   70K

4.54   External fragmentation: 64K; Internal fragmentation: 440K

4.55   21

4.56   512

4.57   23

4.58 $2^{12} = 4096$

4.59   24

4.60   9

4.61   10

4.62   19

4.63 2^{19}

4.64   15

4.65   10

4.66   25

4.67 2^{25}

4.68 (*a*) 2^{14}
(*b*) 2^8
(*c*) 2^{10}
(*d*) 2^{18}

4.69 Six

4.70 144

4.71 70%

4.72
```
int Trans(struct VirtualAddressType virtAddr)
{
    int physAddr = -1;
    if (virtAddr.off >= segTable(virtaddr.seg).len)
        fault();
    else
        physAddr = segTable(virtAddr.seg).loc + virtAddr.off;
    return physAddr;
}
```

4.73 (*a*) 1400
(*b*) Fault
(*c*) 3100
(*d*) 5100
(*e*) Fault

4.74 (*a*) 4
(*b*) 7
(*c*) 9
(*d*) 20

Virtual Memory

On a *virtual memory* system, the logical memory space available to the program is totally independent of the physical memory space. Programs needing 2^{20} bytes of memory can run on a virtual memory system with only 2^{16} bytes of actual memory. Virtual memory frees programs from the constraints of physical memory limitations.

5.1   Demand Paging

Demand paging combines the features of simple paging and overlaying to implement virtual memory. In a demand-paged system, each page of a program is stored contiguously in the paging swap space on secondary storage. As locations in pages are referenced, the pages are copied into memory page frames. Once the page is in memory, it is accessed as in simple paging.

Each entry in the page table has at a minimum two fields: page frame and in/out bit. When a virtual address is generated, the memory management hardware extracts the page number from the address, and the appropriate entry in the page table is accessed. The in/out bit is checked and, if the page is in memory, the physical address is generated by appending the page offset to the page frame number. If the page is not in memory, a *page fault* occurs, transferring control to the page fault routine in the operating system.

When a page fault occurs, the operating system checks to see if any page frames in memory are free. If not, it selects one page for removal. The page marked for removal is copied back out to secondary storage and the in/out bit in its entry in the page table is set to "out". Given a free page frame, the operating system copies the page into the free page frame. The page table entry for the swapped-in page is modified to indicate the page frame number and that the page is in memory. The page fault routine then completes and the hardware reexecutes the instruction generating the trap.

A *dirty bit* can be added to each page table entry. The dirty bit is set by the memory management hardware when there is a write-memory reference to that page. When a page is first loaded into memory, the dirty bit is cleared. If the dirty bit for a page selected for replacement is not set, the page has not been modified since it was loaded into memory. Only replaced pages that have been modified need be written back out to the swapping store.

5.1.1 LOCALITY OF REFERENCE

For reference to swapped-in pages, address translation is performed totally by hardware yielding performance comparable to nonvirtual memory systems. References to swapped-out pages results in page-fault traps, slowing the access time by more than an order of magnitude. Overall performance would be unacceptable if memory reference were random. However, references tend to localize to a small set of pages. This *locality* results in the ratio of "hitting" a swapped-in page versus a swapped-out page being high enough to yield reasonable average access times. The ordered list of page numbers accessed by a program is called its *reference string*.

Locality exhibits itself in two forms. If a memory location has been referenced, there is a good chance it will be referenced again in a short period of time. This is called *temporal locality*. *Spatial locality* refers to the fact that if a memory location is accessed, it is likely that a location near it will be accessed in the next instruction.

Experiments have shown that during the execution of a process, references tend to group together in a number of different localities (Fig. 5-1). For example, a program executing in a loop will access a set of pages that contain the instructions and data referenced in that loop. Calls to functions will tend to increase the numbers of pages in the locality. When the program breaks out of the loop, it may move to another section of code whose locality of pages is virtually distinct from the previous locality.

5.1.2 PAGE LOCKING

The paging system must be able to lock pages in memory so they cannot be swapped out. Much of the operating system must be locked into memory. Most importantly, the code that selects the next page to be swapped in should never be swapped out; it could never execute itself to swap itself back in.

The design of the I/O system may also require some of the pages in a process to be kept swapped-in. If device I/O operations may read or write data directly to a process's memory locations, the pages containing those memory locations may not be swapped out. Although they may not be currently referenced by the process, they are being referenced by the I/O device. Setting a *lock bit* in a page table entry prevents a page from being swapped out.

Although care must be taken to avoid swapping some pages out, a lock bit in the page table is not required in all cases. The system may be designed such that no operating system page is ever swapped out. The I/O system could be designed such that it does not allow I/O directly to a process's address space; all devices would be required to transfer data to and from an operating system buffer. In such a system,

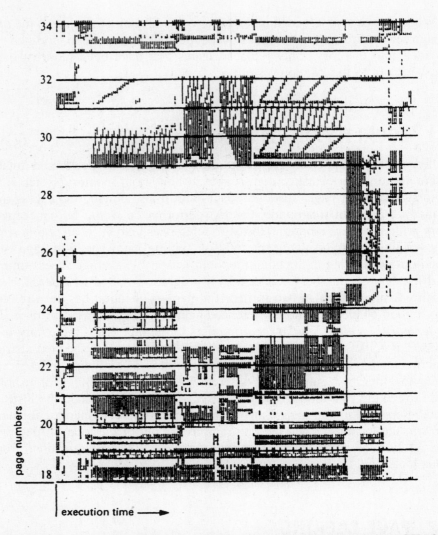

Fig. 5-1. **Locality in a memory reference pattern. (Reproduced by permission of Hatfield, D.,** "Experiments on Page Size Program Access Patterns, and Virtual Memory Performance," *IBM Journal of Research and Development*, **January 1972.)**

swapping is limited to user-process pages, and the system can be designed so that any user-process page can be swapped at any time.

5.1.3 PAGE SIZE

A number of factors affect the determination of the page size.

- The page size is always power of 2, typically ranging from 512 bytes to 16K.
- A small page size reduces internal fragmentation.
- A large page size reduces the number of pages needed, thereby reducing the size of the page table. A smaller page table requires less memory (the space lost to storing page table is sometimes referred to as *table fragmentation*). If

the page table must be loaded into page registers, load time is reduced by having smaller tables.

- A large page size reduces the overhead involved in swapping pages in or out. In addition to the processing time required to handle a page fault, the I/O operation includes the time required to move the disk's read/write head to the appropriate track (*seek time*), the time required for the appropriate sector to spin under the read/write head (*latency time*), and the time to read the page (*transfer time*). Since the seek and latency times are typically more than 90% of the total time, reading two 1K blocks can take almost twice as long as reading one 2K block.

- A smaller page size, with its finer resolution, is better able to target the process's locality of references. This reduces the amount of unused information copied back and forth between memory and swapping storage. It also reduces the amount of unused information stored in main memory, making more memory available for useful purposes.

5.1.4 PAGE REPLACEMENT ALGORITHMS

The algorithm that selects the page to be swapped out is called the *page replacement algorithm*. The *optimal page replacement algorithm* selects for removal the page that will not be referenced again for the longest span of executed instructions. Unfortunately, this algorithm is only a theoretical device. Implementing it would require knowledge of what would happen in the future. Therefore, its use is limited to serving as a benchmark to which other page-replacement algorithms may be compared.

The *First-in First-out* (FIFO) page-replacement algorithm selects the page that has been in memory the longest. To implement this algorithm, page table entries must include a field for the swap-in time. When a page is swapped in, the operating system loads the field with the current time. The page selected for replacement will be the one with the earliest swap-in time. Although easy to implement and inexpensive, FIFO is not very efficient. Frequently used pages, even though they have been in memory the longest, should obviously not be swapped out. FIFO does not consider the amount they have been used and swaps them out anyway.

The *Least Recently Used* (LRU) algorithm keeps track of the last time each page was used, not when it was swapped in. The memory management hardware uses a counter which is incremented during each memory reference. Each page table entry has a field that stores the value of the counter. When a page is referenced, the value of the counter is stored in the page table entry for that page. The LRU algorithm searches the table for the entry with the lowest counter value and selects that page for replacement.

On a system with n page frames, an $n \times n$ matrix provides an alternate method for implementing the LRU algorithm. The matrix is initialized to contain all 0's. When page frame k is accessed, all bits in row k are set to 1. Then all bits in column k are set to 0. If row i contains the lowest binary value, then page frame i is the least recently used. Figure 5-2 shows the matrix for a system with 4 page frames given references to pages in the order 0, 1, 3, and 2.

0	1	1	1
0	0	0	0
0	0	0	0
0	0	0	0

Page 0

0	0	1	1
1	0	1	1
1	0	0	0
0	0	0	0

Page 1

0	0	0	0
0	0	0	0
1	1	0	1
1	1	0	0

Page 2

0	0	1	0
1	0	1	0
0	1	0	0
0	1	1	0

Page 3

Fig. 5-2.   LRU matrix.

Not Recently Used (NRU) is an approximation of LRU. In addition to a dirty bit, each page table entry contains a reference bit. When a page is loaded, the operating system sets the reference bit to 0. When a page is accessed, the hardware sets the bit to 1. In addition, at periodic intervals the operating system will set all the reference bits in the page table back to 0. A value of 0 in the reference bit means it has not been referenced "recently"; a 1 means it has.

The entries can be divided into sets depending on the value in the reference and dirty bits. First priority is to select a page with its reference bit set to 0. Second priority is to pick a page whose dirty bit is 0, since swapping out a dirty page is more time-consuming than swapping out a clean page. The operating system is free to choose any page from among multiple pages with the same reference and dirty bit settings.

Another approximation of LRU called *aging* is achieved by adding a reference byte to page table entries. When a page is accessed, the hardware sets the most significant bit in the reference byte. As in NRU, timer interrupts are used to activate an operating system routine, although the interrupt interval is typically less in this algorithm than in NRU. The operating system shifts all the bits right by one in the reference bytes. A page with the lowest binary value in its reference byte is selected for removal. As with NRU, the operating system may pick any page from among all the pages with the lowest value.

The *Second Chance* replacement algorithm is a combination of the FIFO and NRU algorithms. It selects the oldest page as a candidate for removal and removes it if its reference bit is 0. However, if its reference bit is 1, its load time is reset to the current time, and its reference bit is set to 0. The algorithm then repeats, with the second oldest page now being the oldest. The process continues until a page is selected.

5.1.5 ALGORITHM PERFORMANCE

The performance of the various algorithms can be compared given different sequences of memory references. The list of pages accessed by a process is called its *reference string*. Given an algorithm, a reference string, and the number of page frames, the number of page faults triggered can be determined and used as the basis for comparing the algorithms.

One can also compare performance of a particular algorithm given varying numbers of page frames allocated to a process. One would expect that increasing the number of page frames would result in the same or fewer page faults. This is not always the case. Under some circumstances, a situation called *Belady's anomaly* occurs, and more page frames result in more page faults.

5.1.6 ALLOCATION POLICIES

The hardware of a machine dictates an absolute minimum number of frames which must be allocated to any process. When a page fault occurs, the needed page is loaded into memory and the instruction is reexecuted. If the instruction refers to two addresses but the process is allocated only a single frame, an infinite cycle of page faults would occur. On machines with indirect addressing and instructions with multiple operands, a single instruction can refer to addresses in a number of page frames.

For performance reasons, the minimum number of frames per process is typically higher than the absolute minimum dictated by the hardware. Belady's anomaly notwithstanding, performance usually improves as the number of page frames allocated increases. Whatever the minimum, it can be achieved only by limiting the number of processes that are allocated page frames. This task is performed by the long-term process scheduler. The long-term scheduler limits the. number of processes sharing page frames so that the frequency of page faults results in an acceptable level of performance. Degraded performance because of excessive swapping is known as *thrashing*.

The operating system must decide how many page frames to allocate to each process. One strategy called *equal allocation* divides the available page frames equally among the processes. *Proportional allocation* divides the frames in proportion to the sizes of the processes. In either case, a fixed number of frames are allocated to each process. Fixed allocation can be used with a *local scope* replacement algorithm. A local scope replacement algorithm selects for removal a page from the process that generated the page fault.

Alternatively, an operating system may employ a *variable allocation*, *global scope* algorithm. On such a system, when the replacement algorithm searches for a page for removal, it selects the page from all the processes on the machine. The number of frames allocated to a process would vary as they are measured against the pages from other processes. If the algorithm selects a page for removal that would drop the process below the minimum allocation, either another page is selected or all the process pages are swapped out.

A compromise strategy is to use variable allocation with local scope. The number of pages allocated to a process varies according to the needs of the process. However, the page to be replaced is always selected from the currently executing process. The number of pages allocated to a process is typically based on the process's *working set*.

5.1.7 WORKING SET

The working set of a process at any particular time is the set of pages referenced over some preceding time interval. The working set is frequently expressed using the functional notation $W(t, \Delta)$ where W represents the working set, t represents the time, and Δ represents the interval. Usually it is simplest for time to be measured in terms of executed instructions (a time unit of one means one executed instruction).

The goal is to pick a value for Δ so that the working set reflects the locality of the program. Too small a value for Δ and the working set will not include all the pages in the current locality. Too large a value for Δ and the working set includes pages from a previous locality.

Although knowledge of the pages in the working set of a process is of minimal value to the operating system, knowledge of the size of the working set can be used to determine how many pages to allocate to each process. The number of processes allocated to memory is adjusted so that each process is allocated the number of frames indicated by the working set size.

5.1.8 PREPAGING

If the operating system knows the working set at the time a process was swapped out, it can *prepage* all the pages in that working set when the process is swapped back in. Prepaging prevents the initial reference to the working set pages from generating a page fault. This saves the operating system the extra overhead of processing those page faults. However, some of the pages loaded may never get referenced. Prepaging a page which is not referenced degrades I/O performance and wastes page frames.

Prepaging may also be used at the time of a page fault. In addition to loading the page that generated the fault, the next page in virtual memory may also be loaded. For programs whose execution is primarily sequential, access to one page can be a predictor of an access to the next page. The time cost of swapping both pages is minimal, since disk latency and seek time are the same whether a single page is swapped or two contiguous pages are swapped. The major disadvantage of this form of prepaging is the frames wasted by pages that are brought in but not referenced. Because of this disadvantage, this technique has not been shown to be generally effective.

5.2 Segmentation

Just as simple paging can be modified to create demand paging, segmentation can be modified to create demand segmentation. However, the variability of segment sizes complicates many of the issues encountered in demand paging. In making swapping decisions, the size of the segments becomes a factor in deciding which segment to swap. The entire notion of a working set is distorted by the different sizes of the segments.

A far more practical way to implement segmentation in a virtual memory system is to combine it with demand paging. Either segments are always considered swapped-in, or the swap status of a segment is determined by whether its page table is swapped-in. Thus, handling of segments works basically the same way it works in a simple segmented and paged system. The virtual memory capability is created by demand paging the segments.

Solved Problems

5.1 In this problem, use decimal values, a page size of 2000 bytes, and the following page table.

In/out	Frame
in	20
out	22
in	200
in	150
out	30
out	50
in	120
in	101

Which of the following virtual addresses would generate a page fault? For those that do not generate a page fault, to what physical address would they translate?

(*a*)   10451

(*b*)   5421

(*c*)   14123

(*d*)   9156

Answer:

(*a*)   Fault
  Virtual address 10451 is offset 451 in page 5. Page 5 is "out" resulting in a fault.

(*b*)   401,421
  Virtual address 5421 is offset 1421 in page 2. Page 2 is "in" at frame 200 which is address 400,000. Adding the offset to the frame's starting address yields physical address 401,421.

(*c*)   202,123
  Virtual address 14123 is offset 123 in page 7. Page 7 is "in" at frame 101 which is address 202,000. Adding the offset to the frame's starting address yields physical address 202,123.

(*d*)   Fault
  Virtual address 9156 is offset 1156 in page 4. Page 4 is "out" resulting in a fault.

5.2 In this problem, use binary values, a page size of 2^6 bytes, and the following page table.

In/out	Frame
out	00101
in	00001
in	11011
in	11010
out	10001
out	10101
out	11000
in	00101
...	...

Which of the following virtual addresses would generate a page fault? For those that do not generate a page fault, to what physical address would they translate?

(*a*)   0000101101001

(*b*)   0000010010010

(*c*)   0000100010101

(*d*)   0000001110101

Answer:

(*a*)   Fault
Separating the address into page number and offset yields 0000101,101001. Page 5 is out, resulting in a fault.

(*b*)   11011010010
Separating the address into page number and offset yields 0000010,010010. Page 2 uses frame 11011 to which offset 010010 must be appended, yielding physical address 11011010010.

(*c*)   Fault
Separating the address into page number and offset yields 0000100,010101. Page 4 is out, resulting in a fault.

(*d*)   00001110101
Separating the address into page number and offset yields 0000001,110101. Page 1 uses frame 00001 to which offset 110101 must be appended, yielding physical address 00001110101.

5.3   On a system using demand-paged memory, it takes 200 ns to satisfy a memory request if the page is in memory. If the page is not in memory, the request takes 7 ms if a free frame is available or the page to be swapped out has not been modified. It takes 15 ms if the page to be swapped out has been modified. What is the effective access time if the page fault rate is 5%, and 60% of the time the page to be replaced has been modified? Assume the system is only running a single process and the CPU is idle during page swaps.

Answer:

The percentage of accesses satisfied in 200 ns is 95%. Of the 5% of accesses that result in a page fault, 40% require 7 ms. Thus, 5% × 40% = 2% of all accesses take

7 ms. Similarly, 5% × 60% = 3% of accesses take 15 ms. Converting all times to μs yields the following.

$$\text{Effective access time} = 0.95 \times 0.2 + 0.02 \times 7000 + 0.03 \times 15000$$
$$\text{Effective access time} = 590.19 \,\mu s$$

5.4   On a system using demand-paged memory, it takes 120 ns to satisfy a memory request if the page is in memory. If the page is not in memory, the request takes (on average) 5 ms. What would the page fault rate need to be to achieve an effective access time of 1 μs? Assume the system is only running a single process and the CPU is idle during page swaps.

Answer:

If the page fault rate is p, the percentage of accesses satisfied in 5 ms is p, and the percentage of accesses satisfied in 120 ns is $(1 - p)$. Inserting those figures in the equation to compute effective access time, and converting all times to μs, yields the following.

$$\text{Effective access time} = (1 - p) \times 0.12 + p \times 5000$$
$$1000 = (1 - p) \times 0.12 + p \times 5000$$
$$1000 = 0.12 - p \times 0.12 + p \times 5000$$
$$999.88 = p \times 4999.88$$
$$999.88/4999.88 = p$$
$$19.998\% = p$$

5.5   Assume the amount of memory on a system is inversely proportional to the page fault rate. Each time memory doubles, the page fault rate is cut in half. Currently the system has 32 Mb of memory. When a page fault occurs, the average access time is 1 ms, 1 μs otherwise. Overall, the effective access time is 300 μs. How much additional memory would be needed to cut the effective access time to 100 μs? Assume the total memory in the system must be a power of 2.

Answer:

The current page fault rate can be computed using the following equation.

$$300 = (1 - p) \times 1 + p \times 1000$$
$$299 = p \times 999$$
$$299/999 = p$$
$$29.93\% = p$$

The page fault rate necessary for a 100-μs access time can be computed as follows.

$$100 = (1 - p) \times 1 + p \times 1000$$
$$99 = p \times 999$$
$$99/999 = p$$
$$9.91\% = p$$

The page fault rate of 29.93% must be halved twice to 7.48% to get it under 9.91%. Memory must be increased to 128 Mb.

5.6 If an instruction takes time m if there is no page fault, and time n if there is a page fault, what is the effective instruction time if page faults occur once every i instructions?

Answer:

For every i instructions, $i - 1$ instructions will take time m, and one instruction will take time n. The average instruction time is

$$\frac{(i - 1) \times m + n}{i} = m + \frac{(n - m)}{i}$$

5.7 Give an example of access to variables within a program that results in temporal locality.

Answer:

A program using a variable in a statement is likely to access that variable again in the next few instructions.

5.8 Give an example of access to variables within a program that results in spatial locality.

Answer:

Local variables are typically allocated adjacent memory locations (perhaps locations on a stack). Accessing two local variables typically results in references to memory locations in close proximity to each other.

5.9 Give an example of access to instructions within a program that results in temporal locality.

Answer:

An instruction in a loop will be accessed again in a short period of time when the loop cycles back for subsequent iterations.

5.10 Give an example of access to instructions within a program that results in spatial locality.

Answer:

Sequential execution of instructions results in the next instruction executed being located in a memory location close to the previous location.

5.11 Given a page size of s and an average process size of p in a simple paged system, what is the average amount of memory lost per process due to internal fragmentation?

Answer:

The only space a process wastes is the portion of the last page that is unused. On average, half of the last page will be unused. The average wasted space per process is $s/2$. The average process size does not affect the answer.

5.12 A process has access to f frames, initially all empty. If the process makes m memory accesses to p distinct pages, what is the minimum number of page faults that will occur? The maximum?

Answer:

The minimum number of page faults occurs if each of the p distinct pages is swapped in only once or p times. This is possible, for example, if f is greater than or equal to p. Even if f is less than p, the number of swaps may be limited to p. This occurs when there are subsets of the p pages such that no page exists in more than one subset, each subset contains at most f pages, and all references to pages in each subset occur contiguously. (First, pages only in the first subset are referenced, then the second, etc.)

The maximum number of page faults occurs if each reference results in a page fault or m times. This can occur only when f is less than p. However, if the reference pattern occurs such that the next page referenced is the page previously replaced, each reference will cause a fault.

5.13 Given a system with the following utilization characteristics,

CPU	Low
Swap device	Very high
Other I/O devices	Low

for each of the following, indicate if it is likely to significantly improve, significantly degrade, or have only a minor effect on CPU utilization.

(*a*) Install a faster CPU.

(*b*) Install a larger swap device.

(*c*) Install a faster swap device.

(*d*) Install more memory.

(*e*) Install faster memory.

(*f*) Increase the degree of multiprogramming.

(*g*) Decrease the degree of multiprogramming.

(*h*) Install faster I/O devices.

Answer:

Given the high utilization of the swap device and low utilization of memory, overall system performance is being degraded by excessive swapping.

(*a*) Install a faster CPU.
A faster CPU will probably lower CPU utilization, although the extent it gets lower could be minor.

(*b*) Install a larger swap device.
This would have no effect.

(*c*) Install a faster swap device.
This would probably help because it is probable the CPU is frequently idle, waiting for swap operations to complete.

(*d*) Install more memory.
This would also help by reducing the amount of swapping needed (thereby reducing the frequency of swap device I/O operations).

(*e*) Install faster memory.
This would have no effect.

(*f*) Increase the degree of multiprogramming.
This would probably degrade performance further, by making thrashing worse.

(*g*) Decrease the degree of multiprogramming.
This may be a no-cost way of improving performance. The main objective of multiprogramming is to have enough processes in memory so that all processes are rarely blocked. Given both CPU and device utilization are low, it may be possible to decrease the number of processes (reducing swapping), yet still have ready processes available to run on the CPU.

(*h*) Install faster I/O devices.
Given the already low device utilization, this will probably at best result in a minor improvement.

5.14 Given the average size of a process is p, the page size is s, and the size of a page table entry is e, what page size minimizes wasted space due to internal and table fragmentation?

Answer:

Since the average number of pages required per process will be p/s, the amount of space required by the page table will be pe/s. The amount of space lost to internal fragmentation is $s/2$, making the equation for total lost space

$$\text{Waste} = pe/s + s/2$$

To find the value of s that yields the minimal value, take the first derivative with respect to s and set the resulting equation to zero.

$$0 = -pe/s^2 + 1/2$$

Solving for s yields

$$pe/s^2 = 1/2$$
$$1/2 = pe/s^2$$
$$s^2/2 = pe$$
$$s^2 = pe/2$$
$$s = \sqrt{2pe}$$

5.15 Give a reference string for the FIFO replacement algorithm that causes Belady's anomaly to occur when the number of frames increases from three to four.

Answer:

1,2,3,4,1,2,5,1,2,3,4,5
If three frames are allocated, pages will be swapped as follows.

Before	Page	Fault	After
–,–,–	1	*	1,–,–
1,–,–	2	*	2,1,–
2,1,–	3	*	3,2,1
3,2,1	4	*	4,3,2
4,3,2	1	*	1,4,3
1,4,3	2	*	2,1,4
2,1,4	5	*	5,2,1
5,2,1	1		5,2,1
5,2,1	2		5,2,1
5,2,1	3	*	3,5,2
3,5,2	4	*	4,3,5
4,3,5	5		4,3,5

The number of page faults for three frames is nine. If four frames are allocated, pages will be swapped as follows.

Before	Page	Fault	After
–,–,–,–	1	*	1,–,–,–
1,–,–,–	2	*	2,1,–,–
2,1,–,–	3	*	3,2,1,–
3,2,1,–	4	*	4,3,2,1
4,3,2,1	1		4,3,2,1
4,3,2,1	2		4,3,2,1
4,3,2,1	5	*	5,4,3,2
5,4,3,2	1	*	1,5,4,3
1,5,4,3	2	*	2,1,5,4
2,1,5,4	3	*	3,2,1,5
3,2,1,5	4	*	4,3,2,1
4,3,2,1	5	*	5,4,3,2

The number of page faults for four frames is ten.

5.16 The second-chance algorithm rejects pages that have their reference bit set to 1. What happens if all pages have their reference bit set to 1?

Answer:

If all pages originally had their reference bits set to 1, each in turn will have its load time reset and its reference bit set to 0. After all pages have been processed, the load time order will be the same as it was originally, except all pages will now have their reference bits set to 0. The page that had originally been the oldest will be selected.

5.17 Prove that in matrix implementation of LRU, the value in row k of the matrix is greater than the value in any other row i if and only if page k was accessed the most recently.

Answer:

For any i, matrix location $i \times i$ must contain 0 since all column i entries are set to 0 in any operation that places 1's in a row i (including column i in row i). If the most recent access was to page k, row k will contain a 1 in every column except column k. Moreover, for all values of i, matrix location $i \times k$ will be 0. Thus, for every row i such that $i \neq k$, that row will have a 0 in the only column (k) in which row k has a 0, and will also have a 0 in column i, a row in which row k has a 1. As a result, the value in row k must be less than the value in row i, $i \neq k$. The value in row k of the matrix is greater than the value in any other row i if page k was accessed most recently.

To prove the value is greater only if it was accessed most recently, assume row k contains the largest value, but some other page j was accessed most recently. By the proof above, the value in row j must be greater than the value in row k. But our assumption was the value in k was greater than the value in any other row. By contradiction, the value in row k of the matrix is greater than the value in any other row i only if page k was accessed most recently.

5.18 Given a system with four page frames, the following table indicates page, load time, last reference time, dirty bit, and reference bit.

Page	Load Time	Last Reference	Dirty Bit	Reference Bit
0	167	374	1	1
1	321	321	0	0
2	254	306	1	0
3	154	331	0	1

(a) Which page will FIFO replace?

(b) Which page will LRU replace?

(c) Which page will NRU replace?

(d) Which page will second chance replace?

Answer:

(a) 3
    FIFO selects the page loaded first, page 3 at time 154.

(b) 2
    LRU selects the page referenced last, page 2 at time 306.

(c) 1
    NRU first looks for a clean page that was not recently referenced. Page 1 is the only such page.

(*d*)   2

Second chance first checks the oldest page, page 3. Since its reference bit is 1, it resets that bit to 0 and sets the entry's load time to the current time. The same thing happens to page 0, the next oldest page. The reference bit for page 2 is then checked, and since it is 0 it is the selected page.

5.19   A computer system has four frames and uses six reference bits to implement an aging page-replacement algorithm. At the first clock tick, the reference bits for pages 0 through 3 are 1, 0, 1, and 1, respectively. At the next clock tick, the bits are 0011. Values at subsequent ticks are 1001, 0110, 1100, and 0001. After the last tick, what is the value of the reference byte for all four pages?

Answer:

Values of the counters after each tick would be as follows.

Page Number	Tick 1	Tick 2	Tick 3	Tick 4	Tick 5	Tick 6
0	100000	010000	101000	010100	101010	010101
1	000000	000000	000000	100000	110000	011000
2	100000	110000	011000	101100	010110	001011
3	100000	110000	111000	011100	001110	100111

5.20   Prove that a page-replacement strategy that suffers from Belady's anomaly cannot be optimal.

Answer:

If the algorithm suffers from Belady's anomaly, then for some number of fewer page frames allocated to the process, the algorithm will generate fewer page faults. Running the same algorithm modified to use just the fewer number of page frames (leaving the others unused) will yield better performance. Since the modified algorithm yields better performance, the original is not optimal.

5.21   Given references to the following pages by a program,

$$0, 9, 0, 1, 8, \quad 1, 8, 7, 8, 7, \quad 1, 2, 8, 2, 7, \quad 8, 2, 3, 8, 3,$$

how many page faults will occur if the program has three page frames available to it and uses:

(*a*)   FIFO replacement?

(*b*)   LRU replacement?

(*c*)   Optimal replacement?

Answer:

(a) FIFO replacement

Before	Page	Fault	After
–,–,–	0	*	0,–,–
0,–,–	9	*	9,0,–
9,0,–	0		9,0,–
9,0,–	1	*	1,9,0
1,9,0	8	*	8,1,9
8,1,9	1		8,1,9
8,1,9	8		8,1,9
8,1,9	7	*	7,8,1
7,8,1	8		7,8,1
7,8,1	7		7,8,1
7,8,1	1		7,8,1
7,8,1	2	*	2,7,8
2,7,8	8		2,7,8
2,7,8	2		2,7,8
2,7,8	7		2,7,8
2,7,8	8		2,7,8
2,7,8	2		2,7,8
2,7,8	3	*	3,2,7
3,2,7	8	*	8,3,2
8,3,2	3		8,3,2

8 faults.

(b) LRU replacement

Before	Page	Fault	After
–,–,–	0	*	0,–,–
0,–,–	9	*	9,0,–
9,0,–	0		0,9,–
0,9,–	1	*	1,0,9
1,0,9	8	*	8,1,0
8,1,0	1		1,8,0
1,8,0	8		8,1,0
8,1,0	7	*	7,8,1
7,8,1	8		8,7,1
8,7,1	7		7,8,1
7,8,1	1		1,7,8
1,7,8	2	*	2,1,7
2,1,7	8	*	8,2,1
8,2,1	2		2,8,1
2,8,1	7	*	7,2,8
7,2,8	8		8,7,2
8,7,2	2		2,8,7
2,8,7	3	*	3,2,8
3,2,8	8		8,3,2
8,3,2	3		3,8,2

9 faults.

(c) Optimal replacement

Before	Page	Fault	After
−,−,−	0	*	0,−,−
0,−,−	9	*	9,0,−
9,0,−	0		9,0,−
9,0,−	1	*	1,9,0
1,9,0	8	*	8,1,9
8,1,9	1		8,1,9
8,1,9	8		8,1,9
8,1,9	7	*	7,8,1
7,8,1	8		7,8,1
7,8,1	7		7,8,1
7,8,1	1		7,8,1
7,8,1	2	*	2,7,8
2,7,8	8		2,7,8
2,7,8	2		2,7,8
2,7,8	7		2,7,8
2,7,8	8		2,7,8
2,7,8	2		2,7,8
2,7,8	3	*	3,2,8
3,2,8	8		3,2,8
3,2,8	3		3,2,8

7 faults.

5.22 You have a demand-paged system where intergers are stored in 4 bytes, pages are 256 bytes, LRU page replacement is used, and each process is allocated 3 frames. A process executes the following code.

```
int [] []a = new int[200] [200];
int i = 0;
int j = 0;
while (i++<200) {
  j = 0;
  while (j++<200)
      a[i][j] = 0;
}
```

The code occupies page 0 and, since a location from page 0 is referenced each instruction, page 0 is always swapped-in. Variables i and j are stored in fast registers.

(a) How many pages are needed for the array, assuming all elements of the array are stored in contiguous memory locations?

(b) How many page faults will this program generate?

Answer:

(a) The array has $200 \times 200 = 40{,}000$ elements, each requiring 4 bytes of storage. 160,000 bytes occupy 625 pages.

(*b*)   The program accesses the locations in the array in the order they are stored. Thus, it will swap-in the instruction page, and each of the 625 data pages once, for a total of 626 swaps.

5.23   In the previous problem, how many page faults will be generated if the program was written as follows?

```
int [] [] a = new int[200] [200];
int i = 0;
int j = 0;
while (i++<200)) {
  j = 0;
  while (j++<200})
    a[j] [i] = 0;
}
```

Answer:

Since the program is now varying the first subscript in its inner loop, the references will be to the following locations in the array space:

$$0, \ 800, \ 1600, \dots, 159200, \ 1, 801, \dots$$

Since each reference is to a location in a different page, each reference will result in a page fault. Given, there are 40,000 data references, there will be 40,001 page faults total.

5.24   Given references to the following pages by a program:

$$0,9,0,1,8, \quad 1,8,7,8,7, \quad 1,2,8,2,7, \quad 8,2,3,8,3,$$

what is the working set $W(t, \Delta)$, with t equal to the time between the 15th and 16th references, and Δ equal to 6 references?

Answer:

The 6 references before the 16th reference are 7, 1, 2, 8, 2, and 7. Thus, $W(t, \Delta) = \{1, 2, 7, 8\}$.

5.25   A system using demand-paged segments has a 16-bit virtual address space with 2 segments per process and a page size of 2^{12}. The content of the segment and page tables is specified below (all values binary). Segment length is in increments of the page size.

Segment Table	
Page Table	Length
Pointer to Page Table 0	111
Pointer to Page Table 1	110

Page Table 0	
Frame	In
101011	1
001010	0
001011	1
100110	1
001100	0
110110	1
111010	0
011101	0

Page Table 1	
Frame	In
010100	0
110101	1
110100	0
011001	0
110011	1
001001	0
000101	1
100010	1

For the following binary virtual addresses, indicate what physical address they would be translated into, or if they would generate either a segment fault or a page fault.

(a)   00010100 01010111

(b)   11100100 11111111

(c)   11110100 11000111

(d)   00110010 11000111

Answer:

(a)   Page fault
Divided into its parts, this address is 0,001,010001010111. The entry for segment 0, page 1, is marked as out, resulting in a page fault.

(b)   0001010100111111111
Divided into its parts, this address is 1,110,010011111111. Segment 1, page 6, is located in frame 000101, making the physical address 000101 and 010011111111 concatenated together.

(c)   Segment fault
Divided into its parts, this address is 1,111,010011000111. Segment 1 has a maximum length of 6, and the page specified is 7, so a segment fault is generated.

(d)   100110001011000111
Divided into its parts, this address is 0,011,001011000111. Segment 0, page 3, is located in frame 100110, making the physical address 100110 and 001011000111 concatenated together.

5.26 On a system using paging and segmentation, references to swapped-in locations accessible through an entry in an associative table take 200 ns. If the main memory page table must be used, the reference takes 400 ns. References that result in page faults require 10 ms if the page to be replaced has been modified, 5 ms otherwise. If the page fault rate is 5%, the associative table hit rate is 65%, and 40% of replaced pages are "dirty," what is the effective access time? Assume the system is running only a single process, and the CPU is idle during page swaps.

Answer:

The probability and time, converted to µs, for the various types of accesses are as follows.

Type	Probability	Time (μs)
In, associative	95% × 65% = 0.6175	0.2
In, main memory	95% × 35% = 0.3325	0.4
Out, clean	05% × 60% = 0.0300	5000
Out, dirty	05% × 40% = 0.0200	10000

Effective access time $= 0.6175 \times 0.2 + 0.3325 \times 0.4 + 0.03 \times 5000 + 0.02 \times 10000$
Effective access time $= 350.2565$

Supplementary Problems

5.27   In this problem, use decimal values, a page size of 5000 bytes, and the following page table.

In/out	Frame
out	333
in	300
in	1000
out	100
out	500
in	120
out	412
in	740

Which of the following virtual addresses would generate a page fault? For those that do not generate a page fault, to what physical address would they translate?

(a)   21610

(b)   35410

(c)   27012

(d)   10234

5.28   In this problem, use binary values, a page size of 2^6 bytes, and the following page table.

In/out	Frame
in	00101
in	01011
out	00001
in	11010
out	00011
out	10101
out	11111
in	10101
...	...

Which of the following virtual addresses would generate a page fault? For those that do not generate a page fault, to what physical address would they translate?

(a)   0000001001001

(b)   0000011010110

(c)   0000100000101

(d)   0000000111100

5.29   On a system using demand-paged memory, it takes 250 ns to satisfy a memory request if the page is in memory. If the page is not in memory, the request takes 5 ms if a free frame is available or the page to be swapped out has not been modified, or 12 ms if the page to be swapped out has been modified.

What is the effective access time if the page fault rate is 2%, and 40% of the time the page to be replaced has been modified? Assume the system is running only a single process and the CPU is idle during page swaps.

5.30   On a system using demand-paged memory, it takes 150 ns to satisfy a memory request if the page is in memory. The page fault rate is 10%. To achieve an effective access time of 500 µs, what would the average time need to be to satisfy a request for a page not in memory?

5.31   Assume the amount of memory on a system is inversely proportional to the page fault rate. Each time memory doubles, the page fault rate is reduced by a third. Currently the system has 32Mb of memory. The page fault rate is 2%. When a page fault is not required, the access time is 500 ns. Overall, the effective access time is 300 µs. If memory was increased to 128Mb, what would be the overall access time?

5.32   Given a system with the following utilization characteristics.

CPU	Low
Swap device	Low
Other I/O devices	High

For each of the following, indicate if it is likely to significantly improve, significantly degrade, or have only a minor effect on CPU utilization.

(a)   Install a faster CPU.

(b)   Install a larger swap device.

(c)   Install a faster swap device.

(d)   Install more memory.

(e)   Install faster memory.

(f)   Increase the degree of multiprogramming.

(g)   Decrease the degree of multiprogramming.

(h)   Install faster I/O devices.

5.33   Prove that in matrix implementation of LRU, row k of the matrix is less than row i if and only if page k was accessed less recently than page i.

5.34 Prove the LRU replacement algorithm cannot suffer from Belady's anomaly.

5.35 Consider the two programs in problems 5.22 and 5.23. Assume the fetching and execution of each instruction (including the declarations) take 1 μs (consider testing a loop condition to be executing one instruction) if there is no page fault, and 2 ms if there is. How long would it take the first program to execute? The second?

5.36 Given references to the following pages by a program,

$$0,1,4,2,0, \quad 2,6,5,1,2, \quad 3,2,1,2,6, \quad 2,1,3,6,2,$$

how many page faults will occur if the program has three page frames available to it and uses:

(a) FIFO replacement?

(b) LRU replacement?

(c) Optimal replacement?

5.37 Given references to the following pages by a program,

$$0,1,4,2,0, \ 2,6,5,1,2, \ 3,2,1,2,6, \ 2,1,3,6,2,$$

what is the working set $W(t, \Delta)$, with t equal to the time between the 13th and 14th references, and Δ equal to 5 references.

5.38 On a system using paging and segmentation, references to swapped-in locations accessible through an entry in an associative table take 150 ns. If the main memory page table must be used, the reference takes 400 ns. References that result in page faults require 8 ms if the page to be replaced has been modified, 3 ms otherwise. If the page fault rate is 2%, the associative table hit rate is 70%, and 50% of replaced pages have been modified, what is the effective access time? Assume the system is running only a single process and the CPU is idle during page swaps.

5.39 Given a system with four page frames, the following table indicates page, load time, last reference time, dirty bit, and reference bit.

Page	Load Time	Last Reference	Dirty Bit	Reference Bit
0	227	327	1	0
1	345	367	1	1
2	101	331	1	1
3	234	382	0	1

(a) Which page will FIFO replace?

(b) Which page will LRU replace?

(c) Which page will NRU replace?

(d) Which page will second chance replace?

5.40 Implement a function that chooses the page to be replaced using second chance replacement. The 'pageTable' variable contains the page table.

```
struct PageTableType
  { int  frame;         //  Page  frame.
    char in;            //  In/out bit.
    char reference;     //  Has page been referenced
      recently.
    long loadTime;      //  Time page was loaded or 2nd
      chanced.
  };
struct  PageTableType  pageTable[NUMBER_PAGES];
```

5.41 A system using demand-paged segments has a 16-bit virtual address space with 2 segments per process and a page size of 2^{12}. The content of the segment and page tables is specified below (all values binary). Segment length is in increments of the page size.

Segment Table	
Page Table	Length
Pointer to Page Table 0	100
Pointer to Page Table 1	101

Page Table 0			Page Table 1	
Frame	In		Frame	In
001100	1		010100	1
011101	1		110101	0
100110	0		110100	1
001010	1		011001	1
111010	1		001001	1
110110	0		110011	0
101011	0		000101	0
001011	0		100010	0

For the following binary virtual addresses, indicate what physical address they would be translated into, or if they would generate either a segment fault or a page fault.

(a)   00010100 01010111

(b)   01000100 11111111

(c)   10110100 11000111

(d)   11100010 11000111

5.42 Simulate in a 'C' function the memory management hardware and software in a demand-paged system. Write the function '*Trans*' which takes a paged virtual address and translates it into a physical address (handling page faults as needed), returning the physical address as an **int**. The page size is 2^9. The 'pageTable' variable contains the page table. You may assume the following functions have already been written.

Free: Searches for a free page frame in the free list. Returns the page frame number if a free frame is found, -1 otherwise.

Replace: Selects a page to be replaced using a local page replacement strategy, and returns the number of the page to be replaced.

SwapIn: Takes as parameters a page number and a frame number. Reads the page off the swap device and writes it into the frame.

SwapOut: Takes as parameters a page number and a frame number. Writes the frame into the page's storage on the swap device.

```
struct PageTableType
   { int frame;   // Page frame
     char in;     // In/out bit
     char dirty;  // Dirty bit.
   };
struct VirtualAddressType
   { int page;    // Portion of address specifying page
     int off;     // Portion of address specifying offset
   };
struct PageTableType pageTable[NUMBER_PAGES];
int Free();
int Replace();
int SwapIn(int page, int frame);
int Swapout(int page, int frame);
```

 # Answers to Supplementary Problems

5.27   (*a*)   Fault
           (*b*)   3,700,410
           (*c*)   602,012
           (*d*)   5,000,234

5.28   (*a*)   01011001001
           (*b*)   11010010110
           (*c*)   Fault
           (*d*)   00101111100

5.29   156.245

5.30   4.99865 ms

5.31   133.61

5.32   (*a*)   Install a faster CPU.
           Slight degradation or no effect.

      (*b*)   Install a larger swap device.
           No effect.

      (*c*)   Install a faster swap device.
           No or little effect.

      (*d*)   Install more memory.
           Little or no effect.

      (*e*)   Install faster memory.
           Little or no effect.

      (*f*)   Increase the degree of multiprogramming.
           Probable improvement.

      (*g*)   Decrease the degree of multiprogramming.
           Degradation of performance to some extent.

      (*h*)   Install faster I/O devices.
           Probable improvement.

5.33   In problem 5.17, it was shown that if k was the most recently accessed page, for every row i such that $i \neq k$, every column in row k that contains a 0 will also contain a 0 in row i, and there is at least one column (i) that contains 1 in row k but is 0 in row i. For each subsequent access to a page j such that $j \neq i$ and $j \neq k$, every column in row k that contains a 0 will still also contain a 0 in row i since any column changed to 0 in row k would also be changed to 0 in row i. In addition, since $j \neq i$ column i in row k will still be 0 while column i in row i will be 0. Thus, for any row k accessed more recently than any row i, the value in row k will be greater than the value in row i.

    To prove the value is greater only if it was accessed more recently, then assume row k contains a larger value than some other page j that was accessed more recently. By the proof above, the value in row j must be greater than the value in row k. But our assumption was the value in k was greater than the value in row j. By contradiction, the value in row k is greater than the value in any other row i only if page k was accessed more recently.

5.34   Let $S(n, t)$ be the set of pages in memory at time t using LRU with n frames. For all values of n and t, $S(n, t)$ will be the n most recently referenced pages. Therefore, for any two values $i > k$, $S(k, t)$ is a subset of $S(i, t)$ for all values of t. If a reference generates a page fault when i frames are used because the page is not in the set $S(i, t)$, then the reference would also generate a page fault when k frames are used. The page cannot be in the set $S(k, t)$ if it is not in $S(i, t)$. If every page fault with i frames would also be a fault with k for any $i > k$, the algorithm's performance is never worse with more frames. Thus, it does not suffer from Belady's anomaly.

5.35   First program: 1.331777 s
           Second program: 80.042402 s

5.36 (*a*)   FIFO replacement: 13 faults

  (*b*)   LRU replacement: 14 faults

  (*c*)   Optimal replacement: 9 faults

5.37 $W(T, \Delta) = \{1, 2, 3\}$

5.38 110.2205 μs

5.39 (*a*)   2

  (*b*)   0

  (*c*)   0

  (*d*)   0

5.40
```
int Replace()
{
  lowest = -1;
  while (lowest == -1)
  {
    //----------------------
    //Find earliest loaded page
    //----------------------
    for (int ii = 0; ii < NUMBER_PAGES); ii++)
    {
      if (pageTable[ii].in == 1)
      {
        if (lowest == -1| (pageTable[ii].loadTime
        < pageTable[lowest].loadTime)
          lowest = ii;
      }
    }
    // ------------------------------------------
    // If that page was recently referenced, reset
    // its load time and reference bit, and try again.
    // ------------------------------------------
    if (pageTable[lowest].reference == 1)
    {
      pageTable[lowest].reference = 0;
      pageTable[lowest].loadTime = time(); // Current time
      lowest = -1;
    }
  }
  return lowest;
}
```

5.41 (*a*) 01110101000101011 1

(*b*) 111010010011111111

(*c*) 011001010011000111

(*d*) Segment fault

5.42
```
int Trans(struct VirtualAddressType virtAddr)
{
    int physAddr = -1;
    int page;
    page = virtAddr.page;
    if (pageTable.in[page] == 0)
        // ---------
        // Page fault.
        // ---------
        int emptyFrame = Free();
        if (emptyFrame < 0)
        {
            // ------------------------
            // Identify page to be replaced.
            // Swap out if dirty.
            // ------------------------
            int replacePage = Replace();
            emptyFrame = pageTable[replacePage].frame;
            if (pageTable[replacePage].dirty)
                SwapOut(replacePage, emptyFrame);
            pageTable[replacePage].in = 0;
        }
        // -------
        // Swap in.
        // -------
        pageTable[page].frame = emptyFrame;
        pageTable[page].in = 1;
        pageTable[page].dirty = 0;
        SwapIn(page, emptyFrame);
    }
    physAddr = (pageTable[page].frame << 9) | virtAddr.off;
    return physAddr;
}
```

CHAPTER 6

File System Management

A *file* is a logical collection of information. A *file system* is a collection of files. A file system may also include a variety of other objects that share many of the properties of files (such as I/O devices).

6.1   Directories and Names

File systems allow users to organize files and other file system objects through the use of *directories*. A directory (or *folder*) has been traditionally defined to be a file system object that contains other file system objects. However, that definition is misleading. In most cases, it is more accurate to define a directory as an object that contains the names of file system objects. On systems where there is a one-to-one mapping between names and objects, the distinction between name and object may not be important. But some file systems allow objects to have multiple names or even no name; under some circumstances, the distinction becomes important.

Entries in directories determine the *full pathname* (or names) associated with a file system object. Starting with the root directory, the full pathname is constructed by concatenating the sequence of names traversed. For example, consider the file system in Fig. 6-1. The directory **dir1** contains three names: **file_a**, **dir2**, and **dir3**. The directory **dir2** contains no names. The directory **dir3** contains the names **file_a** and **file_b**. This organization defines six full pathnames. On Unix, those names would be:

```
/dir1
/dir1/file_a
/dir1/dir2
```

Fig. 6-1.   File system contents.

```
/dir1/dir3
/dir1/dir3/file_a
/dir1/dir3/file_b
```

On Windows and DOS, the names would be the same except '\' (backslash) would replace '/' (slash) as the separator character in the filename.

Most systems support the notion of a ***current directory***. Instead of using a full pathname (which can get quite lengthy), a ***relative pathname*** may be specified. The relative pathname is an alias for the full pathname, generated by appending the relative name to the current directory name. In Unix, DOS, and Windows, full pathnames begin with the separator character; relative names do not. With **/dir1** as the current directory, **file_a** is the same as **/dir/file_a**, and **dir3/file_a** is the same as **/dir1/dir3/file_a**.

Some systems permit a file object to be associated with multiple names. On such a system, the names **/dir1/file_a** and **/dir1/dir3/file_b** could refer to the same file.

6.1.1 PARTITIONS

Files are typically stored on secondary storage devices (although system RAM, random access memory, may also be used to store files, such as temporary files, for which quick access is desired). A file system may incorporate the notion of a ***partition*** which determines on which device a file will be stored. On some systems, such as DOS and Windows, the partition is specified as part of the pathname. The DOS/Windows name **C:\rules\section.1** specifies the file system object named **\rules\section.1** in partition **C:**. On other systems like Unix, partitions are ***mounted*** into a single ***unified*** file system name space.

When partitions are mounted, one partition serves as the "root" partition, the partition whose name space serves as the initial unified file system name space. Other file systems can then be spliced into the unified file system name space, typically at any existing directory node. The root directory in the mounted file system then replaces the mount point directory in the unified file system name space. The partition's name space exists in the unified file system name space underneath the mount point.

The operating system must decide what becomes of the contents of the directory where a partition is to be mounted. On some systems, the directory must be empty before a partition may be mounted. On others, its contents become hidden. The designer of the operating system must also decide whether a partition may be mounted more than once. Multiple mounting gives each file in the partition multiple names in the unified name space.

6.1.2 PER-PROCESS ROOT DIRECTORY

On some systems, it is possible to designate a directory that will serve as the root directory for a process. Once such a designation occurs, only the subtree headed by that directory is visible to the process. On a system where no file-sharing is desirable, each user's home directory could be made the root directory for all processes the user executes. To those processes, the root of the file system would be the user's home directory. This capability may also be used by applications to provide additional security. A Web or FTP server may be so configured, limiting its access to a particular subtree reserved for Web or FTP data.

6.1.3 DIRECTORY STRUCTURE

The structure created by the placement of names in directories can take a number of forms: single-level tree, two-level tree, multilevel tree, acyclic graph, or general graph. The simplest structure is a single-level tree. A single-level tree system has only one directory. Names in that directory refer to files or other nondirectory objects. Such a system is practical only on systems with very limited numbers of files.

In a two-level system, only the root-level directory may contain names of directories. All other directories refer only to nondirectory objects. For example, on a multiple-user system, a separate directory could be created for each user on the system (Fig. 6-2).

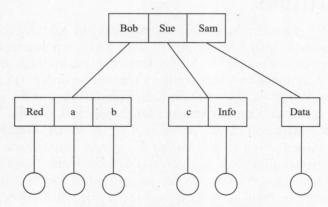

Fig. 6-2.   Two-level directory system.

A multilevel tree system allows growth of the tree beyond the second level. Any directory may contain names of additional directories as well as nondirectory objects.

Figure 6-3 shows the effect of having a nondirectory object with multiple names. Since two links (names) lead to one of the objects, the structure is not a tree; it is a graph. However, if only nondirectory objects can have multiple names, little additional complexity is added. This structure can be referred to as a modified tree. This variant of a tree structure enhances the system's file-sharing capabilities by allowing the same object to be named in separate directories.

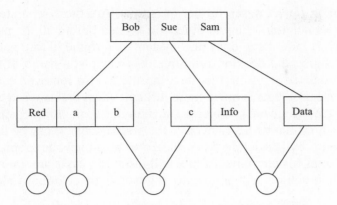

Fig. 6-3.   Nondirectory objects with multiple names.

Further flexibility can be added to a file system by allowing directory objects to have multiple names (Fig. 6-4). This can be especially useful in environments where several users need to share a number of files associated with some project on which they are working. Each user could add a name for the project directory in his or her own personal directory. As files in the project directory are added, deleted, or modified, the project directory named in each user's personal directory would reflect those changes.

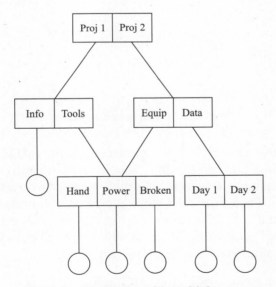

Fig. 6-4.   Directories with multiple names.

While more flexible, graph name structures add complexity. On systems where each object has only one name, the distinction between name and object is seldom significant. Clearly that is not the case when an object has multiple names. One cannot determine whether two names refer to the same file just by comparing the names to see if they are identical.

Deletion of an object raises further questions. Are there separate commands for name and object deletion? Can an object be deleted before all the names for it have been deleted? If not, how does the system determine if all names have been removed? On Unix, the deletion primitive removes just a name. If the name is the only name associated with the file, then the file is also removed.

Solving these problems is much more difficult when the name structure is a graph containing cycles (Fig. 6-5). Objects can now have an infinite number of names (depending on how many times a cycle is traversed). Objects can be limited to a finite number of names by restricting the structure to be an acyclic graph. Unfortunately, general algorithms to determine if a link will result in a cycle are time-consuming. As a result, graph structures, either acyclic or general, are seldom implemented.

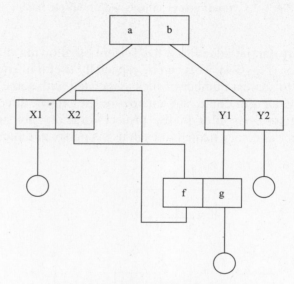

Fig. 6-5.   Cyclic name structure.

Unix uses a limited form of acyclic organization to provide the power of multiple names while limiting the complexity. Nondirectory objects may have multiple names without restriction. However, only the system may create additional names for directory objects. Each time a directory is created, two names are added into the new directory: '.' and '..'. The name '.' is an alias for the newly created directory itself. The name '..' is an alias for the newly created directory's parent directory. The '.' and '..' names create cycles. The names

```
dir1/file,
dir1/../dir1/file,
dir1/./file, and
./dir1/./file
```

all refer to the same file. However, since '.' and '..' are the only names that can create cycles, and those cycles are easily detected, the complexity created by their inclusion is limited.

6.1.4 DIRECTORY ENTRIES

Information about files is stored in a directory entry. The information stored depends on the operating system. Typically a directory entry contains information about the file's ownership, location, size, access rights, times of different kinds of events (last modification, creation). Most operating systems require a file to be *opened* before it can be accessed. The open operation obtains a pointer to the file's directory location so all subsequent reference to the file can be via the pointer rather than the file's name.

On some systems, the directory entry points to a separate file structure where information about the file is stored. For example, on Unix systems, file information is stored in a structure called an *inode*. The directory entry contains only the file's name and its inode number.

6.2   Types of File System Objects

In many operating systems, file system names may refer to objects that are neither files nor directories. Objects that might be found in a file system include the following.

- *Shortcut* (or *soft-link*): A shortcut is a pointer to another name in the file system. In most cases, referring to the shortcut is equivalent to referring to the name pointed to by the shortcut. Deleting the name pointed to by the shortcut typically leaves a dangling pointer.
- *Device*: A hardware device, such as a parallel port.
- *Pipe*: A communication channel between two processes. One process sends data into the pipe, the other process reads that data from the pipe. The pipe buffers data written into it until another process reads the data. Typically the buffer is a limited size, and a process writing to the pipe must be suspended when the buffer is filled. Pipes can be named or unnamed. Since they have no identifying name, unnamed pipes typically may be accessed only by the process that creates them or by processes that are descendants of the creating process.
- *Shared Memory*: An allocation of memory locations for use by one or more processes. Similar to a file on a RAM disk (see Sec. 7.3.8).
- *Semaphore*: A semaphore object that can be used to control synchronization of processes. (See Sec. 3.2.6.)

6.3   File System Functions

The file system must provide users with the ability to perform abstract operations on objects within the file system. At a minimum, the following functions must be provided in some form: creation, deletion, reading, and writing. For example, the following four functions define a very limited but practical set of operations in a file system with a single-level directory structure.

create *name:*
> Creates both an empty file and an entry in the directory which associates the name with the file.

delete *name*:
> Deletes the file named and removes the name from the directory.

read *name location*:
> Reads a byte of information from the indicated logical location within the file named.

write *name location byte*:
> Writes a byte of information to the indicated logical location within the file named. The size of the file is extended as needed.

6.4   Information Types

It is frequently useful to classify the information stored in a file (or other file system object) as being of a particular type: executable program, object file, C++ source file, word processing document, image file, and so on. If the type is known, requests to process a file in an unreasonable way may be denied. For example, executable programs contain machine code which, if sent to a printer, produces unintelligible output (and can waste a large amount of paper). The print spooler program could deny attempts to print executable files.

Three major schemes for identifying file type exist: name extension, magic number, or operating system supported information type. The name extension mechanism identifies the information type by including a particular extension as part of the filename. For example, `'.exe'` or `'.com'` mean executable program, `'.wp'` means Word Perfect document, and `'.asm'` means assembler source file. Name extensions may or may not include operating system support. On DOS, for example, it is possible for any file to have the `'.wp'` extension, not just Word Perfect files. The operating system does not enforce that only Word Perfect files may have `'.wp'` extensions. But DOS does have the restriction that it will only attempt to execute files with the `'.exe'` or `'.com'` extensions (although certainly not a fool-proof protection since nonexecutable files may be given either of those extensions).

The second major scheme identifies information type by looking for a "magic number," a byte or sequences of bytes at a particular location in the file, usually the beginning. For example, the string "GIF8" at the start of a file identifies the content as GIF image data. Operating systems rarely recognize magic numbers; it is up to the individual applications to use them as they see fit. For example, the only magic numbers recognized by the Unix kernel are those that identify executable programs, Unix will execute programs only with those identifiers.

The third scheme uses explicit operating support for information types. The operating system maintains the type as part of the information it associates with a file. The file-create operation includes a mechanism for setting the file type. The Apple operating system goes one step further and not only maintains the file's type but also records the name of the program that by default should be used to process the file. Clicking on the icon representing the file automatically causes the processing program associated with that file to be invoked.

6.5   File System Architecture

File management is organized into a number of levels. At the highest level is the file as it is viewed by the user. The file is considered to be a collection of *records*, where each record is a logical collection of information (e.g., a line of text, information about a person). I/O operations are typically in terms of records. The operating system may support fixed- and/or variable-size record structures. Records may be further divided into *fields*, where a field is a basic element of data (such as name and age). Figure 6-6 depicts the logical file structure.

	Field 0	Field 1		Field f
Record 0	Joe	1952	...	blonde
Record 1	Mary	1982	...	brown
Record 2	Sue	1921	...	red
		.		
		.		
		.		
Record r	John	2001	...	black

Fig. 6-6.   Logical file structure.

Transparent to the user, the operating system considers a file to be a collection of fixed-size *logical blocks*. A block is the basic unit of an I/O operation between the disk and the file system memory buffers. The disk itself is a collection of *physical blocks*. Each physical block stores a logical block and possibly some other administrative data. The block size is a multiple of the basic I/O unit provided by the disk device driver.

6.5.1   ACCESS METHODS

There are two fundamental methods for accessing information within a file: sequential and direct. In *sequential* access, information in the file must be accessed in the order it is stored in the file. Access proceeds sequentially from start to finish. Operations to read or write the file need not specify the logical location within the file, because the operating system maintains a file pointer that determines the location of the next access.

With *direct* access, any logical location within the file may be accessed at any time. Typically, direct access is achieved in one of two ways: by specifying the logical location to be accessed as a parameter to the read or write operation, or by specifying the location in a *seek* operation to be called before the read or write.

Database systems use the two basic operating system access operations to implement a wide variety of higher-level access methods. Some operating systems implement higher-level access methods themselves. Of the higher-level access methods, **indexed** access is perhaps the most significant. With indexed access, each file record has one or more fields. One field serves as the index field. Read and write operations include an index parameter. The record with the matching index value is the record operated on.

For any access method, read/write operations may be synchronous or asynchronous. Synchronous I/O blocks the process until the I/O operation has completed. Asynchronous I/O returns control to the process immediately, leaving the process free to continue executing as the I/O is being performed. If input operations are asynchronous, some mechanism must be employed to notify the process that the operation has completed. This could be accomplished by sending the process a signal, by setting one of the process's variables to a particular value, or by providing a special system call for testing the I/O operation's status. Asynchronous output operations can employ the same notification techniques or offer no notification at all.

Synchronous I/O is the norm, and makes application programming far simpler. The high speed of file I/O operations provides little incentive to use asynchronous I/O. However, asynchronous I/O may occasionally be used with device I/O.

6.5.2 ACCESS CONTROL

Access control limits who can access files and how they can access them. The simplest operating system access control mechanism gives unlimited access to all users. This is the access control scheme used by DOS. On such a system, users wishing to control access to their files must do so by limiting physical (and network) access to their machine.

One aspect of access control is the type of operation to be performed on the file. Controlled operations may include the following.

- *Read*: Read information contained in the file.
- *Write*: Write new information into a file at any point or overwrite existing information in a file.
- *Append*: Write new information at the end of a file only.
- *Delete*: Delete a file and release its storage space for use in other files.
- *List*: Read the names contained in a directory.
- *Execute*: Load the contents of a file into main memory and create a process to execute it.
- *Change access*: Change some user's access rights for some controlled operation.

The other major characteristic of access control is how it determines whether or not to grant access. The most common mechanism is to base the decision on the identity of the user. On a system using an *access list*, the operating system associates with each file the types of operations permitted by each user. In an unlimited access control scheme, an independent set of permissions is maintained for each user. On systems with a number of controlled operations and many users, this represents a significant amount of data.

A limited access control mechanism reduces the amount of data by grouping access permissions for a number of users or files. For example, many operating systems implement the notion of user groups. Each user and each file is associated with one or more groups of users. Instead of having a set of access permissions for every user, each file has only a set of access permissions for its owner and for each group it is associated with. All users in a group share the same access permissions. Another frequently used grouping is requiring all files in a directory to share the same permissions.

The other commonly used basis for determining access is passwords. To perform an operation on a file, a user must specify the file's password associated with that operation (a file password is separate from any possible login password). As with access lists, grouping can reduce the amount of data maintained by the operating system (and reduce the number of passwords a user must remember). For example, all files in a directory may share the same password(s).

An interesting but less frequently used variant of access lists are capabilities. On capability-based systems, instead of access rights being associated with files, they are associated with processes. When file access is attempted, the operating system checks the access rights associated with the process for the appropriate right to the file.

6.5.3 FILE LOCKING

File locking gives processes the ability to implement mutually exclusive access to a file. Three major options exist in the implementation of locking.

- Locking can be limited to files as a whole, or the implementation may allow parts of a file to be locked.

- Locking may apply to any access, or different levels of lock may exist. On some systems, there are both read and write locks. A file locked for reading does not prevent further read access, but write access by other processes is denied. A file locked for writing denies read or write access to other processes.

- Locking may be either mandatory or advisory. With mandatory locking, the operating system prevents access while the file is locked. With advisory locking, the locking primitives only provide information about a file's lock status. Access is restricted only if a process checks the file's lock status and honors any lock that is indicated.

In some circumstances, an operating system may implement an implicit locking mechanism. On Unix systems, write access is denied to any file being executed by a process.

6.5.4 BLOCKING

The I/O subsystem performs I/O in units called *blocks*. The size of a block is typically a multiple of the disk sector size. A file is a collection of block-size units of storage. The **blocking** method determines how a file's records are allocated into blocks.

- **Fixed Blocking**: For files with fixed-size records, an integral number of records are stored in each block. No record may be larger than a block. If the block size is not a multiple of the record size, there will be unused space at the end of the block. The operating system can compute the block and offset within the block of any record given the record and block sizes.

- **Unspanned Blocking**: For systems with variable-size records, multiple records can be stored in each block but no record may span multiple blocks. No record may be larger than the size of a block. Space at the end of a block is wasted if the next record is larger than that space. The operating system cannot compute the location of any record unless it knows the size of all the records that precede it.

- **Spanned Blocking**: Records may be stored in multiple blocks. There is no limit on the size of a record and no wasted space within a block. The only way to compute a record's location is to sum the size of all the records that precede it.

Figure 6-7 illustrates the three blocking methods.

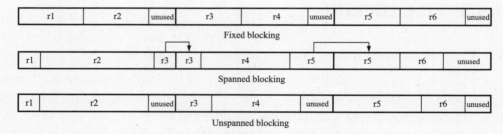

Fig. 6-7. Fixed, spanned, and unspanned blocking.

6.5.5 ALLOCATION

Three basic schemes exist for allocating secondary storage space to files. The allocation scheme is responsible for mapping a file's logical blocks into the actual **physical blocks** on the secondary storage device. In most operating systems, the size of a physical block is a power of 2 between 512 and 4096.

The simplest scheme is **contiguous** allocation (Fig. 6-8). The logical blocks of a file are stored in a partition of contiguous physical blocks. The directory entry need only store the file's starting secondary storage address and its size. The physical location of any byte in the file may be computed by adding the appropriate offset to the file's starting secondary storage address.

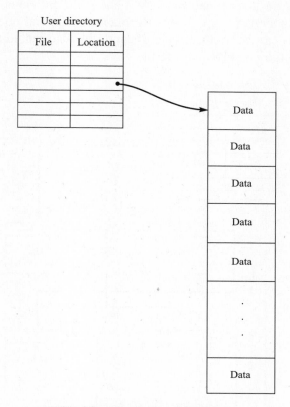

Fig. 6-8.   Contiguous allocation.

When a file is created, contiguous allocation requires preallocation of space for the file. The operating system design may provide for expanding the file's allocation should the need arise. If expansion is permitted and the storage space beyond the end of the file is in use, then one or more files must be moved to accommodate the larger file. The files to be moved must be allocated new partitions on the disk, then copied to those new partitions.

Contiguous allocation of files on secondary storage shares many characteristics with variable partition memory management. The checkerboarding effect leaves storage with a number of unused storage "holes." Some "fit" algorithm (see Sec. 4.4.2.1) must be used to select the hole to which a file will be allocated.

With all the "fit" algorithms, there is a tendency for a large number of small holes to develop, making external fragmentation a significant problem. **Garbage collection** may be used to collect all free space into a single "hole." However, garbage collection is particularly expensive in a file system, given the relatively slow speeds and large sizes involved. For that reason, use of compaction is quite limited.

In *linked* allocation, the physical blocks in which a file is stored may be scattered throughout the secondary storage device (Fig. 6-9). The physical blocks are larger than logical blocks and store both the logical block and a pointer to the physical block where the file's next logical block is stored. The directory entry stores the location of the first physical block. The physical block associated with the Nth logical block may be determined only by reading the previous $N - 1$ blocks and following the links they contain. The performance of append operations (writing to the end of the file) can be improved significantly by also including in the directory entry a pointer to the last block in the file.

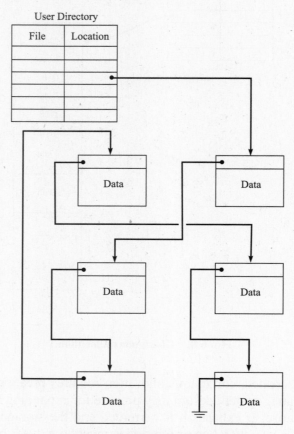

Fig. 6-9. Linked allocation.

Indexed allocation is a variant of linked allocation. The physical block stores only the logical block and is therefore the same size as a logical block. Links to a file's physical blocks are stored contiguously in an index table. The directory entry contains either the index table or a pointer to it (Fig. 6-10).

With contiguous and linked allocation, the file system need only store the starting physical location of the file. All other addresses can be determined from the file's starting location. With indexed allocation, the file system must have an index entry for each block in the file. To minimize the amount of space required in directory structures, multilevel indexing can be used (Fig. 6-11). In such a scheme, indirect index entries point to blocks storing additional indexes. Creating layers of indirect index blocks increases the number of entries exponentially.

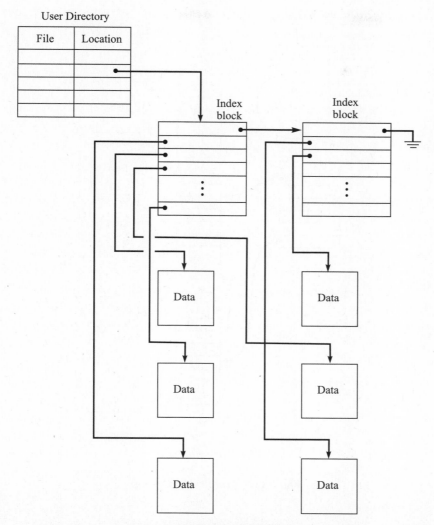

Fig. 6-10. Index allocation.

6.5.6 FREE SPACE

In addition to keeping track of where each file is located on secondary storage, an operating system must also be able to identify those physical blocks that are not currently allocated to any file. A number of mechanisms have been used to maintain the *free list*.

Each block is either in use or not, so its status can be stored in a single bit. Using a series of bits, one bit per physical block, creates a free list *bit-map*. The bits are packed into as few words as possible. Although this mechanism makes efficient use of space, access to information on a particular block is slowed by the extra processing needed to extract information in individual bits from a word.

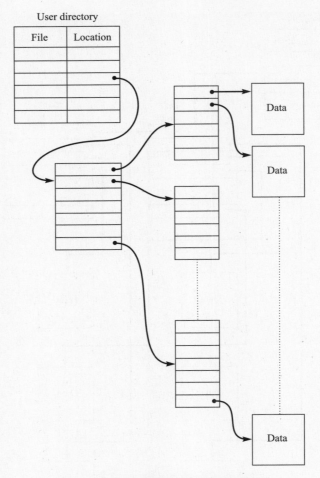

Fig. 6-11.   Multilevel indexing.

A *free list array* stores the addresses of all the free blocks. A block is in use if its address is not in the array. An array allows for efficient implementation of operations to add or remove blocks from the free list.

The free list may also be maintained by creating a linked list of all the free blocks. One advantage of this scheme is efficient use of space; the free blocks themselves store the free list information.

Both the preceding methods can be modified to keep track of groups of free blocks rather than individual free blocks. Instead of a bit-map, each element in a *free hole* array could store the starting block number and number of blocks in a group of free blocks. While each element in the array must be represented by far more than a single bit, fewer array elements are needed. Such schemes can be used to efficiently find a large number of free blocks, particularly if they must be contiguous.

A *linked hole list* scheme involves a similarly modified linked list. The first block in each hole contains the number of blocks in the hole, as well as a pointer to the first block in the next hole in the list.

Solved Problems

6.1   How is a file with two names different from having two copies of a file?

Answer:

With two copies, if one copy gets changed, the other copy stays the same. If there is only one file with two names, changing the file associated with one name also changes the file associated with the other name (since both names refer to the same file).

6.2   On a system that mounts file systems on individual devices into a single file system, a floppy device has been mounted at point **/usr/mount**. If the floppy's file system contains a file by the name of **/data/jan**, what will that file's name be in the overall file system?

Answer:

The root of the floppy's file system merges into the overall file system at the point **/usr/mount**. Thus, **/data** on the floppy becomes **/usr/mount/data** and **/data/jan** becomes **/usr/mount/data/jan**.

6.3   Give one advantage of having the partition specified as part of the filename (as is done on DOS).

Answer:

The filename is readily associated with the device, making it easy for the user to know on which device the file exists. On DOS, a user immediately knows that a filename starting with **A:** is stored on the floppy device.

6.4   Give one advantage of allowing partitions to be mounted into a unified name space.

Answer:

It provides greater flexibility to the person organizing the name space. For example, consider a system with two CD-ROM drives. It may be necessary to move a CD from one drive to the other. After unmounting the first drive, the second drive can be mounted at the same mount point the first drive had been using. All files on the CD can be referred to by the same full pathnames as when it was loaded in the first drive.

6.5   What is the advantage of allowing nonfile objects in the file system structure?

Answer:

It simplifies the abstraction presented to the user. The basic operations that might be performed on the various types of objects are essentially the same, so it is convenient to share a common interface for accessing them. In many cases, it is irrelevant what the type of the object is. For example, when a process is sending output to a file system object, in most cases it is irrelevant to the process whether the object is a device, a pipe, or a file. By having these objects share a common interface, programs can easily be written so they work with any of these objects, yielding greater power and flexibility.

6.6   Add five operations to the four described in Sec. 6.3 to make the file system more useful.

Answer:

rename *oldname newname*: Changes the name of the file from *oldname* to *newname*.
changesize *name size*: Changes the size of the file to *size*. Files increased in size have null bytes added to them; files decreased in size are truncated.
getsize *name*: Returns the size of a file in bytes.
getmodtime *name*: Returns the last time a file was modified.
delname *filename*: The file name specified will no longer refer to the file, but the file will still exist.

6.7   Why would the addition of a *copy* operation provide no increased functionality?

Answer:

The ability to copy a file already exists. By repeatedly reading and writing, one can copy a file using existing operations.

6.8   One could rename a file by copying the file, then deleting the original. Does the existence of a rename operation provide any increased functionality?

Answer:

Yes. In some cases, it may not be possible to copy a file. For example, if one has an 800Kb file in a file system stored on a 1.44Mb an floppy disk, that file could not be copied in an effort to rename it. The rename operation allows the file to be renamed without ever making a second copy of it.

6.9   How does support for having a file with multiple names complicate the deletion operation on a file system?

Answer:

If there is a one-to-one relationship between names and files, it is reasonable for the deletion operation to delete both the name and the file. If a file has multiple names, how should the deletion operation be defined? A number of possible abstractions could be implemented.

- The delete operation deletes the file named and all names associated with the file. To implement this definition, the file system must be able to efficiently determine all names associated with a file.

- Have separate operations for deleting files and names. Only when a file has a single name associated with it may it be deleted. In cases where a file has multiple names, the file may not be deleted. Only the name deletion operation is permitted. This definition only requires the file system to determine the number of names associated with a file.

- Have just one delete operation. Define it to delete a name when a file has more than one name, or to delete both the name and the file if the file has only one name. Again, the file system must be able to determine the number of names associated with a file.

6.10 Is it possible to simulate in software a multilevel directory structure on a system that only supports a single-level tree?

Answer:

If the system allows for sufficiently long filenames, one character could be chosen to act as a directory delimiter. Although all files would be stored in the root directory, a subroutine library could be written that simulated a directory structure based on the delimiter character chosen. The library could implement a change directory command that remembered the name of the current directory and prepended the directory name to the front of any relative name before passing that name to an actual operating system routine.

6.11 If the solution in the previous problem was implemented on a system that limited file names to 10 characters, what is the maximum number of levels a simulated multilevel system could have?

Answer:

Five. If any name could be at most 10 characters, and '_' was chosen as the delimiter character, the most levels that could be achieved in a filename would be by using one character name at each level. For example, _a_b_c_d_e. Since the name ultimately must be a valid filename in the actual operating system, and for each level one delimiter must be used, at most five levels can be achieved. (More levels can be achieved if the set of characters in the simulated file system is less than the set of characters in the real file system. For example, given a system where filenames are case-sensitive. Create a simulated file system with filenames that are not case-sensitive. Choose a delimiter character to be some nonletter. Any character in a simulated system name that is preceded by a directory delimiter would be translated into an uppercase letter. All other letters would be translated into lower case. Thus the simulated name _a_b_c_de_f_g would become ABCDeFG when presented to the actual file system. Since no delimiters would be needed in the actual file system filename, each character could represent a different directory level.)

6.12 The DOS file system considers each file to be just a sequence of 8-bit bytes. Such a system can be described as using what record structure?

Answer:

Fixed-size 1-byte records.

6.13   Give an example of a situation where variable-size records would be useful.

Answer:

A text file with each record containing a line of text.

6.14   Although DOS and Unix recognize file types in different ways (DOS by the extension in the filename and Unix by a magic number at the start of the file), both recognize only executable files. Why?

Answer:

Like most operating systems, DOS and Unix are not concerned with the meaning of a file's contents. They only provide the underlying support structure for various applications to read or write raw data into files. It is up to the applications to interpret, as they see fit, the meaning of the raw data. The only time DOS and Unix are concerned with the meaning of a file's contents is when they are called upon to create a new process and have it execute a program. In that situation, the operating system does want to verify that the file it has been asked to execute does indeed contain an executable program.

6.15   A sequential access file has fixed-size 15-byte records. Assuming the first record is record 1, the first byte of record 5 will be at what logical location?

Answer:

Record 5 is preceded by 4 records, each of 15 bytes. The fifth record will start at byte $(4 * 15) + 1 = 61$.

6.16   A direct access file has fixed-size 15-byte records. Assuming the first record is record 1, the first byte of record 5 will be at what logical location?

Answer:

The answer is the same as for the previous question, 61. The logical layout of the records is the same for both access methods.

6.17   A direct or sequential access file has fixed-size S-byte records. The first byte of record N will start at what logical location?

Answer:

Record N will start at byte $((N - 1) * S) + 1$.

6.18   A program has just read the first record in a direct access file. It next wants to read the tenth record. How many records must the program read to input the tenth?

Answer:

One. Direct access allows the records to be read in any order.

6.19   A program has just read the first record in a sequential access file. It next wants to read the tenth record. How many records must the program read to input the tenth?

Answer:

Nine. Sequential access requires that records be read in order. So before reading the tenth record, records two through eight must be read.

6.20   A program has just read the tenth record in a sequential access file. It next wants to read the sixth record. How many records must the program read to input the sixth?

Answer:

Six. Sequential access typically is one way, from start to finish. To go back to the sixth record, the input would have to start over from record one. Typically, the input stream would have to be reopened or rewound to accomplish this.

6.21   On a system using index access, what should happen if no record matches the index value on a read request?

Answer:

Typically, the read request fails with an error code indicating that no matching record was found.

6.22   On a system using index access, what should happen if more than one record matches the index value on a read request?

Answer:

This may not be possible. The write operation might be defined to fail in attempts to write a record with an index value that matches another record in the file. If multiple records may have the same index, access may proceed sequentially through all the records sharing the same index value.

6.23   On Unix, each file is associated with one user and one group. A limited access list is implemented by assigning a set of permissions for the owner of the file, those in the same group as the file but who are not the owner, and for everyone else. The operations controlled are read, write, and execute access. Assume the system may have up to 2^{16} users and 2^8 groups. How many bits are needed to store each file's access data?

Answer:

The number of users and groups is irrelevant. Each set of three permissions requires three bits to indicate whether or not the permission is granted. There are three sets of permissions. Nine bits total are needed per file.

6.24 On a capability-based system, each file is associated with a unique 16-bit number. For each file, each user may have the read or write capability. How many bytes are needed to store each user's access data?

Answer:

Two bits are needed for each of 65,536 (2^{16}) files. Thus, 131,072 bits or 16,384 bytes would be needed.

6.25 On a system using fixed blocking with 20-byte records and 50-byte blocks, how much space will be wasted in each block?

Answer:

Two 20-byte records can be allocated to each block, leaving 10 bytes wasted.

6.26 Given a system using unspanned blocking and 100-byte blocks. A file contains records of 20, 50, 35, 70, 40, 20. What percentage of space will be wasted in the blocks allocated for the file?

Answer:

The first block can contain the first two records, leaving 30 bytes wasted. The second block can only contain the third record, wasting 65 bytes. The third block can only contain the fourth record, wasting 30 bytes. The last two records will be allocated to the fourth block, which will contain 40 wasted bytes. Thus, of the 400 bytes in the four blocks, $30 + 65 + 30 + 40 = 165$ bytes, or 41.25% is wasted.

6.27 On a system using contiguous allocation, compute the number of the physical block corresponding to the logical block given the file is stored starting at the indicated physical block (assume block numbers start with 1).

(a) Starting physical block: 1000; logical block: 12
(b) Starting physical block: 75; logical block: 2000
(c) Starting physical block: 150; logical block: 25

Answer:

(a) If logical block 1 is stored in physical block 1000, 2 will be stored in 1001, 3 in 1002, and 12 in 1011. $1000 - 1 + 12 = 1011$
(b) $75 - 1 + 2000 = 2074$
(c) $150 - 1 + 25 = 174$

6.28 A file system uses 256-byte physical blocks. Each file has a directory entry giving the file name, location of the first block, length of file, and last block position. Assume the last physical block read and the directory entry are already in main memory. For the following, indicate how many physical blocks must be read to access the specified block (including the reading of the specified block) on a system using contiguous allocation.

(*a*)   Last block read: 100; block to be read: 600

(*b*)   Last block read: 500; block to be read: 200

(*c*)   Last block read: 20; block to be read: 21

(*d*)   Last block read: 21; block to be read: 20

Answer:

The answer for all four scenarios is one. The location of the physical block to be read can be computed from the block number and the location of the first block.

6.29 Repeat the previous problem for a system using linked allocation.

Answer:

(*a*)   Last block read: 100; block to be read: 600
500. Blocks 101 through 599 must be read to obtain the link to the next block.

(*b*)   Last block read: 500; block to be read: 200
200. To find block 200, the chain of blocks starting with block 1 must be read.

(*c*)   Last block read: 20; block to be read: 21
1. Block 20 contains a pointer to block 21.

(*d*)   Last block read: 21; block to be read: 20
21. To find block 21, the chain of blocks starting with block 1 must be read.

6.30 Repeat the previous problem for a system using indexed allocation. Assume the directory entry contains the location of the first index block (not the first block of the file). Each index block contains pointers to 127 file blocks plus a pointer to the next index block. In addition to the last block read, assume the system has in main memory the index block that contains the pointer to the last block read. However, no other index blocks are in main memory.

Answer:

(*a*)   Last block read: 100; block to be read: 600
5. The last block read is pointed to by index block 1, which will also be in memory. The pointer to block 600 is in the fifth index block. Index blocks 2 through 5 must be read before reading block 600.

(*b*)   Last block read: 500; block to be read: 200
3. Index block 4 is in memory. The pointer to block 200 is in the second index block. Index blocks 1 and 2 must be read before reading block 200.

(c) Last block read: 20; block to be read: 21
1. The pointer to block 21 is in the first index block which is the same index block used by block 20.

(d) Last block read: 21; block to be read: 20
1. The pointer to block 21 is in the first index block which is the same index block used by block 20.

6.31   A system uses contiguous allocation. How many read and write operations would be required to add a block to or remove a block from a 101 block file under the conditions specified below? You may assume the following:

- The location of the first block of the file is already in memory.
- The block of information to be added is already in memory.
- In calculating the number of I/O operations, if the location of the first block of a file changes, do not include the output operations needed to rewrite that revised information to the directory entry on the disk.
- There is room for the file to grow at the end of the file but not at the beginning.
- The middle block is the 51st block.
- Do not include any I/O operations needed to add a removed block to the free list.

(a) Add a block at the beginning.

(b) Add a block after the middle block.

(c) Add a block at the end.

(d) Remove the beginning block.

(e) Remove the middle block.

(f) Remove the end block.

Answer:

(a) 203
The entire file must be relocated by one block. All 101 blocks would have to be read and then rewritten. Then the new block could be written.

(b) 101
The 50 blocks after the middle block would have to be read and then rewritten. Then the new block could be written.

(c) 1
Only the new block would have to be written.

(d) 0
Reset the files starting location to be the current location plus 1 block.

(e) 100
The 50 blocks after the middle block would have to be read and then rewritten one block earlier.

(f) 0
Just reset the size of the file to be one block smaller.

6.32 Repeat the previous problem for a system using linked allocation.

Answer:

(a) 1
   The new block would be written containing a link to the block that had previously been at the beginning of the fide. The directory entry is adjusted to point to the new block. No other block need be changed.

(b) 53
   Each of the first 51 blocks would have to be read to obtain the link to the next block. Then the added block could be written containing the link extracted from the 51st block. Finally, the 51st block would need to be rewritten with its link pointing to the added block.

(c) 103
   Each of the first 101 blocks would have to be read to obtain the link to the next block. Then the added block could be written containing the link extracted from the 101st block. Finally, the 101st block would need to be rewritten with its link pointing to the added block.

(d) 1
   Read the first block and extract its link. Store the extracted link value in the directory entry as the file's new starting location.

(e) 52
   Each of the first 51 blocks would have to be read to obtain the link to the 52nd block. Then rewrite the 50th block with a link to what had been the 52nd block.

(f) 101
   Each of the first 100 blocks would have to be read. Then rewrite the 100th block with the null link.

6.33 Repeat the previous problem for a system using linked allocation. Assume all needed index blocks are already in memory. If the content of an index block changes, do not include in the operation count the output operations needed to rewrite that revised information to the disk.

Answer:

(a) 1
   Each pointer in the index block must be moved down one location. Then a new pointer must be added at the beginning. Since the index blocks reside in main memory, no I/O operations are needed except to write the new block.

(b) 1
   Same as above.

(c) 1
   Same as above.

(d) 0
   Each pointer in the index block must be moved up one location. Since the index block resides in main memory, no I/O operations are needed.

(e)   0
     Same as above.

(f)   0
     Same as above.

6.34   For both linked and contiguous allocation, write a function **GetPhysBlock** that returns the physical block number corresponding to a file's logical block number. The function is passed two parameters: the logical block number (**logBlock**) and the physical block number of the file's first block (**physBlock1**). Assume logical and physical blocks start their numbering at 1. For linked allocation, you may make use of a function **GetLink** that, when passed a physical block number as a parameter, returns the number of the physical block pointed to by that physical block.

Answer:

```
// Contiguous
int GetPhysBlock (int logBlock, int physBlock1)
    {
    return physBlock1 + logBlock - 1;
    }
// Linked
int GetPhysBlock (int logBlock, int physBlock1)
    {
    int phsBlock;
    int ii;
    physBlock = physBlock1;
    for (ii = 1; ii < logBlock; ii++)
        physBlock = GetLink(physBlock);
    return physBlock;
    }
```

6.35   Which allocation scheme would work best for a file system implemented on a device that can only be accessed sequentially, a tape drive, for instance.

Answer:

Contiguous allocation. Once the start of the file was accessed, subsequent accesses would be relatively efficient. With linked or index allocation, the various physical blocks in which the file was stored could be scattered all over the device, making access very inefficient.

6.36   Consider a system in which a directory entry can store up to 16 disk block addresses. For files no larger than 16 blocks, the 16 addresses serve as the file's index table. For files larger than 16 blocks, the addresses point to indirect blocks which in turn point to 256 file blocks each. A block is 1024 bytes. How big can a file be?

Answer:

The largest possible file will have $16 = 2^4$ indirect blocks. Since each indirect block can point to $256 = 2^8$ blocks, the largest file has $256 = 2^{8+4}$ blocks. Given a block size of $1024 = 2^{10}$, the maximum file size is $2^{4+8+10} = 2^{22}$.

6.37 How many bits would be needed to store the free list under the following conditions if a bit map were used to implement the free list?

(a)   16 bits per disk address; 500,000 blocks total; 200,000 free blocks

(b)   16 bits per disk address; 500,000 blocks total; 0 free blocks

Answer:

In either case, the number of bits per address and the number of free blocks are irrelevant. The status of each of the 500,000 blocks is stored in a bit. 500,000 bits are needed.

6.38 How many bits would be needed to store the-free list under the following conditions if an array of free blocks were used to implement the free list?

(a)   16 bits per disk address; 500,000 blocks total; 200,000 free blocks

(b)   16 bits per disk address; 500,000 blocks total; 0 free blocks

(c)   16 bits per disk address; 500,000 blocks total; 1,000,000 free blocks

(d) D bits per disk address; B blocks total; F free blocks

Answer:

(a)   200,000 addresses $\times$ 16 bits per address $= 3,200,000$ bits

(b)   0 addresses $\times$ 16 bits per address $= 0$ bits

(c)   500,000 addresses $\times$ 16 bits per address $= 8,000,000$ bits

(d) D addresses $\times$ 16 bits per address $= 16D$ bits

6.39 (a)   On a system with D bits per disk address, B blocks total, and F free blocks, under what conditions will the free list array use less space than the bit map?

(b)   For D having the value of 32 bits, what is the fraction of the disk space that must be free?

Answer:

(a) $D \times F < B$

(b) $32 \times F < B$
$F < B/32$
Less than one thirty-second of the blocks can be free.

6.40   If the information in the free list is lost or corrupted, how can the system recover?

Answer:

Search the file system information for every file on the system and make a list of all blocks used by the files. Reconstruct the free list, including in it all blocks not listed as belonging to a file.

6.41   Most operating systems improve performance by caching some important file system data in main memory. Those operating systems require the computer to be shut down prior to turning the power off. Why?

Answer:

If power were suddenly turned off, the file system stored on the disk could be left in an inconsistent state. For example, consider what might happen after a file write operation that results in a block from the free list being added to a file. Assume the file's information on the disk had been updated to record the added block. But suppose the more frequently used free list information is cached in main memory. Although the free list data in memory no longer includes a reference to the block, the free list information on the disk does. If the power to the system is suddenly lost, when the system is rebooted the block will both be allocated to the file and included in the free list.

6.42   Which of the following inconsistencies in file system information is more serious, having a block allocated to both a file and the free list, or having a block that is not in the free list and not allocated to any file?

Answer:

It is more serious to have a file allocated to both. In time, a second file may be allocated to the block from the free list. Then information written to the corresponding logical block in one file will overwrite the information from the other file. If a block is not allocated to the free list or any file, it effectively ceases to exist. The system loses one block of storage. Given a large number of blocks of storage on a disk, the loss of one block is relatively insignificant.

6.43   On a system using a free hole array, and that has K physical blocks, what is the maximum length of a free hole array? The minimum length?

Answer:

The maximum number of holes is created by having alternating free and used blocks. Thus, the maximum number of holes is $(K + 1)/2$ (where '/' represents integer division). The minimum number of holes is zero, which occurs when all of memory is in use.

Supplementary Problems

6.44 On a system that mounts file systems on individual devices into a single file system, a floppy device has been mounted at point **/mnt**. If the floppy's file system contains a file by the name of **/home/user/data**, what will that file's name be in the overall file system?

6.45 A direct access file has fixed-size 50-byte records. Assuming the first record is record 1, the first byte of record 10 will be at what logical location?

6.46 A sequential access file has fixed-size 32-byte records. Assuming the first record is record 0, the first byte of record 20 will be at what logical location?

6.47 A program has just read the fifth record in a direct access file. It next wants to read the tenth record. How many records must the program read to input the tenth?

6.48 A program has just read the fifteenth record in a sequential access file. It next wants to read the tenth record. How many records must the program read to input the tenth?

6.49 Given a system with up to 2^{12} users and up to 2^{16} files, how many bytes of storage will be needed to store access control data if an unlimited/ access control system is used? The operations controlled are read, execute, write, and append.

6.50 On a system using fixed blocking with 60-byte records and 500-byte blocks, how much space will be wasted in each block?

6.51 Given a system using unspanned blocking and 80-byte blocks. A file contains records of 20, 40, 25, 15, 35, 40, 35. What percentage of space will be wasted in the blocks allocated for the file?

6.52 On a system using contiguous allocation, compute the number of the physical block corresponding to the logical block (assume block numbers start with 1).

    (*a*) Starting physical block: 500; logical block: 432

    (*b*) Starting physical block: 800; logical block: 20

    (*c*) Starting physical block: **P**; logical block: **L**

6.53 A file system uses 512-byte physical blocks. Each file has a directory entry giving the file name, location of the first block, length of file, and last block position. Assume the last physical block read and the directory entry are already in main memory. Indicate how many physical blocks must be read to access the specified block (including the reading of the specified block) on a system using contiguous allocation.

    (*a*) Last block read: 200; block to be read: 50

    (*b*) Last block read: 150; block to be read: 500

(c)   Last block read: 127; block to be read: 128

(d)   Last block read: 128; block to be read: 127

6.54   Repeat the previous problem for a system using linked allocation.

6.55   Repeat the previous problem for a system using indexed allocation. Assume the directory entry contains the location of the first index block (not the first block of the file). Each index block contains pointers to 127 file blocks plus a pointer to the next index block. In addition to the last block read, assume the system has in main memory the index block that contains the pointer to the last block read. However, no other index blocks are in main memory.

6.56   Consider a system using contiguous allocation. How many read and write operations would be required to add a block to or remove a block from a 50-block file under the conditions specified below? You may assume the following:

- The location of the first block of the file is already in memory.

- The block of information to be added is already in memory.

- In calculating the number of I/O operations, if the location of the first block of a file changes, do not include the output operations needed to rewrite that revised information to the directory entry on the disk.

- There is room for the file to grow at the end of the file but not at the beginning.

- The middle block is the 25th block.

- Do not include any I/O operations needed to add a removed block to the free list.

  (a)   Add a block at the beginning.
  (b)   Add a block after the middle block.
  (c)   Add a block at the end.
  (d)   Remove the beginning block.
  (e)   Remove the middle block.
  (f)   Remove the end block.

6.57   Repeat the previous problem for a system using linked allocation.

6.58   Repeat the previous problem for a system using indexed allocation. Assume all needed index blocks are already in memory. If the content of an index block changes, do not include in the operation count the output operations needed to rewrite that revised information index block to the disk.

6.59   Consider a system where a directory entry can store up to 13 disk block addresses. The first 10 addresses point to the first 10 blocks of the file. The 11th address points to an indirect block. The 12th address points to a double indirect block. The 13th address points to a triple indirect block. Each indirect block can contain 256 pointers. A block is 1024 bytes. How big can a file be?

6.60   In version 6 of Unix, one block on the disk, called the super block, stored key information about the file system. Information on the free list originated in two super block variables, the integer **NFR** and the long-integer array **FR**. The Unix documentation described the implementation of the free list as follows.

> "The **FR** array contains, in **FR**[1], ..., **FR**[**NFR** − 1], up to 99 numbers of free blocks. **FR**[0] is the block number of the head of a chain of blocks constituting the free list. The first long in each free-chain block is the number (up to 100) of free-block numbers listed in the next 100 longs of this chain member. The first of these 100 blocks is the link to the next member of the chain. To allocate a block: decrement **NFR**, and the new block is **FR**[**NFR**]. If the new block number is 0, there are no blocks left, so give an error. If **NFR** becomes 0, read in the block named by the new block number, replace **NFR** by its first word, and copy the block numbers in the next 100 longs into the **FR** array. To free a block, check if **NFR** is 100; if so, copy **NFR** and the **FR** array into it, write it out, and set **NFR** to 0. In any event set **FR**[**NFR**] to the freed block's number and increment **NFR**." [from *man S filesys*]

In C, write the functions **allocate** and **deallocate**. The function **allocate** should remove a block from the free list. The function's return value should be the number of the block removed or 0 if the free list is empty. The function **deallocate** should insert the block numbered **N** (passed as a parameter) into the free list.

Assume the **NFR** and **FR** values have already been read from the super block into global C variables by those names. You may use the following routines as required.

```
void rd(long b, long buf[256]);/* Reads block b into buf. */
void wr(long b, long buf[2561);/* Writes buf into block b. */
```

6.61   How many bits would be needed to store the free list under the following conditions if a bit map were used to implement the free list?

(a)   32 bits per disk address; 1,000,000 blocks total; 200,000 free blocks

(b)   32 bits per disk address; 1,000,000 blocks total; 0 free blocks

(c)   **D** bits per disk address; **P** blocks total; **F** free blocks

6.62   How many bits would be needed to store the free list under the following conditions if an array of free blocks were used to implement the free list?

(a)   32 bits per disk address; 1,000,000 blocks total; 200,000 free blocks

(b)   32 bits per disk address;. 1,000,000 blocks total; 0 free blocks

(c)   32 bits per disk address; 1,000,000 blocks total; 1,000,000 free blocks

(d)   **D** bits per disk address; **P** blocks total; **F** free blocks

6.63   On a system using a free hole array, how many holes will exist when no memory is in use?

Answers to Supplementary Problems

6.44 /mnt/home/user/data

6.45 451

6.46 640

6.47 One

6.48 10

6.49 2^{22} bytes

6.50 20 bytes

6.51 12.5%

6.52   (*a*)   931
        (*b*)   819
        (*c*) $P - 1 + L$

6.53   (*a*)   1
        (*b*)   1
        (*c*)   1
        (*d*)   1

6.54   (*a*)   50
        (*b*)   350
        (*c*)   1
        (*d*)   127

6.55   (*a*)   2
        (*b*)   3
        (*c*)   2
        (*d*)   2

6.56   (*a*)   51
        (*b*)   26

(c) 1

(d) 0

(e) 50

(f) 0

6.57 (a) 1

(b) 27

(c) 52

(d) 1

(e) 26

(f) 50

6.58 (a) 1

(b) 1

(c) 1

(d) 0

(e) 0

(f) 0

6.59 $2^{10} \times (10 + 2^8 + 2^{16} + 2^{54}) = 17,247,250,432$ bytes

6.60
```
long FR[100];
int NFR;
int allocate (void)
   {
   int ii;
   long newBlock;
   long buf[256];
   NFR = NFR - 1
   newBlock = FR[NFR];
   if ((newBlock ! = 0)  &&  (NFR == 0))
      {
      rd (newBlock, buf);
      NFR = buf[0];
      for (ii = 0;  ii < 100;  ii++)
         FR[ii] = buf[ii+1];
      }
   return newblock;
   }
void deallocate (long freedBlock)
   {
   int ii;
   long buf[256];
   if (NFR == 100)
```

```
          {
          buf[0] = NFR;
          for (ii = 0; ii < 100; ii++)
            buf[ii+1] = FR[ii];
          wr (freedBlock, buf);
          NFR = 0;
          }
        FR[NFR] = freedBlock;
        NFR = NFR + 1
        }
```

6.61   (*a*)   1,000,000

   (*b*)   1,000,000

   (*c*)   **P**

6.62   (*a*)   6,400,000

   (*b*)   0

   (*c*)   32,000,000

   (*d*) $\mathbf{F} \times \mathbf{D}$

6.63   1

Device Management

Device management is perhaps an operating system's greatest challenge. The operating system must control a collection of devices with multidimensional differences. Wide ranges are found in device speed, information volume, purpose, direction of information flow, and communication protocol. In addition to diversity, the operating system needs the capability to deal with a large number of devices. On some systems, thousands of different devices could potentially be connected to the machine, each of which requires its own unique operating system support. And all of this management must be accomplished in an environment of parallelism. Devices operate mostly independent of the CPU, using their own timing. The operating system, usually running on a single CPU, must deal with concurrent requests for attention from a number of devices.

Although it must deal with a diverse set of devices, the abstraction presented to applications should be as device-independent as possible. The physical characteristics of floppy disks, CD-ROMs, printers, and main memory may vary greatly, but applications should be able to read from or write to them as if they were all the same.

Device management services are provided not just to application programs. File management is built upon the abstract I/O system described in this chapter. Using the device-independent abstraction created by device management software greatly simplifies the task of creating a file system. Similarly, swapping software relies on device management to handle its I/O requirements.

7.1 Hardware I/O Organization

Although the details differ, computers are built around similar architectural designs. The I/O devices, memory, and the CPU communicate with each other by way of one or more communication buses.

The simplest machines have just a single communication bus, to which all devices (I/O, memory, and CPU) are attached (Fig. 7-1). Since communications can occur between only one pair of devices at a time, some kind of protocol is required to control which devices can communicate on the bus at any particular instant. Time is broken up into clock cycles, with one cycle needed to send a piece of information on the bus. A special device called a **bus arbitor** is responsible for making the decision as to which device can communicate during the next cycle. The device selected may communicate with any device it chooses, provided that device is connected to the bus. An addressing mechanism identifies the destination device.

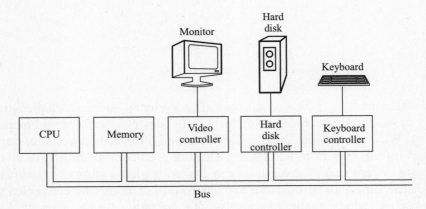

Fig. 7-1. Single-bus architecture.

Normally the bus is allocated to the CPU so it can communicate with memory. Frequent memory accesses and the CPU's relatively high speed results in it having a high bus utilization. Although they need the bus less frequently, the communication needs of I/O devices are usually more time-critical than the CPU requests. Therefore, requests for bus access by I/O devices are usually given a higher priority. Taking the bus away from the CPU and giving it to a device is called **cycle stealing**.

Multiple buses can be found in machines for two principal reasons: parallelism and performance tuning. With multiple buses, multiple communications can occur simultaneously. For example, the CPU could communicate with a serial port on one bus while a disk communicates with memory on another. However, the advantage of multiple buses is limited. Most communications involve either memory or the CPU. Without special multiaccess hardware, they can communicate with only one device at a time.

Performance issues frequently drive the incorporation of multiple buses. Newer PC architectures typically use three types of buses in addition to the CPU's own processor bus (Fig. 7-2). The standard bus for connecting devices is called the **PCI** (Peripheral Component Interconnect) bus. In addition, a special memory bus allows for optimized communication between CPU and memory. An ISA (Industry Standard Architecture) bus is connected to the PCI bus to provide backward compatibility for older ISA devices.

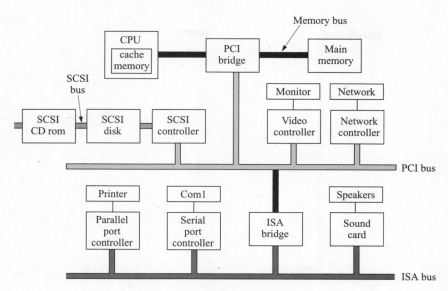

Fig. 7-2.   PCI architecture.

7.1.1 I/O CONTROL

In the simplest model of I/O control, the CPU communicates with the I/O device directly. The CPU is responsible for controlling all the minute details of the device's operation. This type of communication is increasingly rare, perhaps seen in specialized, microprocessor-controlled, embedded systems.

The PC model is for the CPU to communicate with a ***device controller***. A typical command from CPU to controller may start a read operation for a byte of information from a serial device or a sector of information from a disk. The device controller relays to the device the more detailed commands necessary to accomplish the requested operation. By shifting this responsibility to the controller, the CPU is freed to simultaneously perform other processing tasks. Each I/O controller is designed specifically to handle a particular kind of device. Its capabilities are limited and built into the controller. Most controllers can service multiple devices.

On more sophisticated systems, an additional level of I/O control may be employed. The CPU communicates with an ***I/O channel***, which in turn communicates with an I/O control unit (Fig. 7-3). I/O channels are more sophisticated than I/O controllers and may even contain their own CPU. They execute ***channel programs*** that may be loaded in main memory or in the channel's own memory. Communication between CPU and channel can be at a higher level, offloading additional processing into the I/O subsystem.

7.1.2 PORT AND MEMORY-MAPPED I/O

To perform I/O, the CPU must communicate with the I/O module, be it a device, a controller, or a channel. Each I/O module contains one or more registers. The CPU

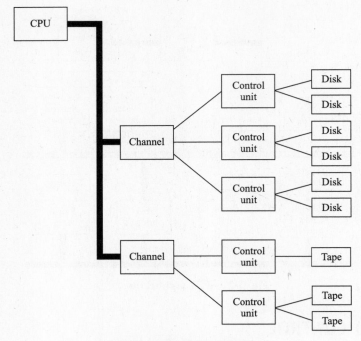

Fig. 7-3.   I/O channel.

communicates by reading from or writing to the module registers. The module communicates with the CPU by setting the registers to appropriate values.

Two approaches have been taken to provide CPUs with the ability to access module registers. With *port I/O*, a limited number of instructions provide I/O capability. One of the instruction operands is an I/O port number. The I/O operation is applied to the I/O module identified with that port.

With *memory-mapped I/O*, any instruction that accesses memory may access an I/O module. A portion of the memory address space is allocated to I/O modules. On systems with limited address space, allocating part of the address space to I/O modules can be a distinct disadvantage. However, on systems like a VAX, being able to use a powerful memory-referencing instruction set to access devices is very attractive.

Some systems provide just one of the I/O capabilities, others both. Regardless of the capability used, port number(s) or memory address(es) must be associated with the I/O module. Permanent assignment by the manufacturer is not practical, since in many cases the I/O address space is limited and there are insufficient addresses to be assigned to all manufacturers. Permanent assignment could be made by module type, but since computer systems frequently have multiple modules of the same type, module addresses would have to be assigned from a set of addresses. Two similar modules with the same address could not coexist in a particular machine. In most cases, the port number or memory address assignment is configurable. Some are set manually using a jumper or a DIP (Dual In-line Package) switch, others using software. In plug-and-play (when it works), the settings are made automatically by the hardware itself.

7.1.3 MODULE REGISTERS

The number and function of module registers depend on the I/O module involved. A module for a simple input device may have two registers: one for data and one for control information. The data buffer would store the input value to be passed to the CPU by the I/O module. The control register would contain bits whose setting by the CPU effectively commands the I/O module. Selected bits may serve to enable the device, reset it, or start a read operation. Other bits in the control register would be set by the I/O module to communicate information to the CPU. Module-writable bits could include bits to signal operation completion, device ready, or different kinds of error conditions.

Modules controlling more complicated devices typically contain more registers. Disk I/O operations require additional information to identify the location on the disk to be operated on and the amount of data to be transferred.

7.1.4 BUSY WAIT I/O

Communication between I/O module and CPU follows one of four basic protocols. In the simplest protocol, the CPU issues to the I/O module a command to start an I/O operation. If an output operation, data is transferred to the module's data buffer. The CPU then goes into a loop, checking with the module to see if the command has completed. Upon completion, status information is checked to verify the operation completed successfully. If an input operation, the data is then transferred from the module buffer. *Busy wait I/O* is inefficient, as processes can make no headway while the CPU waits for the I/O to complete.

7.1.5 POLLED I/O

In *polled I/O*, after starting the I/O operation, the CPU returns to executing processes in the system. However, processing is interrupted at brief intervals to allow the CPU to check back with the I/O module to see if the I/O operation has completed. Polling is more efficient than busy wait, but incurs a high overhead cost of processing frequent timer interrupts. I/O modules have varying requirements of how quickly the CPU must respond to the completion of an I/O operation. Polling is poorly suited for modules that require fast response.

7.1.6 INTERRUPT I/O

Most I/O modules can be set to send an interrupt signal to the CPU upon I/O completion. As with register addresses, the interrupt used by a module is typically a configurable setting. When *interrupt I/O* is used, the CPU is free to ignore the I/O module until the interrupt signal is received. The only added overhead is processing a single interrupt when the I/O operation completes.

The parallelism added in interrupts is both an advantage and a disadvantage. While it improves efficiency, it adds complexity. Code must be carefully written to prevent race conditions.

Interrupts can occur during the processing of other interrupts. Care must be taken to handle them in the proper order. Consider an input device for which fast response to an interrupt is a requirement. While processing an interrupt from this device's I/O module, a string of interrupts for other modules are received and processed. The delay imposed on processing the original interrupt could result in the input being lost. On the other hand, if the system is designed to process interrupts sequentially, an input module could fail if the processing of its interrupt was delayed sufficiently by the processing of previously received interrupts.

A priority scheme is required so that, while processing one interrupt, the CPU may only be interrupted by a higher-priority I/O module. Interrupt processing functions may only execute briefly to prevent failures when concurrent interrupts are received. Designing the operating system to be able to respond with sufficient speed to all possible loads is not an easy task.

7.1.7   DIRECT MEMORY ACCESS (DMA)

Direct Memory Access (DMA) components allow I/O modules to read data from or write data to memory. Without DMA, all I/O data must travel through the CPU. DMA is particularly useful on devices like disks, where many bytes of information can be transferred in single I/O operations. When used in conjunction with an interrupt (which is invariably the case), the CPU is notified only after the entire block of data has been transferred.

7.2   Software Organization

The operating system implements supervisor calls that allow processes to request device input and output services. To enhance generality, the same basic set of primitives may be available for all devices. In some cases, the primitives are the same as the ones for file I/O.

Given the unique characerics of some devices, some device-dependent I/O capability may also be provided. On Unix, the *ioctl* supervisor call performs a variety of functions, depending on the device it is applied to and the arguments specified. For example, it could be used to set the baud rate on a serial line or eject a CD-ROM from a CD-ROM device.

A number of characteristics of devices have an effect on the supervisor call interface provided.

- **Device Speed**: Device I/O can be relatively slow. Some operating systems provide the option of issuing nonblocking I/O operations. Nonblocking input operations can be handled in two ways.

1. Using data received and buffered prior to the system call, return can be immediate using the data in the input buffer. The return value would indicate how much data was supplied. A return value of zero indicates no data was available when the system call was made.

2. The process can be notified when the input operation completes. Notification can be made by sending the process a signal, by setting one of the process's variables to a particular value, or by providing a special system call for testing the I/O operation's status.

For nonblocking output operations, notification can also be used. The other alternative is no notification. In most cases it is irrelevant to the application when the data is actually output by the device.

- **Mutual Exclusion**: Many devices are nonshareable. What kind of protection will the operating system provide to users of those devices? Options include:

  1. Allowing only one process to have the device open at a time.

  2. Assigning ownership of the device to the user who opened it and denying access to other users. This solution allows the owner to override the default and grant access if desired.

  3. Dealing with the problem at the application level by implementing a spooling scheme or some comparable alternative.

  4. Doing nothing. Leave the problem to the users.

- **Unidirectional Devices**: Some devices are input-only or output-only. How should the operating system handle requests that cannot be performed by the device? Typically, devices must be opened before I/O can be performed; the open call can include a parameter indicating the type of access desired. Attempts to open a device for the wrong kind of I/O would fail.

7.2.1 NETWORK I/O

Some operating systems, such as Windows 2000 and Unix, provide a separate abstraction for network devices. Network communications involve complex and often multilayered protocols. Failure to follow the protocol could disrupt all machines on the entire network, so support for the protocols is built into the operating system. Applications are provided with a set of network I/O system calls. One frequently implemented network I/O abstraction is *sockets*.

Picture a socket as a double-sided network jack (Fig. 7-4). On one side is a jack your computer can plug into. On the other side is a jack the remote computer can plug into. System calls allow applications to create sockets, establish connections to sockets on remote machines, detect if other machines have established a connection with a local socket, and send and receive messages on established connections.

7.2.2 LOGICAL I/O

The logical I/O level of device management software implements semi-device-independent kernel I/O objects. The objects are not always totally device-indepen-

Fig. 7-4.   A socket.

dent, as a few classes of I/O objects may exist to better handle the requirements of particular kinds of devices. I/O requests from other modules of the operating system would access the capabilities provided at this level.

Two commonly supported device types are block devices and character devices. For a block device, the smallest unit of transfer is a block. A disk is a block device. I/O operations are in terms of the number of disk blocks (sectors) transferred. Character devices transfer a single character or byte at a time. Modems and printers are examples of character devices.

I/O objects contain necessary information about the I/O operation to be performed.

- Type of operation (read or write)
- Blocking or nonblocking
- Status (pending, in progress, done)
- Error status
- Device
- Logical location to transfer to
- Logical location to transfer from
- Count of bytes to be transferred

- Count of bytes actually transferred
- Scheduling information

For random access I/O, the location on the device where data is to be transferred to or from must be specified. At this level of the I/O system, the address is a block address, not an actual physical device address.

7.2.3 BUFFERING

Logical I/O also provides the buffering required by I/O data. Buffers are needed for a number of reasons.

- Computers have no control over when some I/O devices will start sending input. Even though no process has requested input from the keyboard, there is nothing that the computer can do to prevent the user from typing in characters. The operating system can either ignore those characters or save them until some process issues a keyboard read request. Buffers are used to store unread input.
- Block devices perform I/O in block units. The application interface may permit I/O transfer of any size. Buffers are needed to package the requests into block-size units.
- Some devices use DMA transfers. Buffers are needed as the destination or source of the transfer. Using an operating system buffer ensures the integrity of the transfer.
- If asynchronous write operations are permitted, copying the data into an operating system buffer allows the application to continue executing without concern it will overwrite data that has not yet been written to the device

7.2.4 CACHING

Caching has proven to be an effective performance enhancer under a variety of circumstances. A *cache* is a fast storage device that can hold a copy of some of the data stored on a slower device. If information to be read from a slower device is contained in the cache, the request can be serviced faster by accessing the copy of the data in the cache. I/O caches store device data in main memory.

Systems that implement caches typically create a buffer pool much larger than needed; those buffers become the cache. Additional information must be associated with the buffers, such as the device and location within the device to which the buffer corresponds.

Write operations can be handled by caching systems in a number of different ways.

- *Write-through* caching loads the information to be written into the cache buffer, then immediately writes it to the disk. Blocking write operations do not return until the write is completed.

- *Delayed-write* caching delays the writing of the data to disk until a time the operating system finds suitable. Blocking write operations, however, return as soon as the data has been copied into the cache buffer. A number of strategies may be used to decide when the data will be transferred to disk. The system may wait until a number of unwritten buffers are available to be written, until no I/O operations to the device are pending, until the process performing the write has executed a close operation, or until a system shutdown command has been received. Delayed writes are more efficient but, until the write occurs, the data stored on the disk is inconsistent. A loss of power while in an inconsistent state could corrupt the entire disk contents. One of the reasons systems must be shut down prior to turning off power is to make sure all cached data is written to disk.

Once all cache buffers are filled, additional requests for noncached data requires one or more of the buffers to be reused. The same algorithms used in demand-paging systems can be used to select the buffer whose information will be replaced.

Some disk controllers have their own onboard memory and perform their own disk caching. With such a device, having the operating system also cache data could be counterproductive.

7.2.5 DEVICE DRIVERS

I/O objects generated in the logical I/O software are passed to device drivers, which are customized for the needs of the device they control. Device drivers operate upon one or more closely related devices. The operating system may require that for each device there be a set of functions implemented for that device, such as the following.

open: Perform any startup tasks needed before the device can be accessed.

close: Perform any tasks needed to shut a device down.

schedule: Schedule an I/O request. Some scheduling may be performed by the logical I/O software before requests are passed to the device driver. But the device driver may implement its own scheduling to handle the particular needs of the device it controls.

startio: Check if the device is busy and, if not, start the next I/O operation on the device's scheduling queue.

interrupt: The routine executed when the device sends the CPU an interrupt.

ioctl: Implement any special functions that can be applied to this device.

All device error-checking and recovery should be performed in these routines. Error codes are stored in I/O objects for reporting back to the process that requested the I/O.

Given all the different kinds of devices that might be connected to some computer systems, it would be impractical to include in the operating system all drivers for all possible devices. Most operating systems must be configured for the devices actually present. Only the drivers for the devices specified in the configuration are included in the operating system.

Changes to the configuration require drivers to be added or removed. On some systems, such changes modify an operating system image stored on the disk, and the system must be rebooted to use the new image. In other cases, driver modification can occur dynamically without requiring a reboot. Linux allows device drivers to be configured as present, not-present, or loadable. Loadable drivers can be changed dynamically.

7.3   Devices

A few devices merit closer attention because of the interesting issues raised in their management.

7.3.1   GRAPHICS

The amount of information that must be transmitted to paint the display on modern monitors presents an overall system design challenge. The image on the monitor is generated by controlling the illumination of tiny *pixels*. Early monitors consisted of 200 lines of 320 black and white pixels. In the year 2000, resolutions of 800×600, 1024×768, and 1280×960 are far more common.

The illumination of each pixel is controlled by values stored in video RAM. Basic monochrome displays require only one bit per pixel. Color displays require many more. Each pixel is generated from the primary colors: Red, Green, and Blue (RGB). Using 8-bit color, each of the colors can take on an intensity value between 0 and 255. Combined, 24 bits are needed to express a color pixel value.

For a 1024×768 monitor, 2.3Mb of video RAM is required to store a 24-bit value for each pixel. Indexing schemes can be used to reduce the memory requirement. In one such scheme, the total number of colors that can be displayed at any instant is limited to 256. Pixel values are stored in a single byte, reducing the amount of video RAM needed for a 1024×768 display to well under 1Mb. The pixel values serve as an index into a color palette table of 256 24-bit values. The pointed-to element controls the illumination of the pixel.

To modify a screen image, new data must be written to the video RAM. Given the amount of data that could be involved, this could impose a significant load on the system. Consider the display of full-motion video requiring the display of 25 frames per second. If all 2.3Mb of video RAM must be rewritten 25 times a second, 58Mb of data must be copied to video RAM each second.

Hardware designs have evolved as transfer requirements have increased. PCI bus technology provides personal computers with 132Mb/s transfer capability. The new AGP (Accelerated Graphics Port) has a 528Mb/s transfer rate (Fig. 7-5). Intelligent graphics controllers with graphics accelerators accept commands to manipulate graphics images, modifying the video RAM themselves. Significant performance improvements are obtained by offloading this processing from the CPU. Device drivers must contain the intelligence necessary to take advantage of the capabilities of the graphics accelerator.

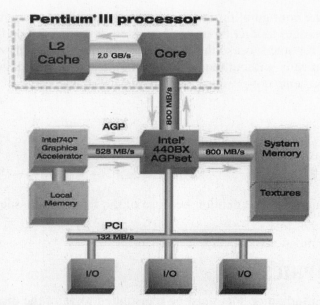

Fig. 7-5. Accelerated graphics port (AGP). (Reprinted by permission of Intel Corporation, Copyright Intel Corporation 2001.)

7.3.2 TEXT-BASED DISPLAYS

Text-based devices are limited to displaying characters in a limited alphabet. Alphabets of 256 characters are common, with the 128-character ASCII alphabet included as a subset. Serial terminals are text-based displays. Monitors and most printers can be used as text-based displays.

The advantage of a text-based display is the speed by which it can be modified. Character values can be represented in a single byte. A display of 25 rows by 80 columns can be specified in only 2000 bytes. For users communicating with a remote system through a modem or even a congested network, the reduced bandwidth needed for the communications is a valuable feature.

Support for text-based devices is typically included in the logical I/O subsystem. Some features commonly found in a text-based interface include the following.

- **Line Editing:** Input is not passed to applications as it is entered. Instead, it is buffered until the *Enter* key is pressed. Limited line-editing facilities are provided. Entering the character that implements the erase function (typically *Backspace* or *Delete*) causes the previous character entered into the buffer to be erased. The editing occurs before the line is passed to the application; thus, the application never realizes the erased character was ever entered. Other line-editing functions, such as a line-erase, might also be provided.

- **End-Of-File:** When an application reading from a file gets to the end of the file, the operating system asserts an End-Of-File (EOF) condition to notify the application there is no additional input to read. The text input EOF character causes the EOF condition to be raised in applications reading from a text device. On Unix, the EOF character is commonly *CNTRL-d*; on DOS, it is *CNTRL-z*.

- **Signaling:** Entering the signal character instructs the operating system to abort all processes taking input from the text device. *CNTRL-c* or *CNTRL-y* are commonly configured as the signal (abort) character.

- **Echo:** A character typed at a keyboard is not automatically displayed on the screen. The computer must echo the character back to the display device for it to be seen. Automatic echo is implemented as part of the text interface, freeing applications from having to provide this functionality. In some situations, like when a password is being entered, an application will turn this feature off.

- **NL/CR Translation:** On most text-based devices, moving the cursor to the beginning of the next line requires a *CarriageReturn* (CR), and a *Newline* (NL) to be received. However, when users enter input, they end a line by pressing the *Enter* key, which sends a CR to the computer. Internally within many applications, the end of a line is represented by an NL character. Depending on the situation, a single NL, a single CR, or a CR/NL represents end-of-line. A text-based interface translates between the various representations as necessary.

- **Case Management:** Some applications and devices exist in a limited case environment, that is, they cannot understand or generate characters in either upper- or lowercase. Case management provides for automatic case translation (upper-to-lower or lower-to-upper).

- **Serial Control:** Text devices are frequently connected through serial lines. The serial interface includes a number of configurable options such as flow control, parity bit checking, baud rate, and modem control. The text interface includes support for these features of serial communications.

7.3.3 STORAGE DISKS

The disk can be considered the one I/O device that is common to every computer. Printers, tapes, mice, network adapters, and sound systems are all optional accessories. Even monitors and keyboards are not required on systems such as servers that are mostly accessed through a network interface. The one I/O device almost all computers require is some kind of disk. Granted, there are diskless workstations and X terminals, but are those computers or just "information appliances"?

Disks come in many sizes and speeds, and information may be stored optically or magnetically; however, all disks share a number of important features. The basic unit of information storage is a *sector*. Contained within a sector is administrative data, identifying the sector and providing redundancy check information, and the actual data to be stored. The sectors are stored on a flat, circular, media disk. This media spins close to one or more read/write heads. The heads can move from the inner portion of the disk to the outer portion. A sector can be read by moving the head in or out to the appropriate location, then waiting for the sector to spin under the head. These characteristics are common to floppy disks, hard disks, CD-ROMs, and DVDs.

DVDs and CD-ROMs differ from the other disks in how sectors are organized. On DVDs and CD-ROMs, the sectors form a long spiral that spins out from the center of the disk (Fig. 7-6). As the circumference of the media increases as the head moves out, the rotation rate of the media must decrease.

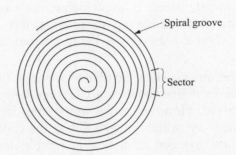

Fig. 7-6.   CD-ROM recording structure.

On floppy disks and hard disks, the media spins at a constant rate. Sectors are organized into a number of concentric circles or *tracks*. As one moves out from the center of the disk, the tracks get larger. Some disks store the same number of sectors on each track, with outer tracks being recorded using lower bit densities. Other disks place more sectors on outer tracks. On such a disk, more information can be accessed from an outer track than an inner one during a single rotation of the disk.

Disks contain one or more media platters. Information may be stored on both sides of a platter (although some multiplatter disk packs do not use the topmost or bottommost surface), with a separate head available for each recording surface. All the heads move together. The term *cylinder* refers to all the tracks at a particular head position. A disk with three platters is illustrated in Fig. 7-7.

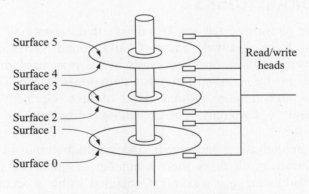

Fig. 7-7.   Hard disk with four platters.

The total capacity of a disk can be calculated by multiplying together the number of cylinders (which is the same as the number of tracks per surface), the number of read/write heads, the number of sectors per track, and the number of bytes per sector (usually 512).

7.3.4 HARD-DISK PERFORMANCE

Three factors affect the time, A, it takes to access data from a disk: ***seek time,*** ***latency***, and ***transfer time***. Seek time, S, is the time required to move a head to a particular cylinder. It is determined by startup delays in initiating head movement, I; the rate at which read/write head can be moved, H; and how far the head must travel, C.

$$S = HC + I$$

Latency, L, is the amount of time it takes the start of information to be accessed to spin under the read/write head. On average, that will be one-half of one revolution. Thus, latency can be computed by dividing the number of revolutions per minute (RPM), R, into 30.

$$L = \frac{30}{R}$$

Transfer time, T, is determined by the amount of information to be read, B; the number of bytes per track, N; and rotational speed.

$$T = \frac{60B}{RN}$$

Total access time is the sum of the three factors.

$$A = S + L + T$$

7.3.5 HARD-DISK SCHEDULING

As should be apparent from the analysis above, the amount of head movement needed to satisfy a series of I/O requests can affect performance. For this reason, a number of algorithms have been proposed for scheduling disk I/O requests.

- **FIFO**: Service requests in the order they are received.
- **Priority**: Service requests according to a priority associated with the requesting process.
- **SSTF**: Shortest Seek Time First services the request whose track position is closest to the current track position. Requests are subject to starvation with this algorithm.
- **SCAN**: Move the read/write head back and forth between the innermost and outermost tracks. As the head gets to each track, satisfy all outstanding requests for that track. Starvation is possible but only if there are repeated requests for the current track.
- **LOOK**: Start the head moving in one direction. Satisfy the request for the closest track in that direction. When there are no more requests in the direction the head is traveling, reverse direction and repeat. This algorithm is similar to SCAN but, unlike SCAN, the head does not unnecessarily travel to the innermost and outermost track on each circuit.

- **C-SCAN and C-LOOK**: "Circular" versions of SCAN and LOOK that only satisfy requests while going in one direction. When the last track has been reached, these algorithms return to the starting track. This reduces the maximum delay before a request will be serviced.

- **N-step SCAN**: The request queue is divided into subqueues with each subqueue having a maximum length of N. Subqueues are processed in FIFO order. Within a subqueue, requests are processed using SCAN. While a subqueue is being serviced, incoming requests are placed in the next nonfilled subqueue. N-step SCAN eliminates any possibility of starvation.

- **FSCAN**: Like N-step SCAN but with two subqueues, each of unlimited length. While requests in one subqueue are serviced, new requests are placed in the other subqueue.

Of these algorithms, the ones designed to improve performance base their decisions on seek time, not latency time. In most cases, it is not possible to predict latency time because rotational location cannot be determined. However, multiple requests for the same track may be serviced based on latency.

In many cases, optimization algorithms are not useful because the disk geometry (sectors per track, number of cylinders, number of heads or surfaces) is not known. Although a disk may publish one geometry, its actual geometry may be quite different. On PCs, limitations built into DOS make it troublesome for a disk to have more than 256 heads or 64 sectors per track. Where possible, the number of cylinders should be less than 1024. PC disks therefore use a virtual geometry to stay within these restraints. The actual geometry may be different.

7.3.6 FORMATTING

Before data can be written to a disk, all the administrative data must be written to the disks, organizing it into sectors. This *low-level formatting* or *physical formatting* is often done by the manufacturer. In the formatting process, some sectors may be found to be defective. Most disks have spare sectors, and a remapping mechanism substitutes spare sectors for defective ones.

For sectors that fail after formatting, the operating system may implement a bad block mechanism. Such mechanisms are usually in terms of blocks and are implemented at a level above the device driver.

The manner in which sectors are positioned on a track can affect disk performance. If disk I/O operations are limited to transferring a single sector at a time, to read multiple sectors in sequence, separate I/O operations must be performed. After the first I/O operation completes, its interrupt must be processed and the second I/O operation must be issued. During this time, the disk continues to spin. If the start of the next sector to be read has already spun past the read/write head, the sector cannot be read until the next revolution of the disk brings the cylinder by the read/write head. In a worst-case scenario, the disk must wait almost a full revolution. To avoid this problem, sectors may be *interleaved*. The degree of interleaving is determined by how far the disk revolves in the time from the end of one I/O operation until the controller can issue a subsequent I/O operation. The sector layout, given different degrees of interleaving, is illustrated in Fig. 7-8.

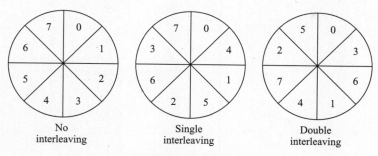

No
interleaving

Single
interleaving

Double
interleaving

Fig. 7-8.   Interleaving.

For most modern hard-disk controllers, interleaving is not used. The controller contains sufficient memory to store an entire track, so a single I/O operation may be used to read all the sectors on a track. Interleaving is more commonly used on less sophisticated disk systems, like floppy disks.

Most operating systems also provide the ability for disks to be divided into one or more virtual disks called *partitions*. On personal computers, Unix, Windows, and DOS all adhere to a common partitioning scheme so that they all may co-reside on a single disk.

Before files can be written to a disk, an empty file system must be created on a disk partition. This requires the various data structures required by the file system to be written to the partition, and is known as a *high-level format* or *logical format*. A file system is not required to make use of a disk. Some operating systems allow applications to write directly to a disk device. To an application, a directly accessible disk device is just a large sequential collection of storage blocks. In such a case, it is the responsibility of the application to impose an order on the information written there.

7.3.7   RAID

A *Redundant Array of Inexpensive Disks* (RAID) may be used to increase disk reliability. RAID may be implemented in hardware or in the operating system. Six different types of RAID systems have been defined. They are described below and illustrated in Fig. 7-9.

RAID level 0 creates one large virtual disk from a number of smaller disks. Storage is grouped into logical units called *strips* with the size of a strip being some multiple (possibly one) of the sector size. The virtual storage is a sequence of strips interleaved among the disks in the array. The principal benefit of RAID-0 is the ability to create a large disk. Its reliability benefits are limited. Files tend to get scattered over a number of disks so, even after a disk failure, some file data may be retrievable. Performance benefits can be achieved when accessing sequentially stored data. On a RAID-0 system, the sequential data is stored on different disks.

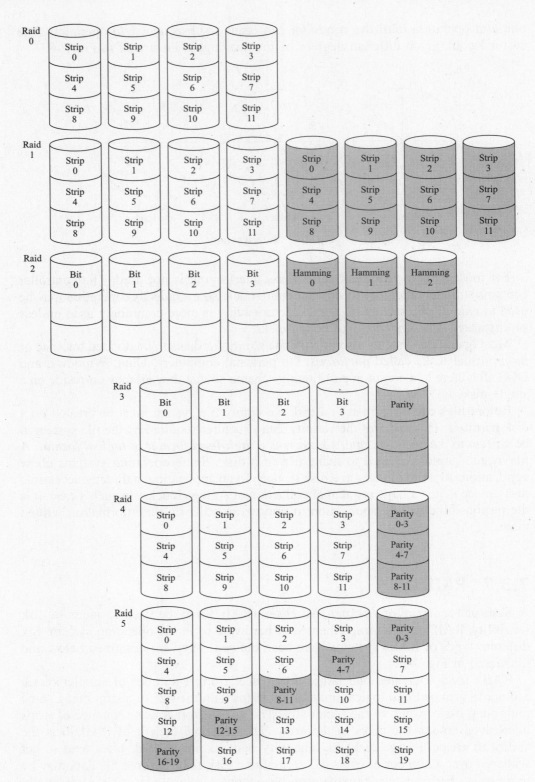

Fig. 7-9.   RAID levels.

While the first disk is in the process of reading the first strip, the second disk can start reading the second strip. If there are N disks in the array, N I/O operations can be occurring concurrently. The process of overlapping requests in this fashion is known as *pipelining*.

RAID level 1 stores duplicate copies of each strip, with each copy on a different disk. The simplest such organization is to have two disks, one being an exact duplicate of the other. Read requests can be optimized to be handled by the copy that can be accessed the quickest. As with RAID-0, under some circumstances requests can be pipelined. Write requests result in duplicate write operations, one for each copy. Writing is not as efficient as reading; completion is delayed until the copy with slowest access time is updated.

In RAID levels 2 to 5, single copies of each strip are maintained. Redundant information maintains functionality despite disk failures. In RAID level 2, an error-correcting code (such as a Hamming code) is calculated for the corresponding bits on each data disk. The bits of the code are stored on multiple drives. The strips are very small, so when a block is read, all disks are accessed in parallel. RAID-3 is similar, but a single parity bit is used instead of an error-correcting code. RAID-3 requires just one extra disk. If any disk in the array fails, its data can be determined from the data on the remaining disks.

RAID level 4 is similar to RAID-3, except strips are larger, so an operation to read a block involves only a single disk. Write operations require parity information to be calculated, and writes must be performed on both the data and parity disks. Since the parity disk must be written whenever any data disk is written, the parity disk can become a bottleneck during periods of heavy write activity.

RAID level 5 is similar to RAID-4, except parity information is distributed across all disks. Figure 7-9 provides an example of how this might be accomplished. RAID-5 eliminates the potential bottleneck found in RAID-4.

7.3.8   RAM DISKS

A RAM disk is a virtual block device created from main memory. Commands to read or write disk blocks are implemented by the RAM disk device driver. Unlike real disks, main memory is direct access. Seek and rotational delays, normally found on disk devices, do not exist. RAM disks are particularly useful for storing small files that are frequently accessed or temporary.

The two primary disadvantages of RAM disks are cost and volatility. To implement a RAM disk, the operating system must reserve a section of memory for RAM disk use. Either memory is lost for use by processes, or additional memory must be purchased for RAM disk use.

The other major disadvantage is that memory loses its contents when power is lost. If the RAM disk is to store a file system, that file system must be remade each time the system is booted. Any files stored on a RAM disk file system will be lost when the system is rebooted. In the event of a power failure, any important data stored on a RAM disk will be lost.

Implementation of a RAM disk is simplified if the memory is contiguous. Allocating a large contiguous section of memory for RAM disk use is easily done when a system is first booted. Depending on the memory management system used, it may be more difficult and inefficient once significant portions of memory have been allocated to processes. For this reason, some operating systems require RAM disks to be defined at boot time. Others allow them to be created dynamically.

 # SOLVED PROBLEMS

7.1 On a computer system with a single 32-bit 100MHz bus (10 ns cycle), the disk controller uses DMA to transfer data to/from memory at a rate of 40Mb per second. Assume the computer fetches and executes one 32-bit instruction every cycle when no cycles are stolen. By what percentage will the disk controller slow down instruction execution?

Answer:

Given the bus is 32 bits wide, the controller can transfer 4 bytes 10,000,000 times per second or 4 bytes every 100 ns. The controller will steal a cycle once every 10 instruction fetches for a slowdown of 10%.

7.2 A computer system that uses memory-mapped I/O has a 16-bit address space. Addresses with ones in the two most significant bits refer to devices. What is the maximum amount of memory that can be referenced in such a system?

Answer:

At most 2^{14} memory locations can be accessed. All addresses 2^{14} and higher refer to I/O devices.

7.3 On a virtual memory system, give one capability that could be provided to users of a memory-mapped system that could not be provided on a port I/O system.

Answer:

On a port I/O system, the instructions that perform I/O are privileged and can be executed only by the operating system. On a memory-mapped system, the operating system could include the address space containing the device registers in a user process's address space. Doing so would give the process direct access to I/O. (In most circumstances, this is not a wise thing to do.)

7.4 How well suited is busy-wait I/O for the following types of systems?

- A system dedicated to controlling a single I/O device
- A personal computer running a single-tasking operating system
- A workstation running as a heavily used web server

Answer:

Busy wait I/O is well suited for the first two systems, poorly suited for the last. On the dedicated system and on the personal computer, the system has nothing else it needs to do while I/O is being performed. The fact the CPU is idle during that time is not a disadvantage. The web server must be able to handle concurrent requests for web pages. It must manage multiple I/O modules controlling network and disk I/O devices as well as perform the computations necessary to process the web service requests. It needs the parallel processing capabilities busy wait I/O does not permit.

7.5 An input device accumulates data in its internal 5120-byte buffer at the rate of 1000 bytes per second. When reading data, the operating system uses polled I/O, emptying all data out of the buffer before returning to normal processing. If the goal is to empty the buffer just before it fills, how long should the polling interval be (assume the polling routine that empties the buffer takes 0 time)?

Answer:

It takes the device 5 s to almost fill the buffer. The polling routine should be executed every 5 s.

7.6 A serial line can receive input at a maximum rate of 50,000 bytes per second. The average input rate is 20,000 bytes per second. If input is handled using polling, the polling routine takes 3 μs to execute, whether or not an input byte is present. Bytes not retrieved from the controller before the next byte arrives are lost. What is the maximum safe polling interval?

Answer:

To make sure no input is lost, the polling rate must be able to handle the maximum input rate of 0.05 bytes per μs or 1 byte every 20 μs. Since it takes 3 μs to execute the polling routine, the maximum polling interval is 17 μs.

7.7 Given the system in the previous problem, assume the input handling was changed to interrupt I/O with an interrupt routine that took 3μs to execute. How much would interrupts decrease the amount of time spent processing the input?

Answer:

Interrupts would only occur when characters were actually received or at a rate of once every 50 μs. Overhead servicing I/O would be 3 μs out of every 50. With polling it was 3 μs out of every 20. Overhead using interrupts would be 40% of that when using polling.

7.8 A disk file contains 32-byte fixed-size records. Physical I/O is in terms of 512-byte blocks that are stored in an operating system buffer. If a process sequentially reads through a file's records, what percentage of the read requests will result in I/O operations?

Answer:

I/O will be in terms of blocks. Each 512-byte block input can hold sixteen 32-byte records. All but one in sixteen I/O requests can be satisfied by information already read into the buffer. 6.25% of I/O requests will result in I/O operations.

7.9 Blocking I/O prevents a process from continuing execution until the I/O is complete. How can processes achieve this functionality on systems with nonblocking I/O? Does the implementation have any disadvantages?

Answer:

A process can block itself by executing in a busy-wait loop until the I/O has completed. However, busy-wait execution makes inefficient use of the CPU.

7.10 A system has two disk drives connected to one disk controller, a line printer connected to a parallel port, and 10 terminals connected to 10 serial lines controlled by a single controller. The disk controller can issue a command to one disk while another disk is processing a command (for example, both disks can be seeking at the same time), but it may have only one disk transferring I/O at a time. The serial controller can handle simultaneous I/O from all its connected devices. All the controllers use DMA. The transfer rates for the devices are: disk device, 1000 Kb/s; printer, 1 Kb/s; and terminal, 5 Kb/s. What is the maximum I/O transfer rate for this system?

Answer:

Only one disk can be transferring at a time but all the terminals' I/O can be handled simultaneously by the terminal controller. The maximum I/O rate is $1000 + 1 + 50 = 1051$ Kb/s.

7.11 Where are the following tasks implemented, in the logical I/O layer, the device drivers, or both?

(a) Checking access permissions

(b) Scheduling the I/O operations

(c) Checking if the requested information is in the cache

(d) Processing a device interrupt

Answer:

(a) Logical I/O

(b) Logical I/O or device driver
Scheduling based on process characteristics such as process priority would occur in the logical I/O software. Scheduling based on device characteristics (such as minimizing seek time on a disk) would occur in the device driver.

(c) Logical I/O

(d) Device driver

7.12 On a system using a disk cache, the mean access time is dependent on the mean cache access time, the mean disk access time, and the hit rate. For the following, what is the mean access time?

(a) Cache: 1 ms; disk: 100 ms; hit rate: 25%

(b) Cache: 1 ms; disk: 100 ms; hit rate: 50%

Answer:

(a) $100 \times 0.75 + 1 \times 0.25 = 75.25$

(b) $100 \times 0.50 + 1 \times 0.50 = 50.50$

7.13 Can you think of a device on a typical PC for which delayed-write caching is a desirable policy? Can you think of a device for which write-through caching would be a better choice?

Answer:

For a hard disk, delayed-write caching is a practical solution. The improved performance is justified by the minimal risk that information will be lost because the machine was improperly shut down. With floppy disks, however, the user may at any time remove the disk from the machine. The risk of such an event corrupting the disk's data may not justify the performance benefits delay-write caching provides.

7.14 On a system using a disk cache, the mean access time is 41.2 ms, the mean cache access time is 2 ms, the mean disk access time is 100 ms, and the system has 8Mb of cache memory. For each doubling of the amount of memory, the miss rate is halved. How much memory must be added to reduce the mean access time to 20 ms? Assume the amount of memory may only increase by doubling (8Mb, 16Mb, 32Mb, 64Mb, etc.).

Answer:

The hit ratio can be computed from the equation

$$2 \times (1 - m) + 100m = 41.2$$
$$2 - 2m + 100m = 41.2$$
$$39.2 = 98m$$
$$0.40 = m$$

Doubling memory to 16Mb would lower the miss rate to 0.20.

$$2 \times 0.80 + 100 \times 0.20 = 21.6$$

An additional doubling to 32 Mb would be needed to lower the mean access time below 20 ms.

$$2 \times 0.90 + 100 \times 0.10 = 11.8$$

7.15　If video memory starts at address A0000000 (hex) for a monitor with 16-bit color for a resolution of 1024 × 768, where will video memory end?

Answer:

A resolution of 1024 × 768 contains 786,432 pixels. Using two bytes per pixel, 1,572,864 bytes of video memory are required. A0000000(hex) + 1572864(dec) = A0180000(hex).

7.16　An application that displays video on a bit-mapped monitor redraws the screen 50 times per second. If the operating system provides the application access to video memory, the application can write the screen image directly to video memory. If the operating system does not supply access to video memory, the application generates the screen image in its own buffer, then makes a system call, passing the operating system the address of the buffer. The operating system must then copy the image from the application's buffer to video memory. The screen resolution is 800 × 600 with 8 bits per pixel. All CPU instructions take 50 ns. There are no memory-to-memory instructions. *LOAD* and *STORE* instructions can be used to move 8 bytes of data between memory and internal registers.

What percentage of CPU time is wasted if the application cannot access video memory directly?

Answer:

The screen contains 480,000 pixels. At 1 byte per pixel, the video image is stored in 480,000 bytes. Without direct access for the application, the operating system must move 24,000,000 bytes per second. At 8 bytes per instruction, 3,000,000 instructions per second must be executed. At 50 ns per instruction, the CPU can execute a maximum of 20,000,000 instructions per second. If direct access is not provided, the percentage of wasted CPU time is 15%.

7.17　What is the principal advantage to building line-editing capabilities into the operating system as opposed to leaving it to the applications?

Answer:

Consistency. By placing the capability in the operating system, all applications are provided the same interface. If implemented in the applications, different applications may implement different conventions or even provide no line editing capability at all.

7.18　Writable CD-ROM media are available in both 650Mb and 700Mb versions. What is the principle disadvantage, other than cost, of the 700Mb version?

Answer:

To record more information on the same sized media, the bits must be recorded at higher densities. The higher-density recording leaves less margin for error and leads to greater failure rates.

7.19　Disks with geometries exceeding the following maximums could not be handled by early DOS systems:

Cylinders 1024
Heads 16
Sectors per track 63

What is the maximum size disk these systems could use?

Answer:

$1024 \times 16 \times 63 \times 512 = 528,482,304 = 528\text{Mb}$

7.20 A disk has 8 sectors per track and spins at 600 rpm. It takes the controller 10 ms from the end of one I/O operation before it can issue a subsequent one. How long does it take to read all 8 sectors using the following interleaving systems?

(*a*) No interleaving

(*b*) Single interleaving

(*c*) Double interleaving

Answer:

The disk makes 10 revolutions per second or one revolution in 100 ms. In 10 ms, less than one sector will have passed under the read/write head.

(*a*) The next sector cannot be read until the disk makes almost a complete revolution. It will require 8 revolutions to read all 8 sectors. At 100 ms per revolution, it will take 800 ms.

(*b*) The next sector will spin under the read/write head almost as soon as the next I/O operation is issued. Two revolutions will be needed to read all 8 sectors, making the total read time 200 ms.

(*c*) A total of 2.75 revolutions will be needed to read all 8 sectors, for a total time of 275 ms.

7.21 A disk has 19,456 cylinders, 16 heads, and 63 sectors per track. The disk spins at 5400 rpm. Seek time between adjacent tracks is 2 ms. Assuming the read/write head is already positioned at track 0, how long does it take to read the entire disk?

Answer:

Each track can be read in one revolution, or 11.11 ms. To read all 19456×16 tracks requires approximately 3459 seconds. Seek time is $(19456 - 1) \times 2 = 39\text{s}$. Total time is $3498\text{s} = 58\text{min}$.

7.22 If the average seek time for the disk in the previous problem is 10 ms, what is the average time to read a sector?

Answer:

Seek time will be 10 ms. Latency time will be 5.55 ms. Transfer time will be 0.18 ms. Total time is 15.73 ms.

7.23 If the disk from the previous problem was used as the swap device on a demand-paged system and the page size was the same as the sector size, the average time to read in a swapped-out page would be the time computed above. Assume that if a page also had to be swapped out, the seek time for the swapped-in page would be only 1 ms. What would be the average time to transfer both pages?

Answer:

The page to be swapped out would take the 15.73 ms computed above. For the pages to be swapped in, seek time is 1 ms, latency time is 5.55 ms, and transfer time is 0.18 ms. Total time is $15.73 + 6.73 = 22.46$ ms.

7.24 On a disk with 1000 cylinders, numbers 0 to 999, compute the number of tracks the disk arm must move to satisfy all the requests in the disk queue. Assume the last request serviced was at track 345 and the head is moving toward track 0. The queue in FIFO order contains requests for the following tracks: 123, 874, 692, 475, 105, 376. Perform the computation for the following scheduling algorithms.

- (a) FIFO
- (b) SSTF
- (c) SCAN
- (d) LOOK
- (e) C-SCAN
- (f) C-LOOK

Answer:

(a) 2013
The tracks traveled to will be 345, 123, 874, 692, 475, 105, and 376, making the total distance $222 + 751 + 182 + 217 + 370 + 271 = 2013$.

(b) 1298
The tracks traveled to will be 345, 376, 475, 692, 874, 123, and 105, making the total distance $529 + 769 = 1298$.

(c) 1219
The tracks traveled to will be 345, 123, 105, 0, 376, 475, 692, and 874, making the total distance $345 + 874 = 1219$.

(d) 1009
The tracks traveled to will be 345, 123, 105, 376, 475, 692, and 874, making the total distance $240 + 769 = 1009$.

(e) 1967
The tracks traveled to will be 345, 123, 105, 0, 999, 874 692, 475, and 376, making the total distance $345 + 999 + 623 = 1967$.

(f) 1507
The tracks traveled to will be 345, 123, 105, 874, 692, 475, and 376, making the total distance $240 + 769 + 498 = 1507$.

7.25 Which disk-scheduling algorithm would best optimize the performance of a RAM disk?

Answer:

All the disk-scheduling algorithms would yield the same device performance. A RAM disk is a virtual device created from main memory. The order in which requests are handled has no effect on performance.

7.26   SSTF favors tracks in the center of the disk. On a system using SSTF, how might this affect the design of the file system?

Answer:

Certain blocks in the file system tend to get heavier usage than others. File system data structures and directories located near the top of the file system tree are referred to frequently. The file system design should place these blocks near the center of the disk.

7.27   When compared to a non-RAID system, which RAID levels offer better performance under almost all typical loads?

Answer:

The ability to access the data in parallel allows all the RAID systems to provide better performance under some circumstances. Given a typical load on a RAID-0 or RAID-5 system, the requests will be satisfied using multiple disks, and pipelining will improve performance. The same is true of a RAID-1 system if data is spread over multiple data disks. On a RAID-2 or RAID-3 system, the data will be read in parallel from multiple disks, achieving a higher transfer rate. A RAID-4 system for which much of the l/O is output will not improve performance, since the performance of the system will be no better than the performance of the parity disk.

7.28   Which RAID levels are useful in cases of head crashes on multiple disks?

Answer:

RAID-1 can be configured to use multiple mirrors of each disk. RAID-2 can be configured to use an error-correcting code that can tolerate multiple-bit failures.

Supplementary Problems

7.29   On a computer system with a single 32-bit 125MHz bus, a disk controller uses DMA to transfer data to/from memory at a rate of 10Mb/s. Assume the computer fetches and executes one 32-bit instruction every cycle when no cycles are stolen. By what percentage will two disk controllers running at full capacity slow down instruction execution?

7.30   Since memory references are slow, relative to the speed of most other CPU operations, one approach to speeding up instructions is to require almost all instructions to access only CPU registers. Only two instructions, LOAD and STORE, would access memory, copying a word to or from a register. On such a system, which is probably used, memory-mapped I/O or port I/O? Why?

7.31   For which device would polling be a better option: an output device such as a printer or an input device such as a mouse? Why?

7.32   A serial line can receive input at a maximum rate of 200,000 bytes per second. The average input rate is 50,000 bytes per second. If input is handled using polling, the polling routine takes 750 ns to execute, whether or not an input byte is present. Bytes not retrieved from the controller before the next byte arrives are lost. What is the maximum safe polling interval?

7.33   Given the system in the previous problem, assume the input handling was changed to interrupt I/O with an interrupt routine that took 1 µs to execute. How much would interrupts decrease the amount of time spent processing the input?

7.34   A disk file contains 256-byte fixed-size records. Physical I/O is in terms of 1024-byte blocks that are stored in an operating system buffer. If a process sequentially reads through a file's records, what percentage of the read requests will result in I/O operations?

7.35   For some applications, it is useful to be able to proceed with execution if a user has not entered input within a certain time limit of being prompted. On a system with only blocking I/O, this can be difficult to implement. However, assume the system does have an *alarm* system call that sends a signal to the process in a specified number of seconds. Upon receipt of a signal, any system call (including an I/O request) returns immediately and the user-defined function *alarm_handler* is executed. Write a program segment and the *alarm-handler* function so the program will reissue its prompt every 5 s until input is received.

7.36   A system has four disk drives connected to two disk controllers and 20 terminals connected to 20 serial lines controlled by two controllers. The disk controller can issue a command to one disk while another disk is processing a command (for example, both disks can be seeking at the same time), but it may have only one disk transferring I/O at a time. The serial controller can handle simultaneous I/O from all its connected devices. All the controllers use DMA. The transfer rates for the devices are: disk device, 700 Kb/s; terminal, 3 Kb/s. What is the maximum I/O transfer rate for this system?

7.37   Where are the following tasks implemented, in the logical I/O layer the device drivers, or both?
   (*a*)   Converting a logical block number to a disk sector, cylinder, and head
   (*b*)   Allocating an I/O buffer
   (*c*)   Checking the ready status of the device

(*d*)   Converting a carriage return character received on input to the generic newline character

7.38 On a system using a disk cache, the mean access time is dependent on the mean cache access time, the mean disk access time, and the hit rate. For the following, what is the mean access time?

(*a*)   Cache: 0.5 ms; disk: 200 ms; hit rate: 30%

(*b*)   Cache: 0.5 ms; disk: 200 ms; hit rate: 60%

7.39 On a system using a disk cache, the mean access time is 80.6 ms, the mean cache access time is 1 ms, the mean disk access time is 200 ms, and the system has 8Mb of cache memory. For each doubling of the amount of memory, the miss rate is cut by 40%. How much memory must be added to reduce the mean access time to 20 ms? Assume the amount of memory may only increase by doubling (8Mb, 16Mb, 32Mb, 64Mb, etc.).

7.40 A system has 16Mb of video memory for bit-mapped graphics with 64-bit color. What is the maximum resolution it can support from the following list: 640×480, 800×600, 1024×768, 1152×864, 1280×1024, 1600×1200, and 1800×1440?

7.41 Given a system using bit-mapped graphics with a screen resolution of 800×600 and 16 bits per pixel. If it takes the CPU one instruction to move 4 bytes into video memory and an instruction executes in 500 ns, what is the maximum number of times per second the video memory can be rewritten without encumbering more than 25% of the CPU time?

7.42 Give an example of a situation where an application would want line editing of input turned off.

7.43 The "staircase" effect occurs on devices for which the CR/NL mechanism is not set properly. What is the staircase effect?

7.44 Disks with geometries exceeding the following maximums cannot be handled by most DOS systems: cylinders, 1024; heads, 256; sectors per track, 63. What is the maximum size disk these systems can use?

7.45 A disk has 16 sectors per track and spins at 1200 rpm. It takes the controller 5 ms from the end of one I/O operation before it can issue a subsequent one. How long does it take to read all 16 sectors using the following interleaving systems?

(*a*)   No interleaving

(*b*)   Single interleaving

(*c*)   Double interleaving

7.46 A disk has 26,310 cylinders, 16 heads, and 63 sectors per track. The disk spins at 7200 rpm. Seek time between adjacent tracks is 1 ms. Assuming the read/write head is already positioned at track 0, how long does it take to read the entire disk?

7.47 If the average seek time for the disk in the previous problem is 9 ms, what is the average time to read a sector?

7.48 Assume the disk from the previous problem is being used as the swap device on a demand-paged system and the page size is twice the sector size. If in the processing of a page fault a page also had to be swapped out, the seek time for the swapped-in page would be only 1 ms. What would be the average time to transfer both pages?

7.49 Which disk-scheduling algorithm is preferable in a single-processing environment that uses blocking I/O? Why?

7.50 On a disk with 1000 cylinders numbers 0 to 999, compute the number of tracks the disk arm must move to satisfy all the requests in the disk queue. Assume the last request serviced was at track 756 and the head is moving toward track 0. The queue in FIFO order contains requests for the following tracks: 811, 348, 153, 968, 407, 500. Perform the computation for the following scheduling algorithms.

(*a*) FIFO

(*b*) SSTF

(*c*) SCAN

(*d*) LOOK

(*e*) C-SCAN

(*f*) C-LOOK

7.51 Show that SSTF favors blocks near the center of the disk.

7.52 Which RAID levels are useful in cases of failure of a single disk?

7.53 Which RAID systems could write the entire disk the fastest? Assume all the RAID systems have N data disks except RAID-5 which has $N + 1$. The disks must be written sequentially.

 # Answers to Supplementary Problems

7.29 4%

7.30 Port I/O is probably used. The principal advantage of memory-mapped I/O is it allows any instruction that accesses memory to access I/O device registers. With just a LOAD and STORE, memory-mapped I/O would give no capability beyond what port I/O offers at a cost of decreasing the size of the address space that references memory.

7.31 The output device would be a better choice since the processing of completed I/O operations is less time-sensitive. Delays in processing output just slow down the printing. Delays in processing input could cause input data to be lost.

7.32   4250 ns

7.33   33%

7.34   25%

7.35
```
int alarm_flag;
void alarm_handler()
{
  alarm_flag = 1;
}
//...
do
{
  alarm_flag = 0;
  alarm(5);
  prompt();
  read(userInput)
} while (alarm_flag == 1);
```

7.36   1460 Kb/s

7.37   (*a*)   Device driver
      (*b*)   Logical I/O
      (*c*)   Device driver
      (*d*)   Logical I/O

7.38   (*a*)   140.15
      (*b*)   80.30

7.39   64Mb

7.40   1600 × 1200

7.41   2

7.42   Line editing collects lines of input and does not provide the application with the input until *Enter* is pressed. Many applications (text editors, mail clients) may at times wish to be in a "command" mode where a single character of input specifies a command to be performed. Line editing would require the user to also press *Enter* before a command could be processed. Turning off line editing gives the application greater control over its interface; in this case eliminating the need for the user to enter an unnecessary extra character of input.

7.43 On devices that do not perform carriage return or newline conversions, newline characters cause the printing to move down one line, carriage returns move the printing to the leftmost column. On a system that uses just a newline to mark the end of a line in a text file, outputting the file without conversions causes just a newline to be output between each line. On a device that does not perform conversions, the output will take on the look of a staircase.

```
line 1
   line 2
         line 3
```

7.44 $8,455,716,864 = 8Gb$

7.45 (*a*) 800 ms

(*b*) 800 ms

(*c*) 143.75 ms

7.46 $3534 s = 59 min$

7.47 13.30 ms

7.48 18.60 ms

7.49 In a single-processing environment that uses nonblocking I/O, each I/O request will be satisfied before another can be issued. With only a single request on the queue, all scheduling algorithms are the same—they select that one request. Whichever algorithm is easiest to implement should be used, probably FCFS.

7.50 (*a*) 2182

(*b*) 1023

(*c*) 1724

(*d*) 1418

(*e*) 1914

(*f*) 1728

7.51 The track at the center of the disk has the shortest average distance to the other tracks. The farther the track gets from the center, the longer the average distance to the other tracks. Given a track picked at random, the closest track on average is the center track. Thus, SSTF will tend to pick tracks toward the center. Once SSTF gets to the center it will tend to remain there, giving preference to the tracks close by.

7.52   All but RAID-0 can recover from the failure of one of the disks.

7.53   RAID-0, RAID-1, RAID-2, and RAID-3 could all pipeline requests so that data was being written to all N disks concurrently. RAID-2 and RAID-3 would be slower to the extent that their I/O would be delayed by parity computation. RAID-4 and RAID-5 would be even slower. Most adjacent blocks access the same parity block, preventing concurrent writes.

CHAPTER 8

Security

Built into the operating system are mechanisms for protecting computing activities. Files, devices, and memory must be protected from improper access, and processes must be protected from improper interference by other processes. Protection mechanisms implement protection policies. In some cases, the policy is built into the operating system, in others it is determined by the system administrator. For example, a protection policy determines which processes are authorized to abort another process. The protection mechanism enforces that policy. Strict protection policies conflict with the needs for information sharing and convenient access. A reasonable balance must be struck between these competing goals.

A system's *security level* is the extent to which all its resources are always protected as dictated by the system's protection policies. Security mechanisms attempt to raise a system's level of security. However, the mechanisms that achieve higher levels of security tend to make the system less convenient to use. Again, a balance must be found between safeguarding the system and providing convenient access.

Security measures attempt to deal with threats to compromise the system's protection policies. Major components of security are authentication, prevention, detection, identification, and correction.

8.1   Authentication

Many authorization policies are based on the identity of the user associated with a process. Operating systems need some mechanism for authenticating a user interacting with the computer system. The most commonly used authentication technique is requiring the user to supply one or more pieces of information known only to the user. Information sources that authentication could be based on include account name or number, Social Security number, mother's maiden name, or date of birth. However, for all the examples cited, the user is probably not the only person who can supply the indicated information. So knowledge of that information does not uniquely identify the individual.

8.1.1 PASSWORDS

Authentication is usually more accurate if it is based on a password. A password is a combination of symbols created for the sole purpose of providing authentication. Since it is only used for this one purpose, it is information that no other individual need be aware of. Passwords also allow a group of individuals to easily be treated as a single entity by the authentication system.

The most commonly exploited vulnerability in password authentication systems is password theft. Passwords can be stolen by guessing them or by observing them. The least sophisticated technique for stealing a password is to try all possibilities until one works. A computer guessing passwords at a rate of one every millisecond can guess over 8.5 million passwords in a day. It would take such a system less than a day to guess all six-digit passwords and only about a month to guess every six-letter password (assuming passwords were restricted to only lowercase letters). Increasing the potential number of passwords and the frequency with which passwords are changed makes a password less susceptible to a ***brute force*** password-guessing attack. The number of password combinations is determined by the password length and by the size of the character set used to construct the password.

Intelligent password-guessing systems reduce the number of combinations by trying passwords containing names or words or even permutations of names or words. An attacker familiar with a user might try names important to the user such as the name of a spouse or a pet (perhaps spelled backward). Users choose name-based passwords because they are easier to remember. A better system for generating easily remembered passwords is to use the first letter in each word of a phrase. The phrase "Schaum's Outline of Theory and Problems of Operating Systems" could be used to create the password "S'OoT&PoOS".

Passwords are also vulnerable to observation. Users frequently write down copies of their passwords. More than once, a piece of paper in a desk drawer has allowed an intruder to break into a user's account. A password can also be stolen by watching the keyboard as a user enters a password. For systems accessed through a network, passwords transmitted over a network are susceptible to devices that monitor network communications (***sniffers***) in an attempt to extract password information.

One-time password systems alleviate some of the weaknesses of password authentication. Each time a user authenticates, a different password is calculated using some function and a seed value. The seed value may be chosen at random by the computer and be supplied to the user, or it may be based on the current time. For example, let the function be to square the seed value, then return the middle five digits of the result. If the computer supplied the user with a seed value of 12345, the user would have to respond with **23990**($12345^2 = 15$**23990**025). Since passwords are only used once, an attacker cannot reuse the password to gain entry to the system.

However, an attacker may be able to deduce the function given one or more copies of inputs and the corresponding results. Functions should be sufficiently complex so they may not be easily deduced. One-time passwords are also vulnerable to theft if a device for computing or recording the function exists and its security is broken.

Smart card systems use both a password (or *passcode*) and a function. The user supplies the card with the passcode. The card calculates a password using the passcode and the current time. The password is presented to the computer which has performed the same calculation. An attacker must obtain both the card and the passcode to penetrate the system.

8.1.2 PHYSICAL AUTHENTICATION

Instead of a password, authentication can be based on possession of some form of key or machine-readable card. Such systems can only be applied in cases where the user has direct access to the computer system. Although this eliminates the need for the users or the computer to remember passwords, key theft still allows an intruder to gain entry into the system.

Far greater security can be achieved by basing authentication on a unique physical, characteristic of the user. Systems for scanning a user's retina or fingerprints are available. Ongoing authentication can even be provided by a system that checks the speed and rhythm of a user's typing.

8.2   Prevention

The most desirable outcome of a security system is for it to prevent intruders from successfully penetrating the system's security. Preventive measures include the following.

- Limiting new passwords to those that pass a series of quality checks. Software exists that can check a password for length, diversity of characters, and the presence of words or permutations of words.

- Requiring passwords to be changed at periodic intervals.

- Encrypting data, either when it is transmitted. or when it is stored. Programs like *ssh* allow communications to and from a remote site to be encrypted.

- Turning off unused or duplicate services. Reducing the number of system entry points reduces the probability of finding an entry point that can be exploited.

- Implementing an internal firewall. Programs like *tcpwrapper* can be configured to deny network access, based on the remote location and/or the service to be accessed.

- Monitoring security advisories and updating software and configuration information as needed. Groups such as CERT and BugTraq provide information on security vulnerabilities and how to fix them.

8.3 Detection

Should a break-in occur, its negative effects may be reduced by prompt detection. Effective detection measures may also discourage intrusion attempts. Constant monitoring provides the best hope for fast discovery.

- Auditing systems record information about system events. For example, the time and user involved in each system login can be logged. Monitoring of system activities can detect unusual activities.

- Virus checkers search the contents of files and boot programs for the presence of known abnormalities.

- The existence of a long-running process in a listing of currently executing processes may indicate suspicious activity.

- The current state of the system can be checked against a previous state. The *tripwire* program can record in its database a fingerprint of any file in the system and later be used to detect changes in the fingerprint for any file in the system.

8.4 Correction

After a system has been penetrated, it is frequently necessary to take corrective action.

- Periodic backups should be performed so a system can be rolled back to a previous state. Backups may be stored offline and even offsite to increase the probability the backup is not compromised during an attack.

- If a backup does not exist or its integrity is unknown, a reload of the entire system may be necessary. An exact record of all currently installed software and updates simplifies the restoration effort.

- It may be necessary to change all resident security information. All users may be required to change their password.

- The vulnerability that allowed the system to be penetrated should be fixed. This may involve deactivating a service, installing a bug fix, or modifying the system configuration.

8.5 Identification

To discourage intruders, it is desirable to identify the source of an attack. Identification is frequently the most difficult security task.

- Audit trails may provide useful identification information. However, depending on the nature of the attack and the location of the log, the information contained in audit logs may have been tampered with by the intruder.

- Systems accessed through modems can keep track of the source of incoming calls using caller-id.

- Systems accessed through a network can record the address of the connecting computer. Attacks relayed through a series of computers must be traced to their origin.

- All services can be configured to require user authentication. For example, a mail server could refuse mail services to any unauthenticated client. If that server is used to relay an email virus, the authentication information may be useful in identifying its source.

8.6 Threat Categories

Threats may be categorized by type of activity or by the type of the attacker. The four categories of attack are:

- **Interruption:** The attack prevents authorized users from accessing system resources (also known as a *denial of service* attack).

- **Interception:** The attackers are able to read information that they should not have access to. While interception problems are normally less serious, they are far more difficult to recover from. Modified data can be recovered from backup. Recovery from the disclosure of confidential information may be impossible.

- **Modification:** Alteration or erasure of information.

- **Fabrication:** Insertion of counterfeit information. For example, adding an account with a large balance into a banking system.

Attackers may be categorized as follows.

- **Masquerader:** A user unauthorized to use the system who is able to obtain the access rights of a legitimate user.

- **Misfeasor:** An authorized user who obtains access rights beyond those to which he or she is entitled, or who uses existing rights for malevolent purposes.

- **Clandestine User:** A user who obtains access rights normally reserved for system administrators and uses those rights to subvert both the protection and the detection systems.

8.7 Program Threats

In many cases, a program is the tool an attacker uses to compromise the security of a system. Benign programs can be used to attack a system if they are misconfigured or contain bugs. Attackers have also created malicious programs to achieve their nefarious deeds. Malicious programs can be classified as follows.

- **Trapdoor:** A secret entry point to a program that bypasses normal protection mechanisms. Some successful attacks on Unix systems left behind a trapdoor that allowed the attackers to easily reenter the system. The *login* program was replaced with a version containing a trapdoor that allowed anyone entering a login name of "toor" ("root" spelled backward) to log in as the superuser without supplying a password.

- **Logic Bomb:** A code segment in a program that causes the program to "explode" when certain conditions are met. An employee could install in an accounting program a logic bomb to check for his or her name in the company payroll. If the employee is terminated, the logic bomb is triggered and the program deletes files or performs some other destructive act.

- **Trojan Horse:** Like the ancient Greek Trojan Horse, a computer Trojan horse hides a nasty secret within a benign exterior. When executed, the apparently legitimate program performs a malevolent act. In some cases, Trojan horses are blatantly destructive. In other cases, they appear to work as advertised, but quietly attack the system. Consider, for example, a Trojan horse version of a program to display the current date. A Trojan horse could be installed to erase all the user's files and display the message "Got you." Or it could display the date normally, but also make a copy of all the user's files in a location accessible to the Trojan horse author.

- **Bacteria:** A program that repeatedly replicates itself. Bacteria do not perform any explicitly destructive acts, but their consumption of resources results in a denial-of-service attack.

- **Virus:** A malicious code segment that, in addition to performing a destructive act, attempts to replicate itself elsewhere in the computer system. Viruses can insert themselves into any executable entity to which they have write access: word processing macros, executable programs, the operating system, or the boot program on the boot sector. Viruses have been a particular problem on DOS and some Windows systems where protection mechanisms are not used to protect system files from modification by users.

- **Worm:** Worms are programs that spread throughout a network. In addition to replicating on the host machine, a worm uses one or more techniques to spread to connected machines. In 1988, a worm unleashed by Robert Morris infected thousands of machines throughout the Internet (a crime for which Morris was convicted in federal court). That particular worm spread by exploiting bugs in two programs that provided network services (*sendmail* and *finger*) and by using a remote command execution facility (*rsh*). It also used sophisticated techniques to break user passwords. It then tried to log in to additional systems using the list of account names and passwords obtained.

It should be noted universal agreement on the definition of these terms does not exist. For some a virus is only a code segment that attaches to a host file. For others, any program that replicates and commits malicious acts is a virus. Table 8-1 summarizes the characteristics of malicious programs as presented in this book.

Table 8-1.   Characteristics of Malicious Programs.

	Needs Host	Replicates	Malicious Acts	Attacks Network	Triggering Mechanism
Trapdoor	Yes	No	Yes	No	Secret entry point
Logic bomb	Yes	No	Yes	No	Specific conditions
Trojan horse	Yes	No	Yes	No	None
Bacteria	No	Yes	No	No	None
Virus	Yes	Yes	Yes	No	None
Worm	No	Yes	Maybe	Yes	None

 # Solved Problems

8.1   How many six-letter passwords can be constructed using lowercase letters and digits?

Answer:

There are 36 possibilities for each of six characters, making the total possibilities $36^6 = 2,176,782,336$.

8.2   What is the minimum, average, and maximum time it would take to crack a six-digit password if one password can be checked every millisecond?

Answer:

The minimum time is 1 ms. If the first guess is correct, only one password need be checked. On average, half the passwords must be checked to find the correct one. There are 1,000,000 six-digit passwords. The average search would take 500,000 ms = 500 s. If the password was not found until all the passwords were checked, the search would take 1000 s.

8.3   On many systems, account passwords are stored in encrypted form using a one-way algorithm. With a one-way algorithm, there is no algorithm for reversing the encryption process (except a brute force testing of all possibilities). How can the system verify a user has entered the correct password if it cannot obtain the correct password from the stored information?

Answer:

The same encryption algorithm is applied to the password entered by the user. If the resultant string is the same as the stored value, the correct password was entered.

8.4   Classify each of the following as authentification, prevention, detection, identification, or correction.

(*a*)   A login program

(*b*)   Scanning for recently modified files in a system directory

(c)   Weekly backups

(d)   Logging all logins and logouts

(e)   Promptly deleting unused accounts

Answer:

(a)   Authentication

(b)   Detection

(c)   Correction

(d)   Identification

(e)   Prevention

8.5   For each of the following threats, classify as interruption, interception, modification, or fabrication.

(a)   Clogging a printer with long phony print jobs

(b)   Adding to one bank account all the fractional cent amounts from all the other accounts

(c)   Monitoring (sniffing) a network wire to obtain account names and passwords

(d)   Sending out phony messages that school or work has been shut down because of snow

Answer:

(a)   Interruption
      The phony print activity prevents other users from using the printer.

(b)   Modification
      The amount of money in the accounts is being modified.

(c)   Interception
      The attacker is reading information he or she are not authorized to read.

(d)   Fabrication
      A counterfeit message has been inserted into the system.

8.6   Why is it easier for a misfeasor than a masquerader to compromise the security of a system?

Answer:

The masquerader must first find a vulnerability that allows access to the system. The misfeasor already has access to the system and therefore has access to a greater number of potential vulnerabilities.

8.7   Which types of malicious programs replicate?

Answer:

Bacteria, viruses, and worms

8.8　When a user enters a command on a DOS or Unix system, the command interpreter searches a sequence of directories for a file whose name matches the command entered. The list of directories searched is configurable and includes the directories where system files are stored. It also often includes the current directory. Explain why it is dangerous to have the current directory searched first.

Answer:

If a user is executing in a directory in which other users can create files, an intruder could install a Trojan horse program with the same name as a frequently used command. Attempting to execute that command in that directory would cause the Trojan horse program to run, not the system command. If the current directory is searched last, the system command would execute. For even a higher level of security, some recommend not searching the current directory at all.

8.9　Explain why reading an email without looking at attachments cannot cause a computer to become infected with a virus (assuming the mail client program is not already infected with a virus).

Answer:

Virus code must be executed to replicate. Reading an email message only executes code in the mail client. Since no code in the email is executed, any malicious content it contains cannot be spread. However, most mail clients have the ability to "view" attachments. If the attachment is a Visual Basic file, the mail client executes the attachment. Thus, viewing an attachment can unleash a virus.

 # Supplementary Problems

8.10　How many eight-letter passwords can be constructed using digits, uppercase letters, and lowercase letters?

8.11　What is the average time in hours it would take to crack a six-letter (lowercase only) password if one password can be checked every 500 μs?

8.12　On some versions of Unix, the one-way password encryption algorithm uses a two-character seed along with the string to be encrypted. For each password stored, a different seed is chosen at random. Why? Does this provide additional protection against an intruder determining the superuser's password?

8.13 Classify each of the following as authentication, prevention, detection, identification, or correction.

    (*a*)   Joining the BugTraq mailing list

    (*b*)   Maintaining checksum values for system files

    (*c*)   Implementing a smart card system

    (*d*)   Generating hard copies of key system documents

    (*e*)   Logging the Internet address of all remote connections

8.14 For each of the following threats, classify as interruption, interception, modification, or fabrication.

    (*a*)   Stealing top-secret weapons information from a Department of Defense computer

    (*b*)   Reformatting an entire disk

    (*c*)   Executing a program that replicates clones of itself as fast as it can

    (*d*)   Creating unauthorized web pages on a web server

8.15 Which types of malicious programs require a host program?

8.16 If a virus must execute to replicate, how can a word processing document transmit a virus?

Answers to Supplementary Problems

8.10 2.1834×10^{14}

8.11 Between 21 and 22 h

8.12 If an intruder obtained a copy of the file containing the account passwords, he or she might attempt to gain access to the system using brute force password guessing. If no seed was used in the encryption algorithm, each guess could be compared with each entry in the file of passwords. By using seeds, each guess is only good at guessing a password encrypted using the same seed.

    Use of the seed helps prevent an attacker from guessing any user's password. It does not help attacks against a particular user's password. The seed does not delay an attempt to crack the superuser's password.

8.13 (*a*)   Prevention

    (*b*)   Detection

    (*c*)   Authentication

      (*d*) Correction

      (*e*) Identification

8.14 (*a*) Interception

      (*b*) Modification

      (*c*) Interruption

      (*d*) Fabrication

8.15 Trapdoors, logic bombs, viruses, and Trojan horses

8.16 Although word processing documents contain text, most word processors also support the inclusion of macros that contain executable code. Viruses are spread in word processing documents by including them in macros.

CHAPTER 9

Bibliography

Anderson, J., *Computer Security Threat Monitoring and Surveillance*, James P. Anderson Co., Fort Washington, PA, April 1990.

Apple Computer Inc., *Apple Technical Introduction to the Macintosh Family*, Addison-Wesley, Reading, MA, 1987.

AT&T, *UNIX Programmer's Manual*, Holt, Rinehart, and Winston, New York, 1986.

Bach, M., *The Design of the UNIX Operating System*, Prentice Hall, Englewood Cliffs, NJ, 1986.

Baer, J., *Computer Systems Architecture*, Computer Science Press, Rockville, MD, 1980.

Bays, C., "A Comparison of Next-fit, First-fit, and Best-fit," *Communications of the ACM*, vol. 20, no. 3, March 1977, pp. 191–192.

Belady, L.A., "A Study of Replacement Algorithms for a Virtual Storage Computer," *IBM Systems Journal*, vol. 5, no. 2, 1966, pp. 78–101.

Belady, L.A., Nelson, R.A., Shedler, G.S., "An Anomaly in Space-Time Characteristics of Certain Programs Running in a Paging Machine," *Communications of the ACM*, vol. 12, no. 6, June 1969, pp. 349–353.

Ben-Ari, M., *Principles of Concurrent Programming*, Prentice Hall, Englewood Cliffs, NJ, 1982.

Bic, L., Shaw, A., *The Logical Design of Operating Systems*, 2d ed., Prentice Hall, Englewood Cliffs, NJ, 1988.

Bourne, S.R., *The UNIX System*, Addison-Wesley, Reading, MA 1982.

Bowles, J., Pelaez, C., "Bad Code," *IEEE Spectrum*, vol. 29, no. 8, August 1992, pp. 36–40.

Brinch-Hansen, P., *Operating Systems Principles*, Prentice Hall, Englewood Cliffs, NJ, 1973.

Brumfield, A.J., "A Guide to Operating Systems Literature," *Operating Systems Review*, vol. 20, no. 2, April 1986, pp. 38–42.

Chen, P., Lee, P., Gibson, G., Katz, R., Patterson. D., "RAID: High-Performance, Reliable Secondary Storage," *ACM Computing Surveys*, vol. 26, no. 2, June 1994, pp. 145–185.

Christian, K., *The UNIX Operating System*, John Wiley & Sons, Inc., New York, 1983.

Coffman, E.G., Elphick, M.J., Shoshani, A., "System Deadlocks," *Computing Surveys*, vol. 3, no. 4, June 1971, pp. 549–576.

Cooper, J., *Computer and Communications Security: Strategies for the 1990s*, McGraw-Hill, New York, 1990.

De Alvare, A., "How Crackers Crack Passwords or What Passwords to Avoid," *Proceedings, UNIX Security Workshop II*, Portland, OR, August 1990.

Deitel, H.M., *An Introduction to Operating Systems*, Addison-Wesley, Reading, MA, 1984.

Denning, P., "The Working Set Model for Program Behaviour," *Communications of the ACM*, vol. 11, no. 5, May 1968, pp. 323–333.

Denning, P., "Virtual Memory," *Computing Surveys*, vol. 2, no. 3, September 1970, pp. 153–189.

Denning, P., "Working Sets Past and Present," *IEEE Transactions on Software Engineering*, vol. SE-6, no. 1, January 1980, pp. 64–81.

Denning, P., *Computers Under Attack: Intruders, Worms and Viruses*, Addison-Wesley, Reading, MA, 1990.

Dijkstra, E., *Cooperating Sequential Processes*, Technical Report EWD-123, Technological University, Eindhoven, The Netherlands, 1965 (reprinted in Genuys [1968]).

Dijkstra, E., "The Structure of the T.H.E. Multiprogramming System," *Communications of the ACM*, vol. II, no. 5, May 1968, pp. 341–346.

Duncan, R., *Advanced MS-DOS*, Microsoft Press, Redmond, WA, 1986.

Enger, N., Howerton, P., *Computer Security*, Amacon, New York, 1980.

Flynn, L.M., McHoes, A.M., *Understand Operating Systems*, Brooks/Cole, Pacific Grove, CA, 2001.

Folk, M., Zoellick, B., *File Structures: A Conceptual Toolkit*, Addison-Wesley, Reading, MA, 1992.

Genuys, F. (ed.), *Programming Languages*, Academic Press, London, 1968.

Grosshans, D., *File Systems: Design and Implementation*, Prentice Hall, Englewood Cliffs, NJ, 1986.

Hatfield, D., "Experiments on Page Size, Program Access Patterns, and Virtual Memory Performance," *IBM Journal of Research and Development*, vol. 15, no. 1, January 1972, pp. 58–62.

Hennessy, J.L., Patterson, D.A., *Computer Architecture: A Quantitative Approach*, Morgan Kaufmann Publishers, Palo Alto, CA, 1990.

Hoare, C., "Monitors: An Operating Systems Structuring Concept," *Communications of the ACM*, vol. 17, no. 10, October 1974, pp. 549–557.

Hoare, C., *Communicating Sequential Processes*, Prentice Hall, Englewood Cliffs, NJ, 1985.

Hoffman, L. (ed.), *Rogue Programs: Viruses, Worms and Trojan Horses*, Van Nostrand Reinhold, New York, 1990.

Holt, R., "Some Deadlock Properties of Computer Systems," *Computing Surveys*, vol. 4, no. 3, September 1972, pp. 179–196.

Holt, R.C., Graham, G.S., Lazowska, E.D., Scott, M.A., *Structured Concurrent Programming with Operating System Applications*, Addison-Wesley, Reading, MA, 1978.

Intel Corp., *Accelerated Graphics Port Technology*, http://developer.intel.com/technology/agp, 2001.

Isloor, S., Marsland, T., "The Deadlock Problem: An Overview," *Computer*, vol. 13, no. 9, September 1980, pp. 58–78.

Knuth, D., *The Art of Computer Programming, Volume 1: Fundamental Algorithms*, 2d ed., Addison-Wesley, Reading, MA, 1973.

Krakowiak, S., *Principles of Operating Systems*, MIT Press, Cambridge, MA, 1988.

Lamport, L., "A New Solution of Dijkstra's Concurrent Programming Problem," *Communications of the ACM*, vol. 17, no. 8, August 1974, pp. 453–455.

Lamport, L., "The Mutual Exclusion Problem," *Journal of the ACM*, vol. 33, no. 2, April 1986, pp. 313–348.

Lewis, B., Berg, D., *Threads Primer*, Prentice Hall, Englewood Cliffs, NJ, 1996.

Liedtke, J., "Toward Real Microkernels," *Communications of the ACM*, vol. 39, no. 9, September 1996, pp. 70–77.

Livadas, P.E., *File Structures: Theory and Practice*, Prentice Hall, Englewood Cliffs, NJ, 1990.

Madnick, S.E., Donavan, J.J., *Operating Systems*, McGraw-Hill, New York, 1974.

Maekawa, M., Oldehoeft, A.E., Oldehoeft, R.R., *Operating Systems: Advanced Concepts*, Benjamin/Cummings, Menlo Park, CA, 1987.

Metzner, J.R., "Structure Operating Systems Literature for the Graduate Course," *Operating Systems Review*, vol. 16, no. 4, October 1982, pp. 10–25.

Microsoft Inc., *Microsoft Windows 2000*, http://www.microsoft.com/windows2000, 2001.

Milenkovic, M., *Operating Systems: Concepts and Design*, McGraw-Hill, New York, 1992.

Peterson, J., "Myths about the Mutual Exclusion Problem," *Information Processing Letters*, vol. 12, no. 3, June 1981, pp. 115–116.

Peterson, J., Norman, T., "Buddy Systems," *Communications of the ACM*, vol. 20, no. 6, June 1977, pp. 421–431.

Pfleeger, C., *Security in Computing*, Prentice Hall, Englewood Cliffs, NJ, 1989.

Pinkert, J.R., Wear, L.L., *Operating Systems' Concepts, Policies, and Mechanisms*, Prentice Hall, Englewood Cliffs, NJ, 1989.

Raynal, M., *Algorithms for Mutual Exclusion*, MIT Press, Cambridge, MA, 1986.

Ritchie, D., Thompson, K., "The UNIX Time-Sharing System," *Communications of the ACM*, vol. 17, no. 7, July 1974, pp. 365–375.

Silberschatz, A., Galvin, P.B., *Operating Systems Concept*, 5th ed., Addison-Wesley, Reading, MA, 1998.

Spafford, E., Heaphy, K., Ferbrache, D., *Computer Viruses*, ADAPSO, Arlington, VA, 1989.

Spafford, E., "The Internet Worm: Crisis and Aftermath," *Communications of the ACM*, vol. 32, no. 6, June 1989, pp. 678–687.

Stallings, W., *Computer Organization and Architecture*, 4th ed., Prentice Hall, Englewood Cliffs, NJ, 1996.

Stallings, W., *Operating Systems: Internals and Design Principles*, 3rd ed., Prentice Hall, Englewood Cliffs, NJ, 1998.

Tanenbaum, A.S., *Modern Operating Systems*, Prentice Hall, Englewood Cliffs, NJ, 1992.

Tanenbaum, A.S., *Structured Computer Organization*, 4th ed., Prentice Hall, Englewood Cliffs, NJ, 1999.

Thompson, K., "UNIX Implementation," *The Bell System Technical Journal*, vol. 57, no. 6, July–August 1978, pp. 1931–1946.

Wiederhold, G., *File Organization for Database Design*, McGraw-Hill, New York, 1987.

INDEX